Keys to the Workplace

Keys to the Workplace
Skills and Supports for People with Disabilities

by

Michael J. Callahan, M.Ed.
Marc Gold & Associates
Gautier, Mississippi

J. Bradley Garner, Ph.D.
Medina City Schools
Medina, Ohio
and
Community Living Associates
Stow, Ohio

·P A U L·H·
BROOKES
PUBLISHING C<u>o</u>

Baltimore•London•Toronto•Sydney

Paul H. Brookes Publishing Co.
Post Office Box 10624
Baltimore, Maryland 21285-0624

Typeset by Yankee Typesetters, Inc., Concord, New Hampshire.
Manufactured in the United States of America by
The Maple Press Company, York, Pennsylvania.

Permission to reprint the following materials is gratefully acknowledged:
Page 38: Gold, M. (1980). An end to the concept of mental retardation: Oh, what a
beautiful mourning. In *Did I say that?* (p. 144). Champaign, IL: Research Press;
reprinted by permission.

Users of *Keys to the Workplace: Skills and Supports for People with Disabilities* are
granted permission to photocopy the blank forms that appear in Appendices A and C
in the course of employment facilitation for individuals with disabilities.

Library of Congress Cataloging-in-Publication Data

Callahan, Michael J.
   Keys to the workplace : skills and supports for people with disabilities /
   Michael J. Callahan, J. Bradley Garner.
      p.   cm.
   Includes bibliographical references and index.
   ISBN 1-55766-276-2 (alk. paper)
   1. Handicapped—Employment.   2. Vocational rehabilitation.   3. Sheltered
workshops.   I. Garner, J. Bradley, 1949–   .   II. Title.
HD7255.C35   1997
331.5'9—dc21   96-37324
                                                                                            CIP

British Library Cataloguing in Publication data are available from the British Library.

Contents

About the Authors

Michael J. Callahan, M.Ed., President, Marc Gold & Associates, 4101 Gautier-Vancleave Road, #102, Gautier, Mississippi 39553; Project Director, United Cerebral Palsy Associations, Choice Access Project. Michael J. Callahan is the project director for United Cerebral Palsy Associations' (UCPA) Choice Access Project. This is a 5-year project to examine the feasibility of providing direct vouchers to people with severe physical disabilities for them to purchase employment services of their choice. Mr. Callahan has worked with the national office of UCPA since 1987. He also has worked with Marc Gold & Associates (MG&A) since 1979, serving as president of the organization since Marc Gold's death in 1982. MG&A is a training company that provides technical assistance to systems, agencies, and families interested in ensuring the complete community participation of people with severe disabilities. He has trained extensively throughout the United States, Canada, and Europe. He is a co-editor of a popular "how-to" book on employment for people with severe disabilities, *Getting Employed, Staying Employed*. He lives in Ocean Springs, Mississippi, with his wife and daughter.

J. Bradley Garner, Ph.D., Medina City Schools, 120 West Washington Street, Medina, Ohio 44256. J. Bradley Garner is Director of Student Services for the Medina City School District and the president of Community Living Associates, an organization that provides training and consultation related to varied aspects of the field of human services. He also serves as an adjunct faculty member at Walsh University in the area of special education. Dr. Garner's professional career and interests have focused on a critical examination of the values and philosophies that we profess in regard to individuals labeled as "severely disabled" and the means by which these values are translated into meaningful supports and opportunities.

Foreword

In 1985, Michael Callahan and I embarked on a conversation that is embodied in this very important book. The conversation started with a question: *How do you resolve the tension between systematic instruction and natural supports in the workplace?* I had come to believe that the traditional job-coach model was not meeting the employment needs of adults with severe disabilities. Michael and his colleagues of Marc Gold & Associates believed that, in part, the failure of the job-coach model was related to inadequate use of systematic instruction. After 3 years of working on a project to help young adults with severe disabilities make the transition into regular community jobs, Michael and I realized that the key to employment for these people was the combination of vocational profiles, natural supports, and systematic instruction. This evolved into an approach that relied on an intensive and personalized analysis of an individual's strengths and preferences to form the basis for job development and placement. In addition, a key feature of the overall employment strategy included a well-trained employment facilitator with the skills to support co-workers and employers responsible for supervising people with severe disabilities in typical jobs and workplaces. This seemingly simple resolution does not capture the intensity of the conversations about natural supports versus job coaching that today are going on across the United States. Nor does it capture the contributions that people with disabilities and their families made to help us understand the conditions of unemployment, underemployment, segregation, job loss, and, albeit too limited, job success and satisfaction. Furthermore, it does not capture the immense contributions of many people across the country who were the first to question the term "unemployable" and to develop a national understanding of the potential of individuals with severe disabilities to be employees.

People with disabilities and their families have been the recipients of employment services, whether those services were good or bad. Providers and professionals have framed the discussions, practices, and disputes about the location and nature of employment supports with little participation from families or people with disabilities. Today, there are new opportunities emerging, pushed by the concept of self-determination. That is, adults with disabilities will be able to purchase their employment supports from whomever is available and competitive. Market forces will help reduce the tensions between natural supports and systematic instruction. Adults with disabilities will choose services and supports that are most likely to get them a job that they want and to arrange for supports that improve the likelihood of job retention and satisfaction.

Marc Gold edited a book entitled *Did I Say That?* It was his own analysis of his ideas and earlier writings. His ability to be reflective and to acknowledge the contribution of knowledge and other forces to new ideas and strategies to support people with severe disabilities had an enormous impact on me. It taught me that today's ideas may be tomorrow's reflections on outdated thinking. Not all of the changes in thinking are the result of a rational evolution of ideas; they are the result of pragmatic responses to social problems. Today, people with disabilities and their families are being confronted with managed care, a decreasing resource base, changes in federal entitlement programs, and increasing waiting lists for services. If we respond with a continued reliance on the service system and do not seek supports in our communities from co-workers and employers, then there will be a severe shortfall of resources. We will be faced with rationing and strict eligibility requirements. This shift to natural supports is not just a new idea; it is a necessity and a valuable tool that will enhance the likelihood of community inclusion and employment for people with severe disabilities.

This book is the culmination of many years of hard work and a first step in helping us to be effective employment facilitators in this new social and fiscal context. I have witnessed the evolution of the ideas. It is the result of working with many people with severe disabilities and having conversations with numerous individuals, families, professionals, and colleagues. It is the result of testing new approaches in different parts of the United States. It will be an important tool for all of us who are in the position of advocating for employment, full inclusion, community supports, deinstitutionalization, desheltering, self-determination and choice, and a positive vision of the future. *Keys to the Workplace* contains ideas and approaches that enhance a positive future for adults with disabilities. It moves us one step closer to a day when activity centers and sheltered workshops are empty and preserved only for the purpose of reminding us of an unfortunate time in history.

Jan Nisbet, Ph.D.
Director, Institute on Disability
University of New Hampshire
Durham, New Hampshire

Preface

Mike Callahan describes his first interactions with Marc Gold in the following manner:

> I first met Marc Gold in early 1976 while I was working at a work activity center in Pascagoula, Mississippi. The work activity center had just landed a major contract, and we discovered that our training skills were lacking in relation to the complex assembly task to be performed and our uncertain expectations of the people employed in the center. Our director had heard Marc speak during a 5-day training he had attended, so he picked up the phone and called for help. In his typical fashion, Marc brashly agreed to do the training for free, if we would sponsor one of his 3-day conferences. Referencing a $30-per-person registration fee (considered outrageously expensive in those days), he said, "If five people come, I'll make $150. If 100 people come, I'll do pretty well!" Over 250 participants showed up for the conference to hear a new way of thinking about people with disabilities.
>
> As important as Marc's perspectives were on the training strategies, values, and competencies that he shared during the conference, I will never forget a simple, personal interaction that occurred while I was guiding Marc through our facility. Marc had asked me to introduce him to the people who worked in our facility. Since I assumed that he meant the staff, we began visiting the various offices and making introductions. Marc quickly stopped me and said, "I really want to meet the people who work here." I began to realize that Marc and I had very different ideas about who "people" were.
>
> Once it became clear to me whom he wanted to meet and talk to, I led Marc through the building to our saw shop. In a foyer next to the back door of the facility, near the restrooms, we were preparing to enter the work floor. Marc noticed a large man with Down syndrome sitting cross-legged on the floor next to the men's toilet. He was rocking gently and did not focus as we walked by. Marc stopped, stuck out his hand, and said, "Hi, I'm Marc Gold." The man kept rocking and did not respond, so I assisted him to stand and said to Marc, "This is Speedy." In the span of less than a few seconds, Marc recognized a dilemma. It was obvious to him that the nickname was not a compliment to Speedy, and he wanted

no part of continuing the insult. However, he had just met me, and Marc was too gentle a soul to embarrass me by lecturing me on thoughtlessness. Before I could apologize, Marc simply smiled and said, "Hi, Speed. How are you doing? It's very nice to meet you." His resolution of the dilemma required no comment, but it hit me like a two-by-four.

I had just received the first of many lessons from Marc on the effort it takes to offer respect to people who desperately need it and who get little of it. I learned, along with countless others, that it is necessary to take great care to look at all of our interactions with people with significant disabilities. He realized how easy it is to slip into practices that feel comfortable, perhaps even natural, which actually rob people with disabilities of their dignity, of their choice, and, ultimately, of their opportunity for a decent life.

But do we really need to be so careful today, in an era of employment, living, educational, and recreational supports that attempt to ensure a valued community role for all people with disabilities? Should a book like this attempt to connect these sentiments and perspective that were necessary 20 years ago? Yes, we absolutely must! Perhaps now more than ever. The reason that this is necessary is that as we get closer and closer to the long-held goals of decent human services, we get further and further away from those poignant issues that clarified our direction in the first place. And it's easier to forget the little things when the big things seem so critical—jobs, homes, rights, entitlements, and the ever-changing political agendas.

It is for these reasons that we were driven in our attempt to link Marc Gold's legacy with every aspect of this book. So far as we know, Marc never uttered the words "supported" and "employment" in the same phrase. The concept crystallized a few years after his death in 1982, and we have been able to draw so much from his body of work and from his spirit:

- The Seven-Phase Sequence was conceptualized by Marc in the early 1970s (Gold, 1980a). In its fourth iteration, it forms the cornerstone of this book.
- Marc always stressed the connection between our values and our practices. We have devoted the entire opening section of this book to a discussion of the perspectives, supports, and relationships that must be in place in order for people with significant disabilities to lead meaningful lives.
- Marc essentially predicted (Gold, 1976) the concept of individualized, negotiated jobs presented in this text by recognizing the strategy of breaking a complete job into teachable tasks that match the skills, needs, and preferences of people with disabilities and then forming the tasks in a newly defined job. The issues of individualized planning and personalized

job development compose the second section in finding the right "keys to the workplace."

- The importance of an effective training technology was asserted by Marc 25 years ago. Even though little has been written on systematic instruction procedures in the last decade, we offer a resolution to the paradox faced by employment support personnel when deciding whether to use natural or human services supports. The third section of this text provides in-depth coverage of powerful training procedures and how they fit in relation to features of naturalness.
- Marc was one of the first researchers to question the unbridled use of behavior modification strategies for training purposes. He felt that an emphasis on reinforcements, even positive ones, led to an unbalancing of the relationship that he thought was so necessary for respect between trainers and learners. As the human services field has moved ever closer to viewing the strategies naturally used in workplaces as a benchmark for acceptable practice, arbitrary behavioral procedures have less and less relevance. This text takes the position that the best place to start when considering motivation and reinforcement strategies is the approach used in each unique workplace.

We invite you into this exploration of the strategies and perspectives necessary to unlock the doors to meaningful employment for all people with disabilities. In our previous book, *Getting Employed, Staying Employed* (Mcloughlin, Garner, & Callahan, 1987; Paul H. Brookes Publishing Co.), we provided a more thorough discussion of the "science of sales" and the general issues relating to employment facilitation. In considering the content of this book, we felt that those issues have held up well over the past decade. We feel that by combining the more timeless features of the original text with the newly emerging issues presented here, facilitators can obtain a practical and effective guide to assist them to fulfill the dream of employment for all people with disabilities.

Section I addresses the primary and critical role of values in the facilitation of employment opportunities for individuals with disabilities. Chapter 1 summarizes the changes that have occurred in the field of human services and how these changes have resulted in improved opportunities for people with disabilities. Chapter 2 emphasizes the role of values in planning for employment. The primary value expressed in this chapter is the importance of listening to the dreams and visions of the individual who is the focus of the planning effort. Chapter 3 illuminates the critical role of supports in the lives of all individuals. Chapter 4 expands this discussion of supports to include the role that families can play in facilitating employment and in generally enriching the quality of life for individuals with disabilities. Chapter 5 extends this discussion to include how friendships and relationships have an impact on individuals with disabilities in the workplace.

In Section II, Planning for Employment, we address several issues surrounding the identification and use of supports to promote community employment for individuals with severe disabilities. In Chapter 6, we present an overall tool for employment planning: The Seven-Phase Sequence. This strategy provides a means for balancing natural supports and individual needs in the process of facilitating employment. Chapter 7 details another important planning tool: The Vocational Profile. The Vocational Profile assists members of the planning team in identifying specific employment outcomes. The Vocational Profile links the individual with disabilities, his or her dreams and goals, and subsequent job development activities. Chapter 8 provides an overview of job development strategies that can be used to promote and respect the desires, goals, and visions of the individual with disabilities. As a final consideration in this section, Chapter 9 summarizes a plan for job analysis within the context of employment settings. The suggested procedures are designed to optimize the value and influence of naturally occurring supports.

Facilitating employment for people with disabilities requires an awareness of the benefits that can be gained from the skillful application of systematic instruction. In Section III, we acknowledge the role of systematic instruction as a *necessary* tool for implementing supported employment. In Chapter 10, the emphasis is placed on strategies for organizing information relative to systematic instruction. Chapter 11 describes various guidelines and strategies for communicating the information "to be learned" in the process of facilitating community employment (e.g., formats for presenting information, when to offer information to the employee, how much assistance should be provided, what kinds of assistance should be provided, where to best teach the task). Chapter 12 provides a mixed bag of observations regarding this process of facilitating employment with a particular emphasis on practical strategies that will either "make or break" the successful nature of this venture. Finally, four appendices provide the reader with sample forms, both blank and completed, that are indispensable in the employment facilitation process.

We encourage our readers to use this book as a practical guide for facilitating employment. Namely, it is suggested that you think of an individual with disabilities for whom employment may be a desired outcome. As you read, apply the principles and strategies to the life of that individual—his or her goals, desires, and visions. In this way, the "keys to the workplace" will become a real part of your relationship to that individual.

Acknowledgments

We have been very fortunate over the years to have had the opportunity to learn and gain insights from a large group of gifted, perceptive, and intuitive individuals who share a common vision and commitment to individuals with severe disabilities. We are extremely grateful for all that we have gained from these experiences.

Thanks to Teresa Callahan for ongoing assistance and support in editing the many versions and editions of this text. Others who have provided us with ideas, challenges, and fresh perspectives on life, people, and this work include Katie Banzhaf, Melinda Mast, Norciva Geddie, Penny Balicki, Rona Leitner, Joy Hopkins, Joan Sweeney, Ellen Condon, Brenda Carson, Milton Tyree, Sarah Wooden and everyone with Training in Systematic Instruction (TSI) in Britain, Karl Elling Ellingsen with VISAR and the trainer's group in Norway, the members of the Ohio Systematic Training Coalition, Steve Zider, Nanci Rhoads Gilbert, Jan Nisbet, Charlie Galloway, Andrew Cosel, Michael and Ronne Cosel, Wade Hitzing, Jack Pealer, John Winnenberg, Sandy Landis, and Pete Flexer.

We also emphasize that many of our most valuable lessons and experiences have been shared with us by people with disabilities and their families. These individuals have served as our mentors and teachers and include Steve Ninemyer; Kim Mitchell; Michael Holsombeck; Ron, Cheryl, and Laurel Volk; Jim, Rosie, and Nick Reed; Cynthia Koch and Kristin Irons; Matt, Eva, and Tom Rettig; Tom, Mary, and Aaron Ulrich; and Whitney Coe.

From Brad, thanks also go to his main sources of support and encouragement: Sydney, Skylar, Ethan, Colin, and Jennifer.

Thanks also go to Theresa Donnelly of Brookes Publishing for believing in the value of this project. We also thank Jennifer Kinard for her good-natured support and editorial assistance. We are also grateful that she did not laugh at us when we made promises about the "absolute last day" that we would have this manuscript ready. And, finally, to Christa Horan, who cheerfully pointed out every typo and patiently waited for responses to her many telephone calls. We appreciate her persistence and insistence on quality.

We also gratefully acknowledge the scores of organizations and thousands of individuals who have participated with us in keeping the work and spirit of Marc Gold alive.

This work ultimately is dedicated to
the lasting presence of Marc Gold,
a visionary whose influence continues to live on in each of us.

Keys to the Workplace

I

Knowing, Believing, and Doing

The Role of Values in Employment

If maximized opportunities for independent and interdependent community living is the ultimate destination for all individuals with severe disabilities, then values must be the road map. From the observation of many individuals, the field of human services—and the values that drive the system—is in a significant state of flux (Schwartz, 1992). What is changing? During the 1980s, the field of human services began to embrace a preference for "community" in the lives of people with disabilities (Bradley, 1994; Schwartz, 1992). This commitment continues. What is changing within the field is a subtle yet powerful movement toward a new definition of community (Bradley, 1994; Knoll & Racino, 1994).

In the past, paid professionals were perceived as diviners of truth. Decisions regarding how, when, and where individuals would be included in the community were dictated largely by clinical judgment, board policy, the professional literature, and the espoused positions of professional agencies. The individual preferences and perspectives of planning teams were heavily influenced by professionals paid to "serve" individuals with disabilities. The change: Human services professionals are now beginning to listen intently to individuals with disabilities as they articulate *their own* individually determined definitions of what is important in community. The role of the professional in human services has, therefore, become more akin to one of a facilitator, a supporter, or a broker—dictated by the vision and preferences of the individual with disabilities. The implications of this new direction are momentous. In this context, human services professionals must join individuals with disabilities—not leading, not following, but working together.

This book focuses on the processes involved in ensuring meaningful and personalized employment opportunities for individuals with severe

1

disabilities. This process involves a methodical blending of two ingredients: 1) the facilitation of personalized supports that emanate naturally from the organizational culture and 2) the skillful use of systematic instruction in a manner that fosters increased levels of work-related skills and performance *and* increased connections between the employee with disabilities and the routines and customs of the workplace.

Section I addresses the critical interaction between values and the process of planning services and supports for individuals with severe disabilities. Chapter 1 provides a retrospective view of the changing role of human services. These changes are analyzed from the perspective of how changes in societal values are reflected in the ways that services are organized and provided. Chapter 2 presents some basic values and directions that should guide planning discussions regarding services and supports for individuals with severe disabilities. The focus of these values is a strong commitment to accepting and honoring the personal histories and dreams of individuals and viewing the role of human services as one of support and assistance in ensuring that these visions and dreams become a reality. Chapter 3 provides an overview of the role that supports play in the lives of all people and the degree to which this issue directly affects the opportunities for employment for individuals with severe disabilities. Two sources of support that have become prominent in the professional literature are family members and friends. Chapter 4 addresses the role that families can play in facilitating employment and in enriching the quality of life for individuals with disabilities. Chapter 5 extends this discussion to include how friendships and relationships affect individuals with disabilities in the workplace.

An important point that is emphasized is that the principles and strategies outlined in Section I apply to all of us—whether or not we have a label. Equally important, however, is the need for communities to work from a position that does not accept a double standard in regard to the availability of living conditions, opportunities, or experiences for individuals with severe disabilities. The availability of supports from a variety of sources, both inside and outside of the human services network, will bring clarity to this vision of community in the lives of people with disabilities.

Values and Employment

—🔑 **1** 🔑—

Concepts and principles can help us to get from one place to another, to move closer to a vision of society based on enduring human values like freedom, community, equality, dignity, and autonomy. Yet they must be viewed in historical context. The concepts that guide us today can mislead us tomorrow.

S. Taylor, 1988, p. 51

If there is one enduring feature that characterizes the issues and controversies that surround individuals with severe disabilities, it is the intense level of emotion and opinion that often emanates from discussions about the "right way" to organize and provide supports and services. Opinions are consistently strong and deep as individuals with disabilities, families, and professionals express their personal perspectives about the most effective strategy for meeting the diverse needs of these individuals. This phenomenon has been especially evident in discussions regarding the definition and delivery of employment-related supports and services. In spite of the many opinions expressed, several questions persistently are asked:

- Should sheltered workshops continue to be an option for individuals with severe disabilities (Schuster, 1990; Weiner-Zivolich & Zivolich, 1995)?
- What expectations are appropriate when discussing wages and fringe benefits for people with severe disabilities who are employed in the private sector?
- How does the human services system meet the expanding need for community job trainers (McGaughey, Kiernan, McNally, Gilmore, & Keith, 1995; Wehman & Kregel, 1995)?
- What is the role of natural supports in the process of employment (Nisbet & Hagner, 1988)?
- When is it appropriate to use systematic instruction as a tool for employment facilitation, and how can this technology be effectively integrated into the culture of the workplace (Callahan, 1993)?

These questions and the surrounding debate become even more significant considering that employment as an outcome for people with severe dis-

3

abilities is a relatively new phenomenon. In the mid-1970s, there was virtually *no* discussion in this area (Pomerantz & Marholin, 1977). Sheltered workshops and activity centers were the only option, and acceptance of this approach generally was widespread among parents and professionals. Since that time, however, the landscape of thought has changed regarding the kinds of opportunities that should be available to people with severe disabilities. As a result, these individuals can now secure and maintain employment and realize many benefits including the opportunity to work alongside other members of the community; earn a paycheck; and experience new levels of freedom, opportunity, and responsibility.

Over this 20-year period, discussions about the "right way" to provide employment services have occurred against the backdrop of overall philosophical changes in several key areas:

- Changes in our view of individuals with severe disabilities
- Changes in our view of "community"
- Changes in organizing and providing supports and services

Readers of this chronology of events, particularly those who were participants in part or all of the process, may remark that this account is incredibly oversimplified and unsophisticated as a description of history. The purpose of this description is not to document the "History of Employment Services for Individuals with Severe Disabilities." Rather, it is to illustrate that the development of those values and ideas that drive the human services machinery continually emerge and change as the years pass. Furthermore, it is to illustrate that no matter how bright and creative we think we are today, we can always do more, and we can always do it better. We hold the hope that in 5 or 10 years we will laugh at the things we are doing today . . . and 10 years after that . . . and 10 years after that . . .

CHANGES IN OUR VIEW OF INDIVIDUALS WITH SEVERE DISABILITIES

From its inception, the field of human services has been based, to a large extent, on a model predominated by an emphasis on deviance (Gold, 1980b). Through the use of standardized, norm-referenced evaluation procedures, people with disabilities are given labels that *presumably* define their abilities, their potentials, and the limits that will be imposed on their futures. This traditional approach to providing supports for individuals with disabilities is based on several *faulty* assumptions:

1. The label that a person is given is a valid guide to the types of services and supports that will best meet that individual's needs (i.e., homogeneity of labeled groups) (O'Brien & Mount, 1991).

2. The skill limitations that an individual may demonstrate are the best indi-
    cators of his or her individual need for supports and services—even in the
    absence of information about the individual's gifts, skills, and capacities
    (O'Brien & Mount, 1991).
3. Trained (i.e., certified or licensed) professionals possess the greatest
    capability to identify and provide those services and supports that would
    best meet the needs of individuals with disabilities (Gretz, 1992).
4. People with disabilities must acquire and consistently demonstrate cer-
    tain prescribed skills and competencies before they can "earn" the oppor-
    tunity to become valued, participating members of the community.
5. It is unlikely that "typical" community members could have any interest
    or ability in establishing an enduring friendship or peer relationship with
    an individual who happens to have a disability.
6. Only trained human services staff members can effectively deal with the
    impact of disability.

Many people may always view individuals with disabilities from a
"deviance" perspective; however, many traditional perceptions, values, and
beliefs regarding people with severe disabilities are undergoing dramatic
change. This change has been characterized as being part of a "conceptual
revolution" (Schwartz, 1992). During this revolution, traditionally valued sensibilities and assumptions are openly challenged, refuted, and disproved. On
a daily basis, increasing numbers of professionals, families, advocates, and
individuals with severe disabilities are openly challenging any status quo
assumptions that promote segregation, isolation, or decreased expectations. In
a spirit of hopefulness, creativity, and expansive thinking, a new set of
assumptions is being forged. This new set of assumptions advocates that individuals with severe disabilities should have friendships and relationships, services and supports, daily routines and experiences, employment opportunities, and guarantees regarding individual rights and protection from harm.

A. Friendships and Relationships
1. Opportunities to establish and maintain friendships and relationships
    with a variety of other community members (Gretz, 1992)
2. Opportunities to form relationships and make those connections that
    will lead to greater levels of autonomy, choice, and independence
    (Beeman, Ducharme, & Mount, 1989; O'Connell, 1988)
3. Opportunities to associate with individuals who accept and value
    their capacities, strengths, and talents (O'Brien & Mount, 1991;
    Snow, 1992)

B. Services and Supports
1. Access to support services from agencies that view inclusive work
    and living as integral rather than component services (Nisbet &

Callahan, 1987a; Sinott-Oswald, Gliner, & Spencer, 1991; Smull & Bellamy, 1991)

2. Access to services that meaningfully replace any services offered by traditionally segregated services (Taylor, 1987)
3. Services and supports that will be available, as necessary, throughout an individual's lifetime (O'Brien & O'Brien, 1994)
4. Services that are planned and provided in a goal-directed fashion (Smull & Bellamy, 1991)
5. Access to services that coordinate and cooperate with any existing natural supports that may affect successful living and working (Rucker, 1987)

C. Daily Routines and Experiences
1. Daily routines that closely approximate those of other members of the community and that reflect personal lifestyle preferences (Klein, 1992)
2. Access to expectations, activities, and instructional experiences that are chronologically age appropriate (Brown, Branston, Hamre-Nietupski, Pumpian, et al., 1979)
3. Instructional experiences that focus on acquiring skills that are functional and meaningful to the individual (Brown, Branston, Baumgart, et al., 1979; Brown, Branston, Hamre-Nietupski, Pumpian, et al., 1979)
4. Participation in inclusive community settings in accordance with natural proportions (Brown, Nietupski, & Hamre-Nietupski, 1976; Brown et al., 1987)
5. Expectations that assume an ability to perform or learn any meaningful activity that is typically performed by same-age peers without disabilities (Brown, Branston, Hamre-Nietupski, Pumpian, et al., 1979)

D. Employment Opportunities
1. Opportunities to fully participate in decisions regarding various employment options (Hagner & Dileo, 1993; West & Parent, 1992)
2. Access to the supports and services that will facilitate employment opportunities in the community (Callahan, 1992; Rehabilitation Act Amendments of 1992; Rusch, Chadsey-Rusch, & Johnson, 1991; Weiner-Zivolich & Zivolich, 1995)
3. Commensurate wages and other benefits for work performed (Bellamy et al., 1984)

E. Individual Rights and Protection from Harm
1. Direct involvement in all activities and decisions that affect their lives (Biklen, 1988; Gerry & Mirsky, 1992; Klein, 1992)
2. A choice among varied services based on their responsiveness to individually identified needs, goals, and desires (Guess, Benson, &

     Siegel-Causey, 1985; Kennedy, Killius, & Olson, 1987; West & Parent, 1992)

3. Humane and nonaversive services and treatment from caring and appropriately trained personnel (Donnellan & Cutler, 1991; McGee, Menousek, & Hobbs, 1987)

4. Evaluations designed and used only for the purpose of gaining the information that is necessary to facilitate meaningful opportunities (Schuler & Perez, 1991)

    This list includes many of the values and principles that are critically important in the design and delivery of supports and services for individuals with severe disabilities. What is infinitely more important than such a list, however, is the opportunity to see these principles become real in people's lives. It is unfortunate that in the field of human services more energy often is spent selecting the precise wording of a policy statement than ensuring that appropriate services are available to the people whom that statement is designed to protect and benefit. It is certainly important to take the time and effort to articulate those critical principles that should serve as the guiding force in supporting and serving people with severe disabilities. We also must commit ourselves to exploring strategies that will ensure meaningful outcomes to larger numbers of people. Although there have been pronounced changes in the way society views people with disabilities, we must consider to what degree these changes have been translated into new opportunities. This chapter emphasizes the issues and strategies that affect the attainment of desired employment outcomes by individuals with severe disabilities.

AVAILABILITY OF EMPLOYMENT
OUTCOMES AND OPPORTUNITIES

What evidence is there to indicate that members of the community at large and human services agencies have altered their views and expectations regarding people with severe disabilities? Three possible responses to this question are 1) the emergence of employment as a desired outcome for individuals with disabilities, 2) the growing impetus for the use of naturally occurring supports in the workplace, and 3) enhanced awareness of quality-of-life outcomes that result from the opportunity to work.

The Emergence of Employment
as a Desired Outcome for Individuals with Disabilities

There was a time in our recent past when sheltered employment was the only option (Mcloughlin, Garner, & Callahan, 1987; Pomerantz & Marholin, 1977; Schuster, 1990). Now, supported employment has become a frequently discussed alternative for individuals with severe disabilities. Consider, for example, the following encouraging excerpt from PL 102-569, the Rehabilitation Act Amendments of 1992:

> (A) Individuals with disabilities, including individuals with the most severe disabilities, are generally presumed to be capable of engaging in gainful employment and the provision of individualized vocational rehabilitation services can improve their ability to become gainfully employed.
> (B) Individuals with disabilities must be provided with the opportunities to obtain gainful employment in integrated settings.
> (C) Individuals with disabilities must be active participants in their own rehabilitation programs, including making meaningful and informed choices about the selection of their vocational goals and objectives and the vocational services they receive. (Section 121 [a][1])

This federal legislation provides a positive and optimistic emphasis on employment for individuals with severe disabilities. To what extent, however, is this optimistic legislative view reflected in agencies and service systems across the United States? The answer to this question provides a good news and bad news scenario: Although data indicate that increasing numbers of individuals with disabilities are participating in supported employment programs, it is difficult to assess the degree to which this trend has affected overall continued enrollments in sheltered work environments (West, Revell, & Wehman, 1992). In addition, it is important to note that "individuals with severe disabilities" are *less* likely than other groups of individuals with disabilities to be considered "eligible" for supported employment services (Kregel & Wehman, 1989). So, although there may be individual agencies that are making attempts to downsize their sheltered workshop services or beginning the process of conversion to a supported employment emphasis, these results have not been observed at a national level to the extent that large numbers of individuals are gaining employment in the community (McGaughey et al., 1995). A comprehensive study by West et al. (1992) yielded the following findings:

> Although there has been growth in the number of supported employment provider agencies, the majority have added supported employment as a service option without decreasing funding, staff, or other resources to alternative segregated day services. Less than one fourth of provider agencies have shifted any resources and downsized alternative day services in order to offer supported employment. This finding confirms *that the majority of provider agencies are filling available supported employment slots while maintaining segregated day services as the primary focus.* (p. 234, emphasis in original)

This finding may indicate that although agencies are beginning to acknowledge and realize the advantages that supported employment can provide, the necessary shift in resources at the agency level continues to be a slow and arduous process (Wehman & Kregel, 1995). This slow evolution is, perhaps, a reflection of both political and financial struggles that often occur within the context of publicly funded agencies and systems (Kendrick, 1994).

The Growing Impetus for the Use of
Naturally Occurring Supports in the Workplace

The growing impetus for the use of naturally occuring supports in the work-place suggests that co-workers, supervisors, and mentors of individuals with severe disabilities can play an increased rolé in facilitating employment. This natural assistance may have an impact on various aspects of the employment process including the identification of employment opportunities, compatibility between the applicant and the workplace, the development and use of task adaptations and modifications, job training support, and general work-site support (Rogan, Hagner, & Murphy, 1993).

The use of natural supports acknowledges that individuals with severe disabilities do not require assistance only from highly trained personnel. It is possible for "regular" people to assist these individuals in much the same way as other members of the community provide assistance and support to one another. In other words, the mystique of disability is, perhaps, being slowly diminished. (Refer to Chapter 6 for an in-depth discussion of the Seven-Phase Sequence, a strategy for supports planning and decision making within the context of a work environment.)

Enhanced Awareness of Quality-of-Life Outcomes
that Result from the Opportunity to Work

With the move into community employment, researchers and practitioners have started to focus their attention on the issues of job satisfaction, social relationships in the workplace, career movement, and earnings as they relate to life outside of the workplace (Rusch, Johnson, & Hughes, 1990; Shafer, Banks, & Kregel, 1991; Test, Hinson, Solow, & Keul, 1993; Wilson & Coverdale, 1993). This is an interesting and encouraging development. When considering supported employment, work must be perceived as an integral part of the person's overall life experience. In this context, work becomes more than simply a service provided by an agency. Workers become more than the recipients of services. As a result, there is now a widened view of the lives of people with severe disabilities; planning activities related to vocation and career go well beyond "job placement" and acknowledge the many ways that lives can be varied and enriched. (See Chapter 2 for a more detailed discussion of values and planning activities.)

Finally, a changing view of individuals with disabilities has resulted in a transfer of "ownership" for planning and decision making and ultimately in the impact of disability. In this capacity, consumers of employment-related services are provided with the opportunity to make decisions regarding a choice of occupations, agency and training staff, training and support methods, and whether to keep a job or resign (West & Parent, 1992). When people assume ownership of decisions regarding their employment, agency personnel are placed in a role of providing advice, technical support, and consultation.

A new type of relationship is formed with a service system in which people are empowered to express, follow, and own their dreams. Consumers and agency personnel become partners in the process of employment. The dreams expressed by the consumer may not be compatible with the philosophies or directions that agency personnel would choose. The tension that results from this new relationship may sometimes result in frustration or failure. The excitement, however, also can result in facilitating new and interesting outcomes that benefit many individuals with disabilities—based on the nature of their individual dreams and goals.

CHANGES IN OUR VIEW OF "COMMUNITY"

Community as a Place

At a time when institutions, segregated schools, and sheltered workshops were the prominent options of the near-sacred continuum of services, opponents and critics of these settings began to correctly suspect that instructional opportunities should incorporate several key components that could not be achieved within isolated or artificial environments (Brown et al., 1986; Brown et al., 1983). Based on this important hypothesis, it was suggested that, to be effective, instructional experiences for individuals with severe disabilities must be "community based." During this formative period, however, community-based instruction was defined primarily by the *location* of instructional experiences. Furthermore, by definition, there was a primary emphasis placed on those skills and competencies that individuals with severe disabilities should be able to demonstrate under certain prescribed conditions. Although these early efforts at community-based instruction promoted an expressed emphasis on the use of "natural cues and consequences," there was relatively little consideration given to the personal, social, or relational aspects of community life. Personal and social skills were portrayed as components of a curriculum rather than as enriching and valued components of a quality life experience.

After this initial movement from facility-based instruction to community-based instruction, the term "community" became synonymous with a rather loosely defined genre of services. Community-based services, like their facility-based counterparts, primarily were defined by the context of their geographic location. Consider, for example, the following definition:

> "Community support services" is used to refer to services to individuals that support them in their adjustment in the community, and services to care providers or natural family members that support them in their attempts to provide necessary care and nurturance for mentally retarded individuals. . . . The services necessary to accomplish this goal fall into several broad categories: education and

training, day activity, leisure, medical care, psychological counseling, and specialized therapies. (Willer, Scheerenberger, & Intagliata, 1980, p. 17)

An understanding of the shape of human services, circa 1980, can be gleaned from this description of "community support services." These services were described as a means to assist individuals with disabilities as they adjusted to life in the community. This phrasing suggests in some fashion, however, an emphasis on providing services to "care providers or natural family members" as they, in turn, worked to provide support to the individual with a disability. This perspective fails to establish any direct connection between the individual with disabilities and other members of the community (other than family members and paid staff members). The role defined here for a person with a disability primarily is that of a recipient of services in a location different from a segregated setting. There is no real emphasis placed on the possibility of extended social relationships or friendships. Once again, it must be noted that this description was made during a formative stage in the move from institutional programs to community opportunities, but it captures an important phase in the development of services and supports for individuals with severe disabilities.

It should be noted that the initial movement from instructional experiences in segregated settings to community-based instruction was a critically important event in the development of services for individuals with severe disabilities. This and other events, in addition to revolutionizing many of the established perceptions regarding instruction, made many families and human services professionals vitally aware of the value and insight that can come from challenging the status quo. Through this process of challenge, new discoveries and new potentials can be identified and realized. This has ultimately become the trademark of services and options for individuals with severe disabilities: progress through challenging and questioning "what we know" to a level that expands "what we do."

Community as an Experience, an Association, a Relationship

The field of human services has started to assign different and more personal meanings to the term "community." The community is no longer seen as simply a *place* in which people live, learn, and work (McKnight, 1990; O'Brien & O'Brien, 1993; Perske, 1993; Wetherow, 1992). Although there continues to be a strong commitment to the belief that people with disabilities must be provided with the opportunity to participate in varied community settings, *community* itself is now portrayed in terms of friendships, relationships, and meaningful connections with a variety of people (Beeman et al., 1989; Mount, Beeman, & Ducharme, 1988a, 1988b; O'Brien & O'Brien, 1992; O'Connell, 1988).

Under the auspices of the "old" definition of community, professionals were committed to teaching individuals with disabilities the skills necessary to participate in a wide variety of community environments. Although there was an implicit commitment to encouraging individuals with severe disabilities to be active participants in their communities, enhanced skill levels were viewed as a means of gaining and maintaining access to those environments and any relationships that may have subsequently been formed in those environments. Furthermore, the skills that would contribute to those relationships would be taught by human services personnel.

The current definition assumes a much more personal interaction between an individual and the community. It is not enough to be able to demonstrate certain skill repertoires within a prescribed physical setting. There is now a realization that it is critical to be a *valued member* of that community, to *share the varied places* that others frequent, to *make decisions* about what is important, and to *grow and develop* in the number and variety of relationships that are experienced (O'Brien, 1987b).

It is difficult to capture in writing the true essence of this somewhat nebulous construct of "community." For each of us, community is embodied in the feelings that we have about our own life experiences, the nature of the individual supports that we require and have available, our relationships with family and friends, the places that we can go where people know more about us than simply our names (if we mutually choose to further establish that relationship), and even opportunities to be alone if we *choose* to be alone. Community is much more than an established list of criteria. Much of what comprises community is difficult to define because of its subjective, individually defined, value-oriented, and uniquely personal nature. The great irony is that although community can only be defined in relation to individual preferences and needs, it can really only ever be achieved in the presence of other people.

Perske (1993), long an observer of the relationship between human services and the lives of the people affected by those services, developed a list of observations about friendships. It can be said that the varying degrees of intimacy, support, warmth, protection, and connection that come from friendships are the core ingredients of the community experience. Perske, in this list, has cogently captured the vast expanse and the limitations of friendships in all of our lives:

- Friendship is a familiar but elusive term.
- Families provide things that friends cannot.
- Families can be limiting.
- Friends can stretch us beyond our families.
- Human services workers can do things friends cannot do.
- Friends help people move beyond human services goals.
- Friends help people rehearse adult roles.
- Friends serve as fresh role models.
- Professionals cannot program friendships.
- The quality of friendships differs in males and females.
- Many aspects of friendships are mysterious.

- A healthy ebb and flow of friends may be more important than "best friends" and lifetime commitments.
- Friendships are reciprocal.
- Good friendships generate their own energy.
- A good friendship is noticeable.
- A good friendship can be attractive.
- Each friendship is unique and unrepeatable.
- Friendships become a haven from stress.
- Some people in authority may frown on friendships.
- Friends are no big deal. (pp. 1–6)

Following is a story about two young women and their experiences with community that serves to connect this discussion to the issue of employment.

Mary and Alice are two young women with disabilities. Both of these young women are employed at a retail store. In the 6 months that Mary and Alice have been employed at the store, they have established many close friendships with their co-workers. This has been a good place to work. Mary and Alice are getting the number of work hours per week that they need financially, they are able to perform their assigned work tasks with skill and accuracy, and they also have a great deal of fun talking and laughing with their friends.

The store that employs Mary and Alice changes management personnel on a frequent basis. The most recent manager decided that it would be necessary to cut costs in order to keep the business in operation. There was a great deal of discussion among the workers about what these cost-cutting measures might be and how they would affect individual employees. Rumors became a frequent fact of life. One of these rumors became a reality when Mary and Alice were given notice of termination from their positions. Conversations with the owners and the managers seemed to focus on the feeling that it was not good for business to have "handicapped people" working in the store.

The manager used the term "handicapped" to describe Mary and Alice. Their co-workers no longer saw them in that manner; the words that they would use to describe Mary and Alice included friends, co-workers, "that girl with dark hair who works in the stock room," or "the young woman who sweeps the aisles—the one who always laughs at my jokes." All of these descriptions and more without using the words "handicapped" or "disabled."

The staff members at the store were outraged when they learned that the store manager planned to terminate the employment of Mary and Alice. What made them most angry was that this decision was made on the basis of their perceived disabilities and not on the basis of their value as employees. In response to those feelings, several of the workers at the store decided to have an informal meeting at a local bar after work. At this meeting, a strategy was developed that included sharing this entire story with the local newspaper.

After the meeting, a few of the workers volunteered to approach the newspaper with information regarding the pending layoffs of Mary and Alice. The newspaper was very much interested in this story, particularly in light of the coverage that they had recently provided on the passage of the Americans with Disabilities Act!

After meeting with a reporter at the newspaper office, another meeting was held with the store manager. In this meeting, several of the employees shared information about their meeting with the newspaper reporter. They informed the manager that if Mary and Alice were terminated from their positions because of their "handicaps," then the newspaper would provide full and extensive coverage of that important event. Needless to say, the store management was caught by surprise and found it necessary to make yet another important business decision. A decision was made that Mary and Alice should keep their jobs.

The most important aspect of this story about Mary and Alice is that human services professionals (who may have wanted to become involved in this situation as a means of protecting the employment of these two women) were not invited to participate in this process. They only happened to hear about this story much later during a casual conversation in the break room with store employees. Those who worked at the store did not really view this whole thing as a "big deal." They also did not feel the need to seek the advice or involvement of human services professionals. They decided to get involved in the lives of Mary and Alice, two individuals whom they valued as friends and co-workers—much as they would do for one another. It seems clear that Mary and Alice were truly valued as members of the group. Stories like this one are the essence of the "new" community for people with disabilities.

Community is largely about feelings and the security that comes from being "members of one another" (O'Brien & O'Brien, 1993). Pealer, Landis, and Winnenberg (1992) focused on the images and experiences that depict and capture the nature of a connected and interdependent life in "community." Think about the feelings and emotions that these images evoke. It may also be helpful to think about the people, places, experiences, friendships, relationships, associations, and so forth that form your own individual experience of being in community:

- Having your co-workers throw a surprise birthday party for you after you all "clock out" for the night
- Always having the coffee pot on because people stop in often and visit
- Sharing dinner together and making a party out of washing the dishes
- Getting a job for someone who has been waiting for a chance to have full-time work

- Getting your first apartment at 21 with a kid you went to high school with—you were the kid in the "multiply handicapped" class, he was the volunteer from the honors program
- Sitting around looking at photos and telling, listening to, and remembering the stories
- Knowing your newspaper carrier by name and having her know yours
- Getting to hold and rock to sleep your neighbor's grandchildren when they come to visit, even though some people still treat you as a dangerous person
- Sitting on a front porch on a street full of front porches, chatting softly with your neighbor on a summer night

These are ordinary things—everyday events. They are examples of the rich pleasure and pain that accompany people living together in community. In their simplicity and variety, these ordinary things represent the kinds of experiences that people with developmental disabilities will increasingly come to have as the vision of community living becomes more real for them. (Pealer et al., 1992, pp. 29–31)

As a result of this redefinition of community, professionals have shifted their attention from simply teaching skills to assisting in the facilitation of friendships and relationships. Gretz (1993) described her experiences in making connections between people with disabilities and others within the community:

The stories that unfolded as people with disabilities and other citizens from their communities came together . . . challenged the very foundation of my human service world. Those who were once clients were now evolving into citizens. Those who were untrained, inexperienced, and, up to now, seen as unwilling were now leading the way for those (including myself) who had viewed themselves as highly professional, experienced, specialized experts. Everyday simple solutions and wisdom replaced professional driven answers. Those who always felt they knew the most knew the least. Specialized training was replaced by human caring. (p. 27)

The Workplace as Community

The redefinition of community and the heightened emphasis on the natural elements of supports have significant implications for facilitating employment opportunities. As a starting point, consider that employment in the community is a desired outcome for individuals with disabilities (where they can be valued members and serve a productive role). The complication that occurs in this scenario is that work environments are somewhat unique in that participants are expected to maintain prescribed levels of performance (e.g., production rates, core job tasks, assigned responsibilities) in order to maintain membership (i.e., employee status) and related benefits (i.e., wages). The workplace presents itself both as an environment that has a rich variety of potential social interactions, friendships, and relationships and as an environment that maintains certain performance expectations (i.e., the tasks that compose the job).

From a differing perspective, we must ask the question, "What is the best way to provide supports to individuals with severe disabilities within the context of a community work environment?" There is a growing body of professional literature that endorses and encourages the notion of using natural supports as a primary means of maintaining employment. Rogan et al. (1993) have defined these "natural supports" as

> any assistance, relationships, or interactions that allow a person to secure, maintain, and advance in a community job of his or her choosing in ways that correspond to the typical work routines and social actions of other employees and that enhance the individual's social relationships. (p. 275)

This definition and other descriptions of the "naturalization of supports" emphasize the role of co-workers, supervisors, and mentors as sources of assistance (Callahan, 1992; Fabian, Edelman, & Leedy, 1993; Hagner, 1992; Hagner & Dileo, 1993; Hagner, Rogan, & Murphy, 1992). Although natural supports have become somewhat popular as a recommended means of facilitating employment, discussions regarding the use of systematic instruction in the workplace have dramatically declined (Hagner & Dileo, 1993). One of the primary issues that is discussed in this chapter is the need to reach a balance between the use of natural features of supports and the individual need for systematic instruction. This premise is based on the belief that natural features of support are a critical ingredient for gaining access into the culture and community of the workplace. There are occasions, however, when natural supports must be augmented by effective systematic instruction procedures. The emerging challenge, as is defined and discussed in this chapter, is identifying and appropriately using natural supports and instructional technology in response to the identified needs of the learner and the culture of the workplace.

CHANGES IN ORGANIZING AND PROVIDING SUPPORTS AND SERVICES

The expectations and values held by community members and agencies have a significant influence on the type, quantity, location, and direction of the supports and options available to individuals with severe disabilities. Not so long ago, the only options available to individuals with severe disabilities were limited to living at home with their families or in large congregate settings—participating in segregated school programs, adult day activities, or sheltered workshops. In general, these settings provide limited opportunities for participants to exercise involvement in community. There also are reduced opportunities in these segregated settings for individuals with disabilities to exercise self-determination, decision making, or personal choice regarding many lifestyle issues (Hagner & Dileo, 1993; West & Parent, 1992). In some communities, it is unfortunate that institutional settings, segregated school programs, adult care activities, or sheltered workshops remain the predominant service options for individuals with severe disabilities.

In times past, and indeed even today in some locations across the United States, people with disabilities often were viewed merely as the "recipients" of services. Decision makers employed by the human services system were charged with the responsibility of allocating available resources, articulating the "agency's" view of the world as contained in a statement of program philosophy, informing individuals with disabilities and their families about what would be the "best placement," and performing the myriad of administrative and bureaucratic tasks required to keep an organization in compliance with regulatory requirements.

We were involved in a project designed to generate strategies that encourage the employment opportunities for individuals with severe disabilities (Mcloughlin et al., 1987). Looking back on that work from today's perspective, much of the emphasis of those well-intentioned strategies centered around a theme of "one directional decision making." In that paradigm, professionals and other people in positions of power made decisions on behalf of others without benefit of personal information or full consideration of their desires, dreams, or wishes. Job development and employment training were conceptualized as highly professionalized procedures involving specific organizational approaches and instructional technologies. Although most of the information contained in that text remains relevant, we have come to realize the critical importance of encouraging personal choice for and receiving direction from people with disabilities. In addition, we have recognized the necessity of incorporating various natural features of support and the values of the workplace culture into the process of employment. Therefore, this update became necessary.

In relation to employment opportunities, the human services system must acknowledge the importance of encouraging people with disabilities to exercise control over their own destinies (Kiernan & Stark, 1986; Rehabilitation Act Amendments of 1992). To operationalize this principle, supported employment programs will be required to perform several very basic functions:

- Maintain a value base that acknowledges the right of all individuals, regardless of the perceived significance of their disability, to fully participate in decisions that affect their lives.
- Develop creative strategies for teaching people how to make decisions and communicate choices.
- Routinely require that people with disabilities be included as participants in discussions and meetings regarding alternative employment options.
- Ensure that there are choices to make. Making choices necessarily requires that the individual has several alternatives from which to select

his or her preferred course of action. One of the major roles of supported employment programs, therefore, will be to identify and, if necessary, develop a range of options that can serve as the template for making choices.

We find ourselves in the midst of yet another shift in thinking. This new era of thinking may be the most exciting and invigorating of all of the stages of change and innovation described previously. Smull and Bellamy (1991) summarized these shifts in thinking to include

- A movement away from defining disabilities in terms of perceived limitations of the individual to a view that analyzes and identifies those ecological realities that affect opportunities for community involvement and participation
- A shift from a model based on an individual's "readiness" for employment and community participation to a model that emphasizes the importance of supports and access to opportunity
- A shift from a model that focuses on diagnosis and prescription to a model that is driven by personal choices and preferences
- A shift from total dependence on human services supports to an emphasis on natural supports

The emergence of an approach that acknowledges and values the rights of individuals with severe disabilities to express and realize their personal preferences and goals will greatly affect the manner in which future services and supports are organized and delivered. Whereas it was formerly accepted that "professionals know what is best," emerging models of support place professionals in a role of facilitating, brokering, and arranging those services and supports that match the expressed preferences and goals of the consumer.

A FINAL THOUGHT

These are exciting and challenging times. The relationships among individuals with disabilities, their families, the professionals who are paid to provide services and supports, and members of the community are taking on new dimensions and directions. As individuals from these various groups begin to interact with one another, learn from each other, and collaborate in accomplishing mutually desired outcomes, there is no limit to what can be learned and accomplished. As has been stressed throughout this chapter, however, the driving force behind those efforts must continue to be a strong value base that promotes the dignity and importance of *all* individuals.

Individualized Planning
A Validation of Personal Histories, Dreams, Visions, and Choices

—⚷ **2** ⚷—

Storytellers and listeners benefit from stories in different ways. Each of us comes to a story—and away from it—with different experiences. Each of us focuses on different details. I don't even expect your story to be absolutely accurate historically, because I understand that you, the storyteller, have selected those parts of your story that mean the most to you, that move you the most.

T. Chappell, 1993, p. 70

The initial step in facilitating employment outcomes for individuals with severe disabilities is effective planning. The process of planning must necessarily take into account a variety of factors:

*   The personal history of the individual
*   The dreams and visions that the individual holds for the future
*   The opportunity to make choices regarding services and supports as they relate to identified outcomes

A natural extension of a planning process that values an individual's personal history is acquiring and organizing services and supports in response to identified needs. The lessons that can be learned from this process of planning and responsive action include 1) the importance of planning activities that take full advantage of the individual's strengths and capacities, 2) that efforts should be made to avoid the occurrence or repetition of experiences that are damaging to the individual, 3) that the individual's own version of his or her story should be told, and 4) that the individual's personal history should be viewed as an extremely valuable learning experience for the writer and the potential reader (Ohio Safeguards, 1990a, 1990b). In this chapter, each of these areas of concern is reviewed and analyzed. This analysis focuses on the activities and strategies that can be used to begin the process of planning for community employment.

19

INDIVIDUALIZED PLANNING
FOR PEOPLE WITH SEVERE DISABILITIES

The advent of state and federal legislation designed to protect and define the rights of individuals with disabilities created a mandate for individualized planning activities (e.g., individualized education programs [IEPs], individualized written rehabilitation plans [IWRPs], individual habilitation plans [IHPs]). Regulations governing the implementation of these laws specified the frequency of planning meetings; the participants who should attend those meetings; and the types of discussions, outcomes, and documentation necessary to meet legal and regulatory requirements. These developments, for the most part, can be placed in the "good news" category as the planning procedures laid down in federal regulations are intended to and do protect the rights of individuals with disabilities.

The "bad news," however, is the strong probability that planning meetings can be designed and conducted in a manner that complies with existing regulations but still does not adequately address those issues that are of primary concern to the individual with disabilities. There are a multitude of books, journal articles, and other media that describe and espouse the various rules and philosophies that *should* govern the design and implementation of individualized planning for people with severe disabilities. The real challenge, however, is transforming these principles and philosophies into workable solutions that respond to the needs of individuals—from the perspective of individuals. Our focus in this chapter is specifically related to planning for employment with a strong emphasis on the values that should be infused into that process.

As a starting point for investigating the benchmarks that should guide the process of individualized planning, there must always be a conscious effort to keep the values of the planning participants in sharp focus (Halpern, 1993; Hasazi, 1991; Ohio Safeguards, 1990b). The practice of using valued cultural experiences as a template for assessing individual life experiences typically is included under the rubric of "quality of life." Gold (1982) asked us to consider what constitutes the "good life" as a way of moving toward a functional definition of quality of life. Although it is difficult to capture an abstraction like "quality of life" in a functional definition, seeking to visualize the exact nature of a meaningful life experience replete with certain identified and valued characteristics is a worthwhile pursuit. It also is sometimes helpful for each of us, when thinking about this concept, to personalize that process and then list those experiences, activities, or opportunities that provide for quality in our own lives. At the same time, we must take great care not to superimpose our own individualized definition of a quality life onto the lives of others.

The parameters for quality of life are shared by all people, with or without disabilities. Knowing this, however, does not reduce the complexity of attempting to define or assess quality of life within the specific context of a person's life. Dennis, Williams, Giangreco, and Cloninger (1993), citing the work of Speight, Myers, Cox, and Hughes (1991), described the "optimal theory" view of quality-of-life values and needs. Optimal theory involves the blending of various perspectives on the life of an individual: 1) *the values and needs of the individual* (i.e., a belief that every person is completely unique), 2) *the values and needs shared by all individuals* (i.e., a belief that all humans share certain values and needs), and 3) *the values and needs shared by certain cultural or societal groups and subgroups* (i.e., there are groups of individuals who share certain cultural values, beliefs, and needs).

These three categories of values provide a basis for discussion and consideration of quality-of-life issues as related to the process of individualized planning. It would be beneficial for those individuals involved in planning activities related to the lives of people with disabilities to maintain an awareness of the values and needs described in the optimal theory model or other models describing quality-of-life issues and criteria. When planning the various supports and services that will be of greatest assistance to an individual with disabilities, it is critical to continually reinforce the following principles:

- Each individual has unique personal characteristics that differentiate him or her from every other person. These characteristics may include a disability but certainly also include many other significant gifts, talents, strengths, interests, and values.
- As members of the human community, we share many common and basic needs.
- Each of us is part of a larger cultural group that shares a common language, traditions, customs, and day-to-day practices (Dennis et al., 1993).

Our planning efforts must celebrate the differences and strengthen the bonds that we all share as people.

A SOBERING PERSPECTIVE ON PLANNING

In the course of their busy and active careers, professionals in the field of human services may be asked to participate in literally thousands of team planning meetings. Participants in these meetings, who often include professionals from a variety of disciplines, are asked to assess the needs of an individual with severe disabilities and then identify desired outcomes and describe appropriate services and supports. As described previously, meeting participants are asked to complete a series of documents designed to meet the conditions of various state and federal laws and regulations (e.g., IEP, IWRP, IHP). During these meetings, decisions are often made that will have a direct impact on the life of the individual who is the focus of the discussion.

It would not be an exaggeration to note that planning meetings often can become rather routine and predictable. There are those occasional meetings in which a controversial issue may be discussed or the individual of concern is represented by an aggressive advocate or a well-informed parent. For the most part, however, these meetings are uneventful and predictable. Professionals frequently develop an immunity (or perhaps a numbness) to the critical nature of these processes. This malaise is brought on by the often routinized and standardized activity of individualized planning. Accepting the routine nature of the planning process can, however, be dangerous.

When feelings of apathy or boredom begin to overcome you during a planning meeting, consider how your life might change if all decisions governing your activities and lifestyle were made by a team of professionals. For example, decisions regarding where you live, the skills and competencies that are important to acquire, whether and where you work, the degree of freedom to explore and expand friendships and relationships, daily schedules, the freedom to come and go as you please, the degree of supervision that you "require," and the frequency with which it will be necessary to assess and quantify levels of performance would all be made by a team of paid professionals.

In such a scenario, imagine that family and friends were invited to participate in the planning process, but the structure and format of the meeting were directed by official agency representatives. Your ideas, dreams, wishes, values, goals, and preferences likely would become secondary to the "best thinking" of the team assembled for the planning process. Most of us would be frightened by the prospect of having life decisions made by a "team." There is good reason to be concerned.

As an overriding principle, individuals involved in planning for people with severe disabilities must continually remind themselves of the significance of those activities. Failing to examine all possible options, to explore new and different perspectives, and to stretch the boundaries of what we know and what we do can be a disservice—one that we would not want to have occur in our own lives.

LISTENING TO DREAMS AND VISIONS

Dreams, visions, and personal goals provide the motivation to keep trying for many people. These hopes also strengthen our commitment to exert that extra effort to attain some desired objective or to give just one more try when things seem their worst. For many people with disabilities, however, the notion of dreaming is too often considered to be inconsistent with the realities of rehabilitation and working. Snow (1992) provided a moving argument for encouraging and heeding an individual's dreams for the future:

> Suppose that the person with a disability is the bearer of a deep and creative dream, and that dream has meaning that can be conveyed to you. Suppose that the dream has the power to enrich your life and the lives of others—that it is a dream we all need—one that would strengthen and enrich our families, schools, communities, churches . . . Bend your will and your inner and outer ear to listen to this dream. Walk into the daily activities and environments of life with this person, as dream and reality mix in a creative dance. May you rejoice in all that you create together. (p. 65)

Acknowledging and valuing that all of us have dreams is critical during any discussions about a person's future. Consider the following example of one individual's persistent pursuit of a dream, often against the best wishes of individuals involved in the planning process.

Katri had always talked about wanting to work with young children in a preschool or child care setting. Professionals, upon hearing of this dream, usually responded (among themselves) by saying, "We all understand that Katri has this dream, but it is unlikely that a young adult with a severe disability could ever get a job in a child care program. Let's be more realistic about this plan."

Katri persisted in expressing her personal goals. In a vocational profile planning meeting, the topic of employment outcomes was, once again, reviewed and discussed. Katri, once again, stated her personal vision of working with small children in a child care center. For some reason, members of the planning team finally listened to Katri's dream. Someone suggested that, as a start, maybe Katri could do some volunteer work in a child care setting. As the discussion proceeded, her father commented that Katri had a former neighbor who operated a preschool program close to their home. A follow-up on this suggestion resulted in the opportunity for Katri to work with children for 10 hours per week. She accepted this position on a volunteer basis. These arrangements were compatible with the needs and conditions that were most important to Katri and her family.

Katri learned the tasks involved in working with young children, demonstrated her ability to be a productive team member, and reestablished her relationship with a long-time family friend (and now, supervisor). Katri required some training to perform the tasks required in her new workplace. Her supervisor believed that these skills should be taught by employees of the preschool program and declined to accept the services of a job coach. As time passed, Katri was assisted and encouraged largely by her co-workers. Her work evaluations were very positive, and Katri demonstrated a high level of motivation to learn new skills in the areas that needed improvement. After several months of volunteer employment, Katri was offered a paid position in the child care program as a classroom aide for 30 hours per week. Her dream had been realized. Today she continues as a successful employee of the child care program.

The dreams and goals that people hold in their hearts must be made an important ingredient in the planning and delivery of employment-related services. Taking this step, however, can be very frightening both for people with disabilities and for professional staff members. It requires that members of the planning team make the commitment to accept and personalize the challenges inherent in those dreams and goals.

> I am signing on to assist this individual to achieve the goals that she personally values in her life. My perceptions and ideas about "what is best" are only opinions. Her visions must become my agenda. I am willing to take the risks of not knowing exactly how to achieve those goals and visions, of making mistakes, and of sharing the ultimate responsibility for those plans that may not work out as we had hoped.

In short, listening to people's dreams and committing yourself to share in those dreams often can require a significant degree of personal courage. As Provençal (1987) observed,

> Our profession is not for timid souls, for people who can only function when they hold all the cards. It takes courage, risk, and the ability to . . . labor conscientiously at any level in this field. When I am most effective I have this package. When I am least effective I have been temporarily separated from it. The difference is within me and what I bring to the encounter. The job owes no obligation. It is not my debtor. (p. 80)

WHEN DREAMS CANNOT BE HEARD

It is important to acknowledge two situations that require distinct consideration during the planning process. The first is when the individual who is the focus of the planning process is physically unable to articulate or express his or her visions and dreams. This may be the result of physical disabilities or other conditions that prevent the individual from using verbal language. Not having access to an assistive communication device exacerbates the situation. This unique challenge requires that participants in the planning process take the time and energy to generate strategies for seeking consensus on the true preferences of the individual. This can be accomplished by

• Taking time in the planning process to determine possible strategies for communicating with the individual (e.g., through some varied type of yes/no response mode, a system for pointing or looking at pictures or representations of preferred activities or choices)

- Allocating extended periods of time for sharing experiences (e.g., places, routines, relationships) to gain some perspectives on the subtleties of how this person communicates his or her likes and dislikes, pleasures and pains, and other forms of preference-related concepts. This process should include a means for validating any hypotheses through the use of multiple observers on multiple occasions.
- Using various strategies for seeking the input of close friends and family members who have known the individual for long periods of time and who already possess some firsthand knowledge of the individual's preferences and desires

A second circumstance involves individuals who have the capability to verbally express thoughts and ideas yet who are hesitant or seemingly unable to articulate any representative picture of what they desire for their future. It may be possible that such an individual has never been asked to express an opinion or make decisions in this area of his or her life. When this occurs, it is recommended that the planning participants provide a cautious and patient response that would provide the following types of support and assistance to the individual with disabilities:

- Activities that encourage the individual to make choices
- Activities that develop a bond of mutual trust between the individual with disabilities and planning team members
- A continuing effort to respect the dignity and uniqueness of the individual with disabilities
- Activities that present varied choices from which the individual with disabilities can choose (as opposed to requiring that the individual "invent" alternatives)

In both situations described here, the emphasis is on ensuring that planning results truly represent the preferences and desires of the individual.

VALUING THE UNIQUE NATURE OF AN INDIVIDUAL'S PERSONAL HISTORY

Each of us is the product of his or her own unique personal history. The experiences that we have had, the successes and failures that we have experienced, the skills and competencies that we have acquired, our individual history of pain and exhilaration, and the nature of our relationships with family and friends combine to create who we are today. When planning services and supports for individuals with disabilities, the effects, results, and outcomes of an individual's personal history should be given full acceptance and consideration.

The degree to which the field of human services has valued the personal histories of individuals with severe disabilities has been extremely limited.

Personal histories largely have been represented by descriptions of an individual's performance on standardized tests, placements in special education programs and facilities, various derived diagnoses, and, for those with challenging behaviors, a listing of offenses and transgressions. Once again we must ask whether those of us who are considered to be "normal" or "typical" would be willing to accept a depiction of our lives primarily or only in terms of statistical and numerical facts (e.g., earned grade point averages or class rankings, yearly earnings, performance on the SAT, number of traffic offenses, number of times that a checking account has been overdrawn). Furthermore, would we be willing to accept that a team of professionals is responsible for making decisions about our lives based on those "relevant" facts and figures?

O'Brien and Mount (1991) provided examples of two contrasting personal histories of the same man, Mr. Ed Davis. The history written by an interdisciplinary team of professionals recounted Mr. Davis's psychometric status and the varied labels that he had been given over the years. The recommendation of this team was that Mr. Davis should undergo a complete psychiatric evaluation. This determination was made after a 20-minute meeting. A personal history compiled by a group of friends and family members (after a 2-hour group meeting with the assistance of a facilitator) presents an entirely different perspective of Mr. Davis. This group of individuals recounted many stories from his life, talked about possible ideas for the future, and voiced their commonly shared connection with Mr. Davis. Within 2 weeks, this group of friends and family members had arranged a work schedule for Mr. Davis within the community doing the things that he liked to do: load vending machines, stack firewood, and do lawn work. Each of these activities, it was determined, could be done without the benefit of a complete psychiatric evaluation.

O'Brien and Mount (1991), in an analysis of the two separate descriptions of Mr. Davis, drew several conclusions about the differences between them. They observed that the descriptions of Mr. Davis were constructed using 1) different rules (in the life of Mr. Davis), 2) different purposes (e.g., complying with regulations versus searching for better solutions), 3) different consequences (e.g., referral for a psychiatric evaluation versus employment and acceptance in the community doing something that he really enjoyed in the company of people who really appreciated his gifts), and 4) different assumptions (e.g., How important are the words of professionals? How important are the bonds of friends and family? Do we learn more from listing an individual's limitations or his or her capacities? Do services exist to change the individual or to help and support the individual?). It is critically important that planning team members continually evaluate the rules, purposes, consequences, and assumptions of decisions made about the lives of individuals with disabilities. As a further test, we must always ask ourselves whether we would like the same rules, purposes, consequences, and assumptions applied to our lives.

Miguel had always been labeled as a young man with "behavior problems." At the age of 22, his frequent displays of aggressive behavior were viewed as a significant source of frustration to human services professionals, and he had always been portrayed as a potential threat to the safety of those around him.

No one was really sure how much Miguel understood. He had always been labeled as "severely mentally retarded," but increasingly there had been attention paid to his deafness and his inability to communicate his feelings, preferences, desires, and wishes to those around him. As a means of exploring this area of concern, an assistant had been employed to assist Miguel through communication with gestures and a modified form of sign language. The person hired for this task was a college student who also was deaf. Miguel and his assistant quickly developed a close, caring relationship. Some people noticed that in the presence of the assistant, Miguel had significantly fewer aggressive outbursts. Could it be that Miguel's aggressive behaviors were his only way of communicating with those around him? Is it possible that access to a means of communication provided an opportunity for Miguel to share his thoughts and feelings? Many of the professionals who worked with Miguel on a daily basis were withholding their judgment on these questions.

There were many discussions about what the future might hold for Miguel. Frequent references were made to enrolling Miguel in "the workshop." Miguel's mother was steadfast in her view that Miguel would never attend a sheltered workshop. Her dream for Miguel included an opportunity for employment in the community. This difference of opinion accelerated to the point that attorneys were engaged as spokespersons. It was suggested that as a means of resolving this issue, all interested parties would be invited to participate in the process of personal futures planning (Mount, 1987; O'Brien, 1987b; O'Brien & Lyle, 1988). Through this collaborative approach to planning, it was hoped that a common vision could be forged for Miguel's future.

As varied human services personnel gathered to meet with Miguel, his mother, and his friends from the community, an interesting thing occurred— Miguel's friends began to describe their relationship with him within the context of the community. One friend discussed that he and Miguel attended various sporting events together. Miguel and his friend found great enjoyment from sharing this experience. This revelation was a great surprise to school personnel, and it challenged their limited perceptions of Miguel as an individual with "behavior problems." They now began to perceive Miguel as a "person" *and* as a member of the community.

Another friend of Miguel's described their weekly trips to the mall and lunches at local restaurants. The descriptions of these events revealed the degree to which they were important to both Miguel *and* his friend. The nature of this friendship was described in tender and caring terms. Once again, those human services professionals in attendance were forced to rethink their attitudes and beliefs about Miguel. As an extension of that analysis, there was a renewed spirit among the planning participants. Options for the future were presented and viewed with an increased level of optimism.

Participants in Miguel's personal futures planning session agreed to pursue the option of supported employment. Miguel ultimately was employed by a company that subcontracts office work and copying services for small businesses. Supported employment services were provided in a blended fashion that included systematic instruction on various aspects of required work tasks and a heavy emphasis on encouraging natural supports that could be provided by co-workers. Miguel continues to be a valued employee of this company and a valued friend to many individuals in his community. His "history" of challenging behaviors was a real concern. This part of his history, however, only reflected a small part of Miguel's total identity.

COMMUNITY CONNECTIONS:
ASSOCIATION, MEMBERSHIP, AND BELONGING

One of the primary goals of individualized planning is to increase the intensity, quantity, and quality of the associations, friendships, and relationships between people with severe disabilities and the people and places that comprise their community. In light of this goal, a major issue emerges: What can or should be the role of professionals and agencies in this "new frontier" of community? This movement has great potential for altering the role of a highly professionalized human services system. During an interview with John McKnight, a thought-provoking observer and critic of the human services hierarchy, he made the following observations regarding this issue:

> It seems to me that the major action necessary for a service system to ensure community incorporation of people with disabilities is for the service system to get out of the way. Service systems represent an economic and psychic wall between the community and individuals who [have disabilities].
>
> A serious question that must be asked by people in the service world is, "How can we stop being the boundary for the lives of people with disabilities?" Once we understand this critical question, then the issue is how to get out of the way. This requires some serious thought about the impact on community perceptions of the notion that if you [have a disability], you are owned by service professionals. (Hasazi, 1991, p. 539)

As reflected in the observations of John McKnight and others (Dufresne & Laux, 1994; Knoll & Racino, 1994; McKnight, 1987; O'Connell, 1988; Schwartz, 1992), there are several issues that must be addressed if the service system is to "get out of the way" and break down the wall between individuals with disabilities and the community. As a starting point, there must be a willingness to *trust* the capabilities of the community (Kendrick, 1994; O'Connell, 1988). Professionals frequently propose that the world at large should acknowledge and accept the gifts and capabilities of individuals with disabilities. At the same time, however, there is an apparent level of unspoken mistrust of the community's capability to treat individuals with disabilities in a fair and humane manner; to establish and maintain meaningful, reciprocal friendships and relationships; and to provide various forms of assistance in response to the issues and concerns of daily life. This perception often is extended to include a belief that the community may have capabilities to perform certain functions for people with disabilities but only under the watchful eye of human services professionals (e.g., service coordination). A transformation of thought and action regarding a movement to community will be observed when professionals begin to embrace the fact that regular, ordinary, run-of-the-mill, next-door, down-the-street, untrained, uncertified, unlicensed people can significantly enrich the lives of individuals with severe disabilities. This necessitates trust as a starting point—and there is no substitute.

After developing a trust in the capability of community, the second imperative in building connections is to *invite* a wider range of people to become active participants in the planning process. It makes little sense for a group of human services professionals to sit alone around a table and try to determine the best means to create community connections and supports for an individual with disabilities. Planning, from the outset, must include and involve members of the community. *It is our position that the supply of people in the community who, given the opportunity, would actively participate in the life of a person with disabilities far exceeds the demand for those supports.* What is lacking in the implementation of this equation, however, is the ability of human services personnel to effectively invite the participation of the community. A starting point for all planning discussions should be examining the natural supports that are currently a part of the individual's life. From that point, planning participants can begin to assess the need to augment or intensify support services or to leave well enough alone and be available only as a resource for additional information or consultation on an as-needed basis. It is important to allay the human services inclination to immediately fill any gaps that may exist in an individual's skill or performance repertoire with extreme levels of instructional support and highly trained personnel.

A third factor in the movement toward community connections is an acceptance of the confusion and uncertainty that are just a part of the process. It is not possible to control or predict every possible contingency that may exist in a person's life or in a workplace. Surprising and unexpected events undoubtedly will occur. In response to this uncertainty, several key attitude adjustments are necessary: 1) a willingness to adjust and modify current courses of action, 2) a willingness to be flexible to an entirely new course of action, 3) a spirit of adventure in regard to new and untried solutions (this can be contagious), and 4) a view of each potential "crisis" as a new opportunity.

The final consideration that should be remembered when moving into the community is the bitter reality of time investment. This process will take time. It is unreasonable to assume that workable connections that will last can be built in a short period of time. There is no shortcut to the hard work and energy required for this task. At the same time, however, experience is a great teacher and, over time, effective strategies will emerge.

THE OVERRIDING ISSUE OF PERSONAL CHOICE

That human services professionals provide opportunities for individuals with severe disabilities to exercise personal choice in their lives is an excellent indicator of progress and change in the field. The pervasive trend and practice for professionals or agencies to make decisions "on behalf" of people with disabilities has a long-standing tradition. Guess, Benson, and Siegel-Causey (1985), in an analysis of issues related to personal choice and autonomy among people with disabilities, concluded that

> There exists among many professionals and practitioners the belief that persons with severe disabilities are not capable of making choices and decisions—or at least the kind of choices that attending adults would perceive to be in the best interest of the persons with a handicapping condition. Indeed, the . . . technology used with learners who have severe handicaps has historically been predicated on a deviancy model wherein . . . service providers assume to know what will enable the recipients of these efforts to better function in our society. . . . Necessarily, the act of choosing, and allowing persons with handicaps to make choices and express preferences, carries with it a certain element of risk. Yet, this is what personal autonomy is all about, and persons with handicapping conditions have the same right as others to acquire autonomy. They need to learn, as do persons who are not handicapped, that wrong choices can sometimes have unpleasant consequences. (pp. 79–80)

As a means of examining the issue of choice, visualize a visit to your favorite restaurant. Your choices (i.e., the food items that you have to choose from) are outlined before you in the form of a menu. From this listing, you can exercise personal choice only within a defined range. For example, you may only choose the meat dishes that are listed. At the same time, however, you may have the option to request that your chosen meat dish be cooked in a certain manner (e.g., rare, medium-rare). Depending on the procedures and preferences of the restaurant management, you also may have the choice of certain combinations of side dishes that are offered on the menu. In any event, the choices that you have largely are defined by the constraints imposed by the menu.

At those times when the menu of choices available to us seems to restrict or limit our actions, we must remember that there is always "another way" if we are willing and motivated to look for it (Gold, 1980a, 1980b). For example, in the film *Five Easy Pieces* (Rafelson & Wechsler, 1970), actor Jack Nicholson portrays a man who wants to order a piece of plain white toast in a restaurant. The waitress, who views one of her primary roles as being the defender of the menu, indicates that plain white toast cannot be ordered from the menu. Undaunted by this arbitrary rule, Nicholson proceeds to order a bacon, lettuce, and tomato sandwich on white toast. The waitress is infinitely more comfortable with this conventional order from the menu. Nicholson then proceeds, however, to stipulate that he would like his bacon, lettuce, and tomato sandwich on white toast *without* bacon, lettuce, and tomato (i.e., white toast).

It is not possible for a human services agency to provide a fixed list of services and supports that are responsive to the needs of *all* individuals with disabilities. The menu of choices available to individuals with disabilities varies greatly across geographic locales, agencies, school districts, and individual disabilities. The challenge for planning teams is to make the most creative use of available options and resources *and* to create new and different configurations with those resources. If Jack Nicholson had been in the mood to totally exasperate the waitress, there are a large number of different sandwich combinations that could have been ordered from three different types of bread (e.g., white, rye, wheat) and three different ingredients (e.g., bacon, lettuce, tomato). It seems quite likely that not everyone will like all of the combinations that are created from these available resources. At the same time, however, the greater the number of combinations that are created, the greater the possibility of matching the preferences of an individual customer.

If the human services system is to seriously address the issue of choice in the lives of individuals with severe disabilities, then we must find and use a variety of strategies to seek out the actual preferences, dreams, visions, and choices held by people with disabilities. We cannot assume to know a person's individual preferences unless he or she is given the opportunity to express those preferences. Also, we must view the primary mission of the human services system as assisting people to realize their dreams and exercise their personal choices. Finally, it is critically important that we encourage opportunities for each individual to make decisions and choices about employment issues including preferred occupations, the types of services and supports received from human services agencies and training staff, the methods and intensity of supports, and decisions regarding keeping or resigning from a job (West & Parent, 1992). Allowing people to make these types of decisions about their lives may result in a conflict between the choices that the person with a disability makes and the direction preferred by professionals or family members. The opportunity to choose, however, is a validation of individuals' capacities and capabilities and an indication that we value them for who they are, as they are. This is, perhaps, one of the most important messages that we can ever share with anyone.

Ferguson (1976) summarized the importance of "giving" people control over the choices that guide their lives and the liberation that can occur during this process:

> We are not liberated until we liberate others. So long as we need to control other people, however benign our motives, we are captive to that need. Giving them freedom we free ourselves. And they are free to grow in their own way. (p. 105)

ALLOWING OUR HEARTS TO BE MOVED AND OUR BELIEFS TO BE CHALLENGED

There is strong and overriding emotion that surrounds work in the field of human services. Provençal (1987) eloquently described the intense nature of this phenomenon:

> This business is a mother-lode of hurt. But there is also a terrible beauty within our grasp, if we choose to use the pain and not run from it. Most of us are within just minutes of being moved by the drama of our work, if we put ourselves in position to be moved. It is our obligation to do so. (pp. 82–83)

Accepting the challenge of being moved by the drama of people's lives involves risk. This risk often first emerges during the process of planning when professionals are willing to listen to dreams as they are first expressed, then nurtured, and later formed into a course of action. Participating in the planning process inserts the human services professional into the life of an individual with disabilities in a very unique manner. This involvement can be performed in a detached and impersonal fashion or, if we choose to accept the challenge posed by Provençal, with passion, caring, and active commitment. The former approach requires little investment of personal energy and entails minimal risk. The latter presents an opportunity to acknowledge our own vulnerabilities to the needs of other people. This vulnerability also may extend to acknowledge the limits that exist in our own skills and expertise when juxtaposed against the real-life needs of a person who may have many complex emotional, behavioral, physical, and learning challenges. The risk is heightened even further when we make commitments to overcome those challenges and enhance the opportunities and experiences of the individual. At these times, we come face to face with our own fallibility and ignorance, particularly at those moments when our limited knowledge base does not contain the necessary components to meet these presented challenges.

Another aspect of risk taking occurs when the knowledge and practices that guide professional activity are challenged and overturned by new developments, emerging theories, and promising practices. Responses to newly developed professional practices often are met with resistance and skepticism. This cynicism often is unrelated to the real or perceived validity of the newly developed technique and more frequently is associated with the prospect that a change may be required within the arena of standard practice of the professional (O'Brien, 1987a; Peck, 1991).

The emergence of new technologies does not need to be viewed as a threat to the sensibilities and long-standing beliefs of professionals. It can prove to be an invigorating and renewing factor. This is a certain energy that emanates from a description by Schwartz (1992) of the influence that Marc Gold had on his perceptions, beliefs, and professional experience:

> "Try Another Way" was an expectation-shattering challenge to the beliefs of vocational potential upon which the enterprise of sheltered work was built. [Marc] Gold provoked great excitement as well as great resistance by traveling around the country showing how people with severe retardation, dismissed as having "no vocational potential" and left to rock on some ward, could be quickly taught to perform such complex tasks as assembling an intricate bicycle brake. He did it in front of my eyes in front of an audience of several hundred, with a person whom he had never met before using a simple sorting board. It was astonishing. It was magic. I returned home to the workshop and built a sorting board just like his. I got hold of a bunch of old heavy institutional door locks, took them all apart, broke down the assembly into small gestures, and practiced assembling them so they would work until I knew the job intimately. Then I got Mitch, the person in the workshop whom we all believed to be the least capable of learning there, and who spent all day sanding (often across the grain), and asked him if he would work on putting together locks with me. After a very short time it was completely clear that Mitch could learn to put locks together, tiny reversible parts and all, and that I could teach him to do it. (p. 101)

This experience obviously had a lasting effect on the writer. We can only hope that change also made a difference in the lives of Mitch and others who were formerly viewed as the "least capable." The starting point in this episode was Schwartz's willingness to take a chance and use a promising technique for the purpose of improving the life of another person.

A FINAL THOUGHT

Our obligation should be clear: to provide the best available (i.e., most current, most valid, most responsive) techniques, strategies, and resources to the individuals with disabilities with whom we work. Individuals who step into the role of assisting, advising, or supporting individuals with severe disabilities have a clear responsibility to undertake this obligation. During the initial stages of planning, this responsibility can be observed as active involvement in activities that acknowledge the importance of the process. As plans proceed and the time comes to begin providing supports and services, this responsibility can be observed in a flexible and dynamic approach to selecting strategies and resources. This open, dynamic view acknowledges that we do not have "all of the answers" and that we can always learn new and better ways to do everything.

The Dynamic Nature of Supports

3

If the endeavor of providing individualized support is to succeed, providing support cannot be just an esoteric activity. . . . It must become the core of a new system marked by a clear sense of mission that challenges the current boundaries of what is called human services.

J.A. Knoll and J.A. Racino, 1994, p. 321

Supporting individuals with disabilities as they are included in the community is not a new idea. As described in this chapter, the major changes we are experiencing in human services are not related to a new awareness that people need supports; rather, the changes are related to the manner in which the delivery of supports is being conceptualized, negotiated, and implemented. In simple terms, there is a movement away from "agency services" in the traditional sense (e.g., facility-based program options, certified or licensed personnel as the main source of intervention, undue influence of the diagnostic testing model in the definition of an individual's needs and the response to those needs, a clinical orientation) and a movement toward individualized supports. Luckasson and Spitalnik (1994) observed that this movement has forced human services personnel to look beyond the traditional "one size fits all" mentality that plagued the field for so many years. Instead of talking casually about "slots," "openings," or "programs," each of which carries a connotation of fitting individuals into an existing program or service, we are now thinking about the needs of individuals; the environmental demands of the places they frequent; and the supports that respond to their individually defined strengths, talents, and needs. The first steps are being made to learn more about this process. Within this movement toward a supports-oriented approach, there are many potential benefits that can be realized within the lives of people with disabilities.

The field of human services has slowly acknowledged that appropriate supports are a pivotal component in determining the quality of life available to individuals with disabilities (Bradley, 1994). It has been uplifting to observe the degree to which the term *supports* has crept onto the scene as a central theme in the areas of education, employment, and community living.

In the professional literature, for example, there are many references to supporting individuals with severe disabilities in a variety of community environments and in their associations with the community (Bartholomew-Lorimer, 1993; Bradley, Ashbaugh, & Blaney, 1994; Giangreco & Putnam, 1991; Hagner, 1992; Klein, 1992). At the same time, however, there has been a variety of descriptors used to clarify and specify the exact nature of these supports. For example, in the professional literature there are references to *natural supports* (Callahan, 1992; Gerry & Mirsky, 1992; Nisbet & Hagner, 1988), *indirect supports* (Rogan, Hagner, & Murphy, 1993), *instrumental supports* (Hagner & Dileo, 1993), *formal and informal supports* (Klein, 1992), *individual supports* (Bradley et al., 1994), and *job supports* (Hagner, 1992). Throughout these publications, there is a common vision of *supports* as a range of alternative strategies and resources that can be used to assist individuals with disabilities in the community. In addition, there are several other common themes: 1) strategies for organizing, securing, and providing supports for individuals with disabilities; 2) varied opinions as to the exact nature of appropriate supports, their definition, and their use; and 3) issues and convictions expressed in the professional literature must bear a direct relationship to the concerns of practitioners who deal with this question on a much more basic level—day after day, in the real lives of people with disabilities. Despite a slight degree of cynicism regarding the perpetual gulf that exists between theory and practice, we also would quickly add the need to solidify and approach consensus on a workable model for planning and delivering supports *and* a common terminology for describing supports in terms of how they are provided, by whom, and for what purpose.

SUPPORTS: A NEW VARIATION ON AN OLD THEME

In 1992, the American Association on Mental Retardation (AAMR) issued a new procedural manual designed to describe and define the parameters of mental retardation (Luckasson et al., 1992). This document presents itself as a vast departure from the five previous manuals on the "classification and terminology in mental retardation" (Grossman, 1973, 1977, 1983; Heber, 1959, 1961). The newest definition of mental retardation is as follows:

> *Mental retardation* refers to substantial limitations in present functioning. It is characterized by significantly subaverage intellectual functioning, existing concurrently with related limitations in two or more of the following applicable adaptive skill areas: communication, self-care, home living, social skills, community use, self-direction, health and safety, functional academics, leisure and work. Mental retardation manifests before age 18. (Luckasson et al., 1992, p. 1)

Although not immediately evident from the actual wording of the definition, reviews and commentaries of the supporting documents make frequent references to the "paradigm shift" that has taken place in the *field* of mental retardation (Luckasson & Spitalnik, 1994; Schalock et al., 1994). The significance of this new definition was described by one reviewer in the following manner:

> The publication of the new American Association on Mental Retardation classification manual has brought the definition, and more importantly, AAMR, in line with an evolving paradigm shift referred to by some as the "support revolution" (Schwartz, 1992) in the way people with mental retardation are viewed and served. This paradigm shift, to a large extent grounded in the philosophy of normalization, involves a move away from a defect orientation focused primarily on deficits in particular domains (IQ and adaptive behavior) and towards a more outcome or role-based orientation that asks the question, "What supports are needed to function in specific age-relevant social roles and community contexts?" This definition is congruent with a world in which people with mental retardation are studying, living, working, and even parenting in independent, although sometimes supported, settings. (Greenspan, 1994, p. 545)

As expected, the perceived change in direction presented in the 1992 definition of mental retardation has evoked controversy and debate within the field of human services. There has been ongoing discussion and debate regarding the psychometric integrity of this system (Jacobson, 1994; McMillan, Gresham, & Siperstein, 1993). Interestingly, it has been reported that during the field-test phase of the AAMR publication, 75% of the respondents identified problems with the new definition, yet 95% felt that this new definition reflected current directions in the field of mental retardation (e.g., use of a supports model) (McMillan et al., 1993). This may just be a reflection of the disagreements that perpetually plague the field of human services or a growing awareness that changes are rearranging long-standing allegiances to many of our sacred icons such as IQ scores. Perhaps there can be some reason for optimism in that many professionals are beginning to look beyond bestowing labels on individuals with disabilities and defining the types of supports or services received by that individual based on the label. Rather, based on the initial assumption that the community is where people belong, efforts will be directed toward developing necessary and appropriate supports.

There is a certain irony to the publication of a "new" definition of mental retardation. Consider, for example, the definition of mental retardation proposed by Gold (1980a) many years ago: "Mental retardation refers to a level of functioning which requires from society significantly above average training procedures and superior assets in adaptive behavior on the part of society; manifested throughout the life of both society and the individual" (p. 148). This definition speaks clearly to the interdependent relationship between individuals with disabilities and society. Perske (1987) provided an account of the events surrounding this proposed definition and the manner in which it was received:

> In 1974, he [Marc Gold] made a frontal attack on the generally accepted definition of mental retardation. He argued that the standard definition generalized too

much, and that it was derived from test numbers that froze a person into a terrible, permanent classification. The definition ignored a person's areas of normal capability, failed to measure a person's real potential, and denied the fact that development in a person is a lifelong process. Gold also pointed out that the standard definition tended to be psychological and medical in nature, while his own definition tended to be sociological. Then Gold offered his own definition. . . . One would think that this definition would be enough. Not for this man. He even tried to get it across with—believe it or not—a poem:

An End to the Concept of Mental Retardation:
Oh, What a Beautiful Mourning
by Marc Gold

If you could only know me for who I am
Instead of for who I am not.
There could be so much more to see
'Cause there's so much more I've got.

So long as you see me as mentally retarded,
Which supposedly means something, I guess,
There is nothing that you or I could ever do
To make me a human success.

Someday you'll know the tests aren't built
To let me stand next to you,
By the way you test me, all they can do
Is make me look bad through and through.

And someday soon I'll get my chance,
When some of you finally adapt.
You'll be delighted to know that though I'm MR
I'm not at all handicapped. (Gold, 1980a, p. 144)

A member of the committee responsible for revising the *Manual on Terminology and Classification in Mental Retardation* discussed the definition with Marc and a copy was submitted. Later, the man wrote to Marc: "Thanks for sending the definition, which was considered by the Terminology and Classification Committee and was most helpful. Looking forward to talking with you in the near future about this" (Gold, 1980a, p. 146). Marc hoped that his sociological definition might indeed be used as an adjunct to the psychologically and medically oriented standard definition. The committee member never wrote again. The 1977 edition of the manual came out without one word in the definition being changed from the 1973 edition. (p. ix)

In addition to psychometric and definitional differences, the most significant departure from tradition presented in the 1992 publication is the description of a multidimensional approach to viewing individual strengths and weaknesses and a beginning emphasis on the need to identify the supports required for participating in the community. Luckasson and Spitalnik (1994), relying heavily on the AAMR model and definitional framework, conceptualized supports as

resources and strategies that promote the interests and causes of individuals with or without disabilities that enable them to secure access to resources, information, and relationships as part of inclusive work and living environments and that result in enhanced interdependence, productivity, community inclusion, and satisfaction. (pp. 88–89)

One of the most important features of this definition is that it applies to all people, not just individuals with disabilities. This definition stabilizes the concept that we *all* are in need of varying levels of support during the course of our lifetimes.

The foundation of the importance of supports is solidly tied to the essential characteristics of desirable, positive, and meaningful community experiences for people with disabilities (Luckasson & Spitalnik, 1994). These characteristics, drawn from the work of O'Brien (1987b) and O'Brien and Lyle (1988), include 1) *community presence* (i.e., sharing ordinary places in the community), 2) *competence* (i.e., opportunities to demonstrate acquired skill repertoires), 3) *respect* (i.e., having a valued role as part of the community), 4) *community participation* (i.e., being part of a social network that includes a variety of friendships), and 5) *choice* (i.e., a degree of autonomy in the everyday matters of life). The objective, then, is to sustain the use of supports in a manner that encourages the realization of these events for every individual with disabilities.

It also is assumed that to achieve these valued outcomes, many individuals will require an infinite variety of individually designed supports. The categories used to describe *support resources* include the individual and his or her personal resources, other people, technology, and services. This delineation of support resources acknowledges several important points: 1) there is no one quick and easy response to the needs of individuals with disabilities; 2) supports can come from a variety of sources including friends, family, co-workers, supervisors, fellow students, church members, fellow club members, next-door neighbors, the regulars at the local tavern, the people whom you talk with at the bus stop each morning, the waitress at the restaurant that you frequent, and so forth; and 3) technology and formal services do play a role as mechanisms designed to assist people with disabilities—a balanced role that complements and amplifies the other, more natural, resources and strategies.

Descriptions of the AAMR model have been very carefully crafted to specify that supports should *not* be characterized as a continuum. As examples, supports have alternatively been described as a "constellation" (Luckasson et al., 1992) and as an "array" (Luckasson & Spitalnik, 1994). We might even suggest the term *cornucopia*. It is gratifying to observe that many writers in the area of disability are squeamish about using the word *continuum*. This reluctance has been particularly noticeable since Taylor's (1987, 1988) critical analyses of this long-time foundation for planning and implementing human services programs. The concerns of Taylor and others are primarily related to the fact that under the auspices of a continuum-based approach to services, individuals with disabilities must earn their way into the community. The traditional criteria for inclusion have been dictated by the varied steps on the continuum. *We strongly assert that inclusion and participation in community must be assumed as the constant outcome for all individuals with disabilities. Supports merely serve as a means to that end.* To arrange supports into some type of linear, continuum-based progression would be largely useless and counterproductive. We therefore refrain from using continuum for fear of being misinterpreted in regard to our feeling about services designed on a continuum-based model.

According to the AAMR model, support can serve a variety of functions within people's individual lives. These functions include befriending, financial planning, employee assistance, behavioral support, in-home living assistance, community access and use, and health assistance (Schalock et al., 1994):

- *Befriending*—socializing and enjoying the company of another individual or group of individuals
- *Financial planning*—managing income, paying bills, saving for the future
- *Employee assistance*—facilitating supports in the workplace, direct instruction, negotiation with employers, and so forth.
- *Behavioral support*—assistance in modifying varied environments/situations in response to personal and behavioral needs of the individual
- *In-home living assistance*—attendant care, architectural modifications, meal planning, housekeeping assistance
- *Community access and use*—linkages with social organizations and activities, securing services and supports from generic resources
- *Health assistance*—medical assistance, dental care, awareness of the effects of diet and exercise on health, and so forth

It is encouraging that the terminology used to describe these support functions is general in nature in that it refers to the various support functions that *any* individual may need at some time in his or her life.

A final aspect of the AAMR model relates to the levels of intensity of supports. The relative intensity of supports can be judged to be intermittent, limited, extensive, or pervasive. Several observers (Borthwick-Duffy, 1994; McMillan et al., 1993) have queried whether these "intensities of supports" are just a clever disguise for the discarded levels of mental retardation (e.g., intermittent = mild, limited = moderate). According to Schalock et al. (1994), there are several key ways in which the supports model differs from the former use of levels of mental retardation: 1) four dimensions—intelligence and adaptive behavior, psychological and emotional status, physical/health factors, and environmental factors—are evaluated in relation to individual strengths and difficulties as a means of determining the required levels of supports as opposed to the traditional dependence on the intelligence quotient and adaptive behavior; 2) the evolving supports in the life of an individual are determined by a team of individuals that could include representatives from varied disciplines, the individual, and his or her family and friends; 3) supports are determined in relation to strengths and weaknesses; 4) supports are viewed as being fluid and changeable in response to the needs of the individual and the environment; 5) support predictions are not ability predictions; and 6) varied levels of support will be needed across environments making any global summary label a meaningless term.

The fact that this model has been promulgated by this particular organization and that there has been a theoretical departure from the traditional definitions could be significant factors in the history of human services. The AAMR supports model provides an excellent theoretical foundation for further thought and development in the area of supports for individuals with disabilities. Ultimately, however, the measure of any model of service is the degree to which the implementation process affects the lives of individuals in a positive and constructive manner. It is suggested that the initial impact of the AAMR model largely will be observed within the academic community. Many university faculty and other human services theoreticians will expend great levels of energy debating the positive and negative features of this model and its departure from "tradition." The degree to which this approach meets the needs of individuals with disabilities will depend on the practitioners who will ultimately have the greatest opportunities to breathe life into the approach. It may take years to realize, understand, and appreciate the real impact.

SUPPORTS PLANNING BASED ON
THE FEATURES OF NATURALNESS

As described previously, the AAMR model provides a sound theoretical foundation for conceptualizing the role of supports in the lives of individuals with disabilities. The remainder of this chapter describes an approach to supports planning that is roughly based on the constructs of the AAMR model but also incorporates the values and approaches from a variety of other sources (Bartholomew-Lorimar, 1993; Callahan, 1993; Gretz, 1992; Kendrick, 1994; McKnight, 1987; Mount, Beeman, & Ducharme, 1988a, 1988b; O'Brien, 1987b, 1988; O'Brien & O'Brien, 1993). The primary purposes of this approach are 1) to emphasize the role of supports in the wide variety of situations that constitute a person's life experience, 2) to encourage divergent and creative thinking about the possible applications and alternatives for supports design, and 3) to avoid or reduce the need to "label" or categorize supports in a rigid manner.

The process of supports planning occurs on two levels: the *organizational level* and the *relational level*. At the organizational level, an emphasis is placed on two critical factors: 1) approaches to planning and securing supports that are responsive to the individual needs of people with disabilities and 2) approaches to providing those supports in a meaningful, productive, and unobtrusive manner. The relational level of supports planning focuses on varied types of interactions that occur among the applicant, the employer, and co-workers.

Supports Planning at the Organizational Level

There are two critical aspects of supports planning at the organizational level: 1) an awareness of the varied approaches that can be used to secure supports that are responsive to the individual needs of people with disabilities and 2) an awareness of the varied types of supports and how they can be used in a meaningful and productive manner.

As depicted in Figure 3.1, these dimensions have been arranged to form the two axes of an overall supports planning matrix. The axis entitled "Approaches to Securing Supports (Means)" includes those supports that originate from inside of the work environment (i.e., internal) and those that are provided by sources outside of the work environment or organization (i.e., external). The axis entitled "Approaches to Securing Supports (Ways)" includes possibilities ranging from those supports that are typical for all employees to those that are uniquely applied to the learning and work situation of a particular employee.

Approaches to Securing Supports   In this proposed approach, there are two diverse views of planning, organizing, and securing supports. These are the *means* of providing supports. The term *internal supports* refers to those resources and procedures that emanate from within the environment, location, or associational group of which the individual with disabilities is viewed to be a member or participant (e.g., from within the company where the individual is employed, from within a club or organization). Internal supports emerge when an individual or a group of individuals from within an environment or associational group decides to provide support to assist an individual with disabilities. As examples of internal supports (with emphasis on the source from which the supports emanated), consider the following:

- Members of a church congregation decide to renovate a portion of their building so that it is fully accessible to Mary, who experiences difficulties with mobility.
- A carpool is formed by a group of workers for Allen, who does not have access to other means of transportation.
- A group of people at work get together to take meals to Kyle, a co-worker who has been ill.

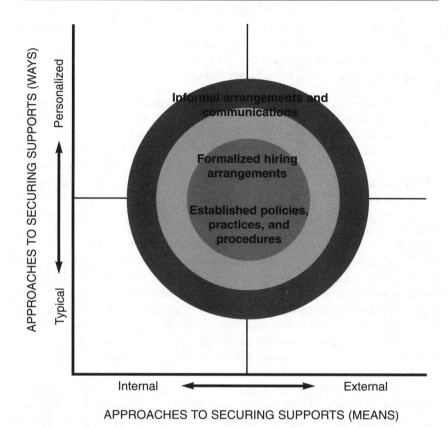

Figure 3.1. A model for individual supports planning.

- Someone is always naturally available to help Kate carry her tray from the lunch line to the table in the factory cafeteria, as her mobility difficulties make this task extremely difficult.

External supports are those that emanate from outside of the environment, location, or associational group of which the individual with disabilities is a participant. These are the *ways* in which supports are provided. This factor in supports planning has been the traditional and customary strategy for assisting individuals with disabilities. So, for example, a rehabilitation agency will "send in" an individual to provide systematic instruction, redesign a work station, or provide attendant care services. As a general rule, external supports are more technologically based and professionalized. The following are examples of external supports specifically related to individuals with disabilities:

- A case manager from the county disability services agency visits John every payday and assists him in making deposits and bill payments.

- An employment specialist[1] visits Meredith at work once or twice a month to troubleshoot issues related to production.
- A van provided by the vocational rehabilitation services transports Louis each day as he travels to and from work.

Historically, the process of designing and organizing supports has been interjected into the environment from the outside (i.e., external supports). This trend, however, appears to be changing. The predominant and growing direction clearly is toward the further development of skills and strategies that will promote the increased use of supports that are generated from *within* the environment or associational group (i.e., internal supports). Although the use of external supports has been the fashion in human services, the times are changing.

There is a definite need to hone the skills and thinking of practitioners toward the wider use of internal support strategies that draw upon the features of naturalness. In many ways, generating direct supports is one of the most challenging tasks facing those responsible for supports planning. For each individual and for each environment, planners must observe the interaction between these two variables and create (often) from scratch a creative and unique approach to organizing supports. Although lessons learned in one setting or with one individual who has certain types of difficulties may be somewhat transferable or generalizable, there is a large amount of regeneration that occurs every time supports are discussed for a specific individual or environment.

The Types of Supports Received   When discussing varied strategies for providing supports for individuals with disabilities, there is continued concern regarding the degree to which the established support relationships are promoted, paid for, monitored, evaluated, assisted, facilitated, and so forth by individuals or agencies other than those directly involved (i.e., the individual with disabilities and the provider of supports). These are the *ways* in which supports are provided. Given this particular qualifier, there are two additional aspects of providing supports that require further discussion and examination. The term *typical supports* refers to the varied types of assistance, intervention, working conditions, and so forth that would be made available to any employee of the organization. In the genre of supported employment, typical supports often are referred to as "natural supports" (Callahan, 1992; Gerry & Mirsky, 1992; Hagner, Rogan, & Murphy, 1992; Jorgenson, 1992; Murphy & Rogan, 1994; Williams, 1992) For example, in the Senate Report related to the Rehabilitation Act Amendments of 1992, the following definition of *natural supports* was provided:

---

[1]Throughout this text we will use the term "employment specialist" to refer to a human services professional responsible for providing on-site support or training services to an individual with disabilities. This term is considered to be synonymous with the terms *job coach*, *employment facilitator*, *job trainer*, and so forth.

The term natural supports is a broad term meant to include having a supervisor, co-worker, or other employer(ee) provide supervision and support at the worksite; using college students, friends, or other volunteers/mentors from work or the community to provide needed services or supports; or using family members in a support role. (Senate Report, 102–357)

This definition seems to rely heavily on the fact that natural supports are provided by friends, family, co-workers, and other apparently nonpaid individuals. Another definition, provided by Rogan et al. (1993), stipulates that natural supports

> may be described as any assistance, relationships, or interactions that allow a person to secure, maintain, and advance in a community job of his or her choosing in ways that correspond to the typical work routines and social actions of other employees and that enhance the individual's social relationships. (p. 275)

There are purists who speak often about the absolute necessity that all supports be "natural." In fact, within this chapter, we will make frequent references to a generalized type of assistance known as "natural supports." It should be noted, however, that a *natural* support is not necessarily an organically grown, fat-free, cholesterol-free, nutritious, vitamin-laden, fiber-filled relationship between people that springs from nowhere and meets the varied needs of all people. This utopian event may occur, but not very often— certainly not as often as would be needed in order to meet the support needs of all people with severe disabilities. Forest and Pearpoint (1992) addressed the issue of "purity" in planning for supports in the following manner:

> Our critics say, "But it SHOULD be natural. It SHOULD be spontaneous." Who made that rule, we wonder? When people say, "It should happen naturally," we start to worry. We do not believe anything in life just happens naturally. Nor do we believe we can make everything we want happen. Life just does not work that way.
>   We do believe we can set the stage, create conditions for good relationships, good health, and optimal learning. Then we can hope and continually work for the best possible outcome. . . .
>   Let's not romanticize the notion of . . . supports. When we look at people with disabilities who actually are managing in this society and have a circle of support, we see that they are few and far between. We also see that it was blood, sweat, and tears that brought them to that circle and not simply good luck. (pp. 70–71)

This spin on natural supports does not address this issue in quite the same way, but it does make a strong inference that natural supports are embedded within the typical work routines and social actions of other employees. This implies a kind of "nothing special" approach to providing support (Hagner, Cotton, Goodall, & Nisbet, 1992). We strongly concur that natural supports are, by definition, those that evolve and grow out of the typical and ongoing routines of the environment (i.e., the culture of the workplace). From this perspective, naturalness can be assessed by asking the following question: If another individual, one without a disability, were in this same situation, is it likely that this type of support would be necessary, evolve, and become a reality? In some ways, this may not be a fair question as the essence of a natural support is that, from the viewpoint of an outsider, it just happens. The outsider cannot truly assess the nature of the linkage between the recipient of the supports and the providers of the supports and for what reasons this relationship may have emerged. This mystery is critical to a full understanding of the process. As to whether the support is viewed as being "typical," the issue of "disability" may not even be a relevant ingredient of the discussion.

Examples of typical supports include the following:

- Tom, a friend and co-worker of Carlos, holds a place in the lunch line for him. Carlos has difficulties with mobility and often does not arrive at the cafeteria in a timely manner. Tom decided *on his own to provide this assistance to Carlos.*
- Bill often completes his assigned work tasks a few minutes before the end of his scheduled shift. *He decided to approach his supervisor* and request permission to help Leslie, a young woman with disabilities who just began working in his office building. He will help her with some last-minute filing that always occurs near the end of the workday. Bill provides this assistance *whenever he is able. Bill says that he just "likes helping out."*

Another dimension of the proposed paradigm is found in the provision of *personalized supports.* This term refers to supports that are uniquely required by an employee to facilitate learning of work skills or to maintain required quality or quantity standards of the position. For example, an individual with physical disabilities requires assistance in using the restroom. A co-worker is paid by a rehabilitation agency to assist the individual with disabilities at those times of the day. This assistance is provided on the basis of a formal agreement between the individual providing the supports and the agency. It is presumed that this support would not continue without the benefit of the financial agreement. In this sense, the supports are "personalized" (i.e., uniquely required by an employee).

Personalized supports often are the easiest to define and identify. There are several distinguishing characteristics that make personalized supports so identifiable:

- An agreement exists between the individual providing the supports and either the recipient of the supports or a third-party agency that in all likelihood provides the funding for this arrangement.
- Some exchange of money or in-kind contribution occurs for providing the supports.
- A means of accountability is in place for providing the specified supports.

Examples of personalized supports include the following:

- Jed works in a large retail store stocking shelves. *One of his co-workers is paid extra to remain a few minutes after her regular shift to check the accuracy of Jed's work. The cost for this extra time is reimbursed by the vocational rehabilitation service.*
- Loretta needs assistance in rearranging her clothing after using the restroom. Milly has been asked to provide assistance in this area. *With the permission of her employer and under the condition that this assistance will not interfere with her regular tasks, Milly is given a small stipend by the county disability services agency.*
- An employment facilitator, *provided by a private contract agency*, has been assigned to visit the workplace to provide assistance to Larry as he learns newly assigned work tasks.

Personalized supports are those most similar to traditional vocational training and rehabilitation services. This is not meant to be a criticism. In fact, there are situations in which specialized types of support are necessary. In those instances, the most effective and expedient approach to support may be to simply hire someone to perform the required tasks. For example, an individual with disabilities has an opportunity to work in a local factory. Before this can happen, however, there are a number of jobsite renovations and adaptations that are necessary. For this purpose, the local rehabilitation agency contracts with a rehabilitation engineer who has demonstrated expertise in this area. In this scenario, it is believed that this personalized support is necessary and cannot be secured by any other means.

Supports Planning at the Relational Level

An overlay to the entire process of supports planning is the relational aspects of working. The *relational level* of supports planning refers to the variety of mechanisms used to communicate information to the employee, which clarifies or stipulates the conditions or contingencies of employment. This includes the most formal forms of communication (e.g., adopted and established policies and procedures), specific and personalized communications between the employer and the employee (e.g., memoranda describing compensation or fringe benefit agreements), and informal communications between the employee and co-workers or supervisors.

It is assumed that the process of planning and implementing supports for individuals with severe disabilities will require extensive communication between the employee, the employment specialist, and co-workers. In many instances, the quality of these communications will be the single greatest variable in determining the ultimate success of the employment process.

As illustrations of supports planning at the relational level, consider the following situations:

- In making efforts to find employment for Maria, an individual with a disability who comes from a family in which the primary language of the home is Spanish, the employment specialist finds a jobsite where many of the other employees speak Spanish in their interactions with one another during the workday (e.g., in the break room, during casual work-related interactions during the day). The employer does not require or even encourage the employees to speak Spanish. Maria's familiarity with the language and her ability to respond to this language appropriately, however, may greatly affect the degree to which supports can be provided by the other employees.
- Employees have established a practice of assisting one another to meet the production standards required by the employer. This type of assistance is never mentioned or documented during the job analysis process. It is something that is only known and practiced by "insiders."

In summary, effective supports planning must include an awareness and consideration of several key factors including the various approaches that can be used to secure supports, the various types of supports that are available or that can be developed, and the relational issues that affect all areas of the employment process.

THE FIVE QUESTIONS

Before any decisions are made regarding the nature of the supports that may be needed to assist an individual with disabilities, five critical questions must be addressed. These questions are intended to focus the energies of planning team members. They also are intended to clarify the thinking of these planning participants to include new and as yet undiscovered strategies to provide supports for people with severe disabilities. The five questions that should be reviewed during the supports planning process are the following:

1. Where are supports needed?
2. What are the outcomes that are sought through the supports that will be provided?
3. How will the necessary supports be provided?
4. Who will be responsible for ongoing organization and provision of the identified supports?
5. When will the identified supports be provided?

The following is an examination of each question and how the questions relate to the design of individual support options for individuals with severe disabilities.

Where Are Supports Needed?

Where supports are needed relates to the environments in which supports may be needed or will be provided. Responses to this issue may include the places in which an individual resides, works, shares time with his or her friends engaged in leisure activities, goes to school, participates in religious worship, purchases groceries, prepares meals, secures medical or dental care, and so forth. To address these issues, supports planning participants must become aware of the physical aspects of the identified settings that may have an impact on the performance of required tasks/activities.

Within the context of the personal futures planning format (Mount, 1987; O'Brien, 1987b; O'Brien & Lyle, 1988), there is a discussion activity that asks participants to construct a "Places Map." This matrix identifies several important factors regarding the environments in which an individual with disabilities might participate. Environments are classified either as being part of the "community" (i.e., places frequented by other members of the community) or as a "human services" environment (i.e., places restricted to individuals with disabilities). As might be expected, for many individuals with disabilities, participating in human services–based environments is a predominant factor in their lives. An important goal, of course, is to increase the number of community environments in which the individual is able to participate as a valued member (O'Brien, 1987b). The final activity of completing the Places Map is to identify settings and environments that potentially are valuable and meaningful for future participation.

Some of the supplementary questions that might guide an investigation of the "where" question are as follows:

- Is it necessary for this support to be provided by human services personnel?
- Could the same support be provided by someone who is a natural and ongoing part of the selected environment or associational group?
- If supports are provided by individuals from within the environment, then is there any concern about their reliability and longevity (i.e., will this individual provide the types and quantity of supports needed, will the individual continue to be associated with the particular environment)?
- Have the perspectives and opinions of individuals within the environment been fully explored when considering how to deliver supports?

What Are the Outcomes that Are Sought Through the Supports that Will Be Provided?

Determining the skills and competencies that are needed in environments in which individuals with disabilities might participate requires a knowledge about the routines, activities, and demands of these varied settings. Just as it is critically important to know a task before you attempt to teach that task to someone else (Gold, 1972, 1980b; Mcloughlin, Garner, & Callahan, 1987), it is equally important to have a thorough awareness of the subtle intricacies of a setting or environment before attempting to speculate on the "possible" need for supports.

There are several strategies that can be used to assist in answering the "what" question. Brown, Branston, Baumgart, et al. (1979) have suggested using an "ecological inventory." The ecological inventory provides a listing of the skills, activities, and tasks performed by the participants in a given environment (i.e., what people typically do in this setting). In the area of employment, this inventory process takes on a more comprehensive view in the form of a job analysis. (See Chapter 9 for a complete discussion of the job analysis process.)

As Yogi Berra once remarked, "You can observe a lot just by watching." The environmental analysis that results from an ecological inventory or job analysis requires that someone visit the designated setting and make a list of the activities that occur in that setting. Perhaps one of the most critical factors in this strategy is requiring that someone actually visit the chosen environment in order to generate the inventory. It is not appropriate to speculate on the task or skill requirements of an identified environment. In the work context, for example, to take the position that "all fast-food restaurants are alike" would be a major mistake. Even with an effort to maintain uniformity in products and procedures, each fast-food restaurant has subtle, distinctive features (e.g., management style, other employees, clientele) that make it different from every other. The same is true of all other work environments that often are perceived to be like every other in their category (e.g., hospitals, factories, retail stores). The visitation and observation must be made on a firsthand basis—there is no substitute for the experience of the sights, sounds, smells, people, and so forth. The time spent on a visitation is especially critical when there is a desire to facilitate the use of typical supports; it is critically important to assess the informal aspects of the work culture and to begin establishing relationships with co-workers and supervisors who will be interacting with the new employee with disabilities.

To assist in the process of determining the skills and activities that routinely occur within an environment, the following clarifying questions can be asked:

- Is support in this setting considered to be a short-term or long-term need?
- Is it possible to view the provision of supports as an intermittent rather than continuous process (i.e., encouraging opportunities for the individual with disabilities to exercise areas of independent performance and receive supports only when necessary)?

How Will the Necessary Supports Be Provided?

Another way of asking how the necessary supports will be provided is, "What are the strategies and resources that will be employed to ensure that the identified outcomes are achieved in a timely and efficient manner?" In many ways, this may be the most important question during the planning process. In this phase of the planning process, team members are actually creating the interrelated supports that may be required.

There are individuals with severe disabilities who will require what are considered to be pervasive levels of support if they are to be employed in the community. Even in those circumstances, however, it is recommended that employment specialists begin their analysis of support needs with a strong preference for using the processes that are naturally available, a solution to the paradox created by the need to initiate and maintain employment as naturally referenced as possible and the extensive support needs of people with severe disabilities. The approach recommended here uses a modification of the Seven-Phase Sequence for training originally developed by Gold (1980b) and revised for natural work environments by Callahan (1991a) to help answer these questions. This sequence represents a conceptual model designed to balance the natural capacity of community workplaces and the individual needs of employees. The Seven-Phase Sequence provides a clear direction to employment specialists to initiate instruction using the natural ways, means, and people available to any new employee (see Chapter 6).

Supplementary "how" questions that may guide the planning process include the following:

- If technology is the support of choice, then will the approach selected be durable and easily maintained?
- If systematic instruction is the support of choice, then what are the long-range prospects?
    1. Will skill acquisition reduce the need for long-term instructional supports?
    2. Are long-term instructional supports available?
- Will the type of support selected serve as an interference or detractor in the area of social interactions and relationships between the individual with disabilities and others in the environment (i.e., the presence of an individual who provides direct, systematic, instruction deters co-worker interactions in an employment setting)?
- Is it possible to combine varied sources and means of supports (e.g., internal sources, external sources, natural and conditional) rather than view the provision of supports as a one-directional issue?
- If required, which types of support activities will be the least disruptive and obtrusive in this particular environment?

Who Will Be Responsible for Ongoing Organization and Provision of the Identified Supports?

The "who" question is not intended to identify specific individuals who will provide supports to individuals with disabilities. Rather, this question addresses the issue of whether the needed supports will be organized and provided from within the environment or through an external source. In this regard, there is an ongoing concern that the provision of supports does not serve as a barrier between the individual with disabilities and other individuals in the environment. On occasion, extraordinary levels of technology, instruction, and other supports have been used to "include" an individual with disabilities within an environment. Although the individual who was a recipient of these supports was, in fact, "in" the environment of choice, he or she was not a part of the environment (e.g., involved with the other people there, a participant in the informal culture of the setting). The technology and instructional support designed to assist an individual can inadvertently turn into barriers that preclude him or her from fully participating in the culture of the workplace.

To increase the likelihood that supports will emphasize the features of naturalness, it is critical that employment specialists always begin with the assumption that supports can be provided by naturally occurring people in the workplace (e.g., co-workers, supervisors). Beginning with this assumption increases the likelihood that the planning process will follow a logical progression beginning with those that are the least intrusive and the most natural.

A couple of questions designed to assist in ensuring that supports serve in a supportive rather than a restrictive manner include the following:

- Will the individual who is identified as a source of supports be predictably available to provide necessary supports?
- What are the "encouragers" that can be used to promote the continuation of supports provided by people in the workplace (e.g., acknowledgment of the effort provided by individuals, commendation by the employer, a written or verbal "thank you")? Caution must be exercised here as there are individuals who simply want to help out but are adamant about not wanting any kind of recognition for their efforts.

When Will the Identified Supports Be Provided?

The "when" question is primarily a question of intensity—how often and to what degree is it necessary to provide a given support? Of the questions that have been asked, this is perhaps the least-considered issue. Supports do not need to be an around-the-clock, perpetual feature of the environment. It is likely that an individual with disabilities can exert his or her own personal influence over situations and requirements in an environment with the assistance of occasional or episodic supports in specific instances and can perform narrowly delineated tasks and activities. Supports are not intended to be a blanket that covers every aspect of an environment and the tasks and activities that occur within that setting. Supports should be applied in a cautious and systematic fashion in direct relationship to the individual involved and the specific demands of the environment. Intensity is a variable term.

To consider the issue of intensity of supports (i.e., "when"), planning team members are encouraged to consider the following questions:

- If this is a support that is only required on an episodic basis (i.e., unpredictably needed but critical), then is there a backup when the primary source of supports is unavailable?
- If primary sources or backup sources do not materialize when needed, then will the employment opportunity be at risk, *or* will the safety of the individual be in jeopardy?

A FINAL THOUGHT

It is important to remember that the design and implementation of supports for individuals with severe disabilities is not a "one shot deal." None of us has the wisdom or insight necessary to predict the exact effects or level of success that will be realized through the implementation of various support strategies. For this reason, developing and nurturing supports is an ongoing process. Circumstances change, and the needs and availability of people and other resources change. Therefore, those individuals involved in planning or providing supports must be ready and willing to make adjustments, modifications, and alterations as necessary. In fact, we would suggest that maintaining a continuously high level of flexibility toward supports may be one of the most important attributes that effective planning participants can bring to the process.

The Role of Families
in the Employment Process

⚜ 4 ⚜

The little world of childhood with its familiar surroundings is a model of the greater world. The more intensively the family has stamped its character upon the child, the more it will tend to feel and see its earlier miniature world again in the bigger world of adult life.

C.G. Jung, 1913/1953, p. 83

For many individuals with severe disabilities, their family is a mainstay of support and security. This support and security can take numerous forms and be evidenced at various levels of influence and intensity. As a general rule, however, the extent of family involvement may largely dictate the number of options and opportunities that will be available for individuals with severe disabilities during adulthood. Involving the family in planning and the process of transition into employment clearly is important, yet it must be balanced with an emphasis on protecting the dignity and decision-making rights of the individual with disabilities. This delicate balancing process—encouraging family involvement while encouraging independence—requires the human services professional to assume many roles, including facilitator, counselor, motivator, coach, and mediator. Primarily, however, the professional becomes a guide to family members as they travel the maze of services, supports, and eligibility requirements that are major considerations in planning for community employment. This chapter examines the various roles that families can play in the process of facilitating community employment and strategies that can be used to encourage participation and support for this desired outcome.

THE ROLE OF FAMILIES

Although it is often assumed that employment is the ultimate goal, we must continually caution ourselves to view the lives of people with disabilities in a larger context of community living. Any discussion of community employment for individuals with severe disabilities must include a serious consideration of the role that families play in this process. Although human services agencies do play a critical role in organizing and planning the activities surrounding community employment, their involvement often is not sufficient for success; families also must play a crucial role. A significant number of adults with disabilities either live with their natural families or have families who continue to be involved in their daily lives (Blalock, 1988; Mallory, 1995). For this reason, it is important to consider strategies for involving families in a manner that respects the role of families but that also maintains the dignity and status of adults with disabilities.

Before examining the role of families in the lives of adults with disabilities and community employment, it is important to make a disclaimer: In the field of human services there often is a tendency to make sweeping generalizations about the characteristics and practices of families that include a member with a disability. We do not want to perpetuate this practice. For this reason, readers are encouraged to consider the following guidelines when reviewing the information and strategies recommended in this chapter:

- All families, regardless of whether they contain an individual with disabilities, are a collection of individuals with varying personalities, needs, dreams, and skills.
- There are differences among all families, whether they happen to contain a member with a disability or not. These differences should be respected and valued as distinctive reflections of the individuals who comprise a family.
- It is not the role or responsibility of the human services professional to "change" the family. The primary responsibility of the human services professional is to the individual with disabilities who is the focus of planning, services, and supports. The individual's family can and should be involved in this process. This involvement should enlist the strengths and support of the family. At the same time, however, it is critically important to protect the autonomy and dignity of the individual with disabilities.

Bellamy, Rhodes, Mank, and Albin (1988) proposed seven alternative roles for the families of people with disabilities who are preparing for community employment: 1) set family goals, 2) participate in the individual program-planning process, 3) develop and share information, 4) influence program management, 5) influence the system, 6) provide supports directly, and 7) share information concerning supported employment experiences. Examples in each of these areas include the following:

1. **Set family goals**
   - Determine how employment will affect the family's routines.
   - Identify the types of commitments that may be necessary in order to facilitate this process (e.g., providing transportation).
   - Serve as an advocate for the family member with disabilities.

2. **Participate in the individual program-planning process**
   - Identify critical instructional goals and outcomes.
   - Identify required specialized and general services.

3. **Develop and share information**
   - Respond to questions and concerns regarding program development and implementation.
   - Identify training issues.
   - Review past experiences in work or community situations that may be relevant to the current employment-planning activities.

4. **Influence program management**
   - Serve as a member of the board of directors for agencies providing supported employment programs.
   - Participate on committees, task forces, and systemic advocacy efforts.
   - Ensure that program personnel are accountable to promises made within the context of the individual's service plan (e.g., individualized education program, individual habilitation plan, individual written rehabilitation plan).

5. **Influence the system**
   - Communicate with legislators regarding regulatory and policy matters.
   - Participate in advocacy or consumer organizations.
   - Write letters or testify on key pieces of legislation that affect the lives of individuals with severe disabilities.

6. **Provide supports directly**
   - Locate potential worksites.
   - Assist in purchasing appropriate work clothing.
   - Provide transportation to and from work.

7. **Share information concerning supported employment experiences**
   - Provide public speaking services to parent organizations.
   - Make presentations at conferences sponsored by professional organizations.
   - Consult with other families.

Quite obviously, families must carefully assess their interests and abilities relative to participating in any or all of these potential roles. Human services personnel should take the responsibility to advise families and friends of the varied roles that they can serve in developing a supported employment plan for their son, daughter, brother, sister, or friend. Families have always played an important role in assisting family members to get jobs. Employment training personnel, by involving willing families at a level that encourages participation without jeopardizing personal choices and personal dignity, will greatly enhance the probability of success.

Family Transitions

For most parents, the process of watching their children mature and assume adult roles and responsibilities often is difficult and confusing. Families want what is "best" for their children and hope that they will avoid the mistakes that sometimes occur as young adults begin to make choices. This period causes questions regarding when to let go and when to get involved—the troublesome and bewildering dilemmas that all parents face. For parents who have an adult son or daughter with a disability and who may have only infrequently thought of the possibility of community employment, the prospect of the risks associated with this independence is frightening. Employment specialists must maintain an awareness of these realities and deal with parents in a sensitive and supportive manner. To imply that we have all of the answers and that the process of employment is entirely predictable is untrue and may jeopardize desired outcomes.

The degree to which the transitions of life can affect a family often is a function of the family's overall level of adjustment:

> Difficult developmental transitions in the life cycle of a person with a disability cause stress for the entire family. . . . Job loss, career changes, divorce, retirement, deaths, and similar transitions in the family's life cycle can also be particularly stressful.
>
> Transitions often reflect the cyclical nature of many of the family's stresses. For example, parents who grieved at the birth of a disabled child may find that sadness recurs when the disabled person finishes an educational program and the parents are reminded that their child is different and will not be leaving for college with the others in the fall. Such transitions also explain how previous efforts at coping influence how current problems are handled. . . . For example, parents who received little support from others when their child with a disability was born are more likely to rely on their own resources when additional problems arise later in the child's development. (McCallion & Toseland, 1993, p. 580)

Mallory (1995) analyzed the social policy issues that surround the life cycle transitions of families that include a member with a disability. A distinction was drawn between *developmental transitions* and *institutional transitions* in the life of a family. Developmental transitions are those "associated with maturation and increased competence and are essentially independent of rules governing social institutions" (p. 214). Institutional transitions are those that "mark a change in status for the individual as a function of moving from one institutional environment to another" (p. 214). The term *institutional* in this context refers to an organizational structure rather than to a physical setting. Mallory also observed that the differences that exist between these two types of transitions and their respective influence on the family are not addressed or acknowledged within the context of current social policy. So, although the concept of "transitions" has become part of the social policy language, the impact of these experiences has not been fully understood by policy makers or, perhaps, service providers.

Ferguson, Ferguson, and Jones (1988) provided an interesting and useful approach for examining the types of transitions that occur in a family as a son, daughter, brother, or sister with disabilities moves into adulthood. These transitions are described as bureaucratic transitions, family life transitions, and status transitions. The changes that occur in each of these areas can determine the degree to which the family as a unit or individual members will become effectively and productively involved as employment opportunities are developed and implemented.

Bureaucratic Transitions   A bureaucratic transition is "the process whereby the agencies and professionals involved with a family change from representatives of the special education system to representatives of the adult service system" (Ferguson et al., 1988, p. 180). These transitions may be observed in a variety of forms including surrendering to the unquestioned expertise and decision-making power of professionals, accepting that no help is available, assuming the role of professionals in the absence of other forms of available support, and engaging with professionals to achieve those outcomes that were most important for the family member with a disability. This type of transition is particularly noticeable as families move from the mandates of special education during the school-age years into the permissive world of adult services. The guarantees of the Individuals with Disabilities Education Act (IDEA) of 1990 (PL 101-476) often are replaced with a spot on a waiting list or the opportunity to enter a sheltered workshop. This abrupt change often is a surprise to families. It is anticipated that the requirement for transition planning beginning at age 16 will facilitate a better understanding of how the system operates and the establishment of smoother passage into adult services.

Family Life Transitions   Family life transitions "cover all the changes and/or disruptions in established routines and accepted responsibilities that make daily life manageable within family units" (Ferguson et al., 1988, p. 182). Family life often can require that individuals juggle various responsibilities, acknowledge and resolve interpersonal conflicts, assume various responsibilities, and occasionally adjust their own personal needs for the benefit of the family. As changes occur in the lives of individual members and, consequently, within the relationships between family members, adjustments and transitions become necessary. Quite often, these transitions are difficult and disruptive. The degree to which the family can remain a cohesive, functioning unit during these times of change is one measure of the family's internal strength.

Status Transitions   A status transition is the "process as constructed by the parent whereby the status of a son or daughter changed from child to adult" (Ferguson et al., 1988, p. 184). These transitions are observed at the time when "children" become adults and begin to exercise various levels of independence and autonomy. This can be a difficult and confusing time in the life of a family. For years, the parents may have been told that their son or daughter probably would never achieve any level of independence and certainly would never be able to seek community employment. Although these predictions may have been difficult to accept, many parents and families had unwillingly done so, often with the encouragement of professionals. Now, as expectations have changed and as emerging technology for community employment becomes more widespread, parents are being asked to readjust their perceptions and expectations for their sons and daughters once again. This change often is difficult as parents are being asked to alter long-standing assumptions concerning their relationship with their children. Assistance and understanding are necessary as parents and other family members make this transition.

I Want More than that for My Daughter

There is much to be learned from listening to the stories told by parents as they describe their experiences and aspirations for their sons and daughters with disabilities. The second author of this book was asked to participate on a panel presentation, which included a group of parents who were being honored for their active involvement and advocacy on behalf of their own children. One of the participants was describing her efforts to promote community employment as an outcome for her adult daughter Jessica. Her descriptions of these experiences were filled with emotion and conveyed strong feelings of frustration. Promises had been made and broken many times by human services professionals.

As this mother described Jessica's aspirations to gain employment in the community and the difficulties that had been encountered, she began to explain some of the internal conflicts that she was feeling at that time in her own life. She was keenly aware that her friends' sons and daughters were graduating from college and entering the job market. She did not particularly resent or lament her own daughter's disability—her animosity was more correctly directed toward professionals who did not "buy the dream" and who seemingly felt no urgency to take the steps necessary to facilitate Jessica's employment in the community. Summarizing her feelings about the current situation and the future, she remarked,

> I want my daughter to have her own life. This will give her the sense of freedom and independence that she deserves. I must also admit that it will also give me a new level of independence. At this point, we each need to begin living our own lives. I do not want Jessica to have a career as my best friend and companion. She needs her own job and her own identity.

At that moment, she visualized a time in the near future when Jessica would be finished with school and unemployed, with no connections in the community. This episode reflects the frustration that parents and families often feel when their dreams (i.e., the dreams of the parents/family and the individual with disabilities) are not heard or accepted by the professionals who are employed to assist in making those dreams become a reality. It has been our experience that many of the parents and families who previously had fought the system to ensure that their sons and daughters would be included in general education settings are now advocating for community employment as their children have become adults. Furthermore, many of these families have grown tired of waiting for adult services agencies to catch up with what are known to be recommended practices in community employment. Conversations with these families, much like the one just described, reflect a certain weariness toward the process. At the same time, however, there is a drive and a commitment that motivates them to continue and to try one more time to move the system on behalf of their son or daughter.

STRATEGIES FOR INVOLVING FAMILIES

The degree to which the families of individuals with severe disabilities are included in the process of employment often is based on conscious decisions by human services professionals. Granted, there are family members who will ensure that they are involved and included in every aspect of planning and implementing community employment for their son, daughter, brother, or sister with severe disabilities. *They* will make the effort to attend meetings, gather information, generate alternative solutions to problems, ensure that all necessary procedures and "paperwork" are completed in a timely manner, and so forth. These family members insert themselves into the process without invitation from the professionals responsible for the details and steps necessary for successful employment. This often is a different and more contentious arrangement than situations in which family members are actively recruited and welcomed participants. In fairness, we also must acknowledge that there are families and family members who will actively avoid involvement, indicating little or no interest in the issues surrounding community employment. They agree that employment in the community would be a "nice" thing to do but express no interest in involving themselves in the process. Still another possible consideration is the family that openly opposes any efforts to facilitate community employment. This is typically the case when employment is viewed as a challenge to the comfort and safety of a sheltered workshop placement.

For each of the situations just described, the employment specialist and other professionals have an obligation to invite involvement by welcoming families on the families' terms. Families can be powerful allies and collaborators in the development of employment outcomes for individuals with disabilities. It behooves the professional community to find alternative methods for engaging families in a manner that promotes a team approach to community employment. In developing strategies for involving families in the process of employment, it is critically important that human services personnel maintain sensitivity to family matters and a primary focus on the individual.

A sensitivity to family matters requires an awareness of the total family structure. For the family, the issue of employment may be affected by other things that are occurring in the lives of individual family members (e.g., marital discord, personal health, their own employment-related problems, divorce, financial difficulties). Personal difficulties in any of these areas may preclude full, active involvement in the development of employment plans for a son, daughter, brother, or sister.

Family members may have some doubts or concerns about the feasibility of movement into community employment. For example, the perceived risks may be of great personal concern to parents who have never really considered this employment outcome as an option for their son or daughter. In some cases, the individual assigned to facilitate employment may be the first professional who has suggested this as a serious option. In such an instance, it is important for the employment specialist to remain patient and work through this issue *with* the family.

As the employment specialist interacts with the family, a balance must be sought between inviting the family to participate in the process and ensuring that the individual with disabilities remains the focus of the planning and decision-making process. This requires a commitment to always protect the dignity and importance of the individual who is the focus of the employment process. That individual must always be given the opportunity to make choices, express preferences, and make decisions. In addition, it is critical to maintain an awareness of situations in which the desires and wishes of family members may be overshadowing or minimizing the feelings and opinions of the individual with disabilities.

Approaches to involving families can be addressed when there is a commitment to empower and include families. These areas of involvement can include 1) involvement in planning activities, 2) involvement in decision making, 3) the family as a source for employment leads, and 4) the family as a source of supports.

1. **Involvement in planning activities**
   - Arrange meetings at a time that is convenient for family members.
   - Respect and value the information that family members can provide regarding the individual who is the focus of community employment efforts.
   - Make sure that attendance at scheduled meetings does not provide an overwhelming presence of "professional expertise."
   - If acceptable to the family, occasionally conduct planning meetings and activities in their home setting. Respect the family's wishes and preferences in this area.

- Refrain from using "disability jargon" (Hagner & Dileo, 1993) to describe the activities and technology involved in supported employment.

2. **Involvement in decision making**
   - Provide family members with readable, practical information and data regarding supported employment.
   - Be available to answer questions and concerns, in a factual, straight-forward, and individualized manner.
   - Always remember that the decisions reached by individuals with disabilities and their families *belong to them.* Professionals have the right to express their opinions and share relevant information from their training and experience that have an impact on the planning and implementation of the employment process. The final decision, however, always belongs to the person who is the focus of the discussion. Respect his or her right to choose and to assume responsibility for his or her own life.

3. **The family as a source for employment leads**
   - It is likely that the family has visualized the types of work situations that may be best suited to the needs, skills, and personal goals of the individual who is the focus of employment facilitation. Listen carefully to these ideas as they may contain many excellent leads and directions for the job search.
   - Throughout the planning process, invite family members to suggest possible employment locations. Before pursuing any activity in this area, be sure to check with the individual who has identified a possible lead for job development activity.
   - There may be some difficulties associated with having family or friends as employers. This situation may tend to place that employer in an awkward position—especially if there are problems related to employment, and he or she is uncomfortable mentioning these problems or taking some type of job action (e.g., firing or laying off the employee). A recommendation to pursue employment with a family member or friend should be considered very carefully before implementing.

4. **The family as a source of supports**
   - There may be a need for various kinds of supports that can be provided by the family. If transportation is a problem, for example, then there may be some advantage to seeking potential employment locations along the route followed by another family member as he or she goes to work. This can provide a relatively easy solution that does not cause a major inconvenience for anyone.
   - When considering individual family members as sources of support, be sensitive to when someone may "volunteer" out of a sense of duty

or obligation. It is important to honestly assess whether this individual will truly be able to provide the identified support over a long period of time or when other competing difficulties arise.

A FINAL THOUGHT

Families play a continued and important role in the lives of many adults with severe disabilities. In planning for employment, the family may be a valuable resource and a source of important insights. Human services professionals involved in the employment process are encouraged to respect the potential contributions that families can make and to invite them to be active participants in the planning process. This involvement should not be portrayed or viewed as a way of placating the concerns of family members or merely as a matter of protocol. It is important to remember that the role of professionals often is to advise and to make recommendations regarding the "best" options for an individual. This role sometimes extends to implementing those options. The recipient ultimately must live with the consequences of the recommended course of action. The seriousness of this area of an individual's life absolutely requires that we seek and encourage maximum levels of involvement in all phases of the employment process.

People Issues
Friendships, Relationships, and Human Nature

5

*People experience different ways of belonging to each other. They speak
of others as kin, as friends, as co-workers, as neighbors, as belonging to
the same association or congregation, as sharing a common interest, as
being "regulars" (like a regular customer in a tavern or a regular visitor to a park). Shaped by culture and personal history, each of these different relationships implies privileges and obligations specific to its participants. Most people identify someone as a friend, but each friendship
takes its own shape and meaning. For each person, these different kinds
of belonging form the context for social support.*

J. O'Brien & C.L. O'Brien, 1992, p. 18

The professional literature contains an overwhelming amount of rhetoric that
espouses the many and varied benefits of community employment (Albin,
Rhodes, & Mank, 1994; Bellamy et al., 1984; Hagner & Dileo, 1993; Kregel
& Wehman, 1989; Mcloughlin, Garner, & Callahan, 1987; Rhodes & Drum,
1989; Rhodes, Mank, Sandow, Buckley, & Albin, 1990; Rusch, Chadsey-
Rusch, & Johnson, 1991; Sinott-Oswald, Gliner, & Spencer, 1991). These dis-
courses are eloquent, impressive, and incredibly convincing. Although there
are many reasons why community employment is frequently promoted as the
preferred outcome for people with disabilities, one of the foremost reasons is
the opportunity to work and interact with other members of the community.

Interactions that occur in the workplace can take a variety of forms. These
interactions often are portrayed as only applying to individuals with disabilities
as they enter employment. Nothing could be further from the truth. Think about
current or former work experiences, and answer the following questions:

- When you arrived at work the first day, how were you greeted or welcomed?
- Who introduced you to the other employees?
- Was someone assigned to give you a formal introduction to the rules, procedures, and expectations of the work setting?

- Were there unwritten workplace habits and customs, not part of the "formal" orientation, that you learned by observation or experience?
- Were you ever invited to participate with your co-workers in social activities that extended beyond the workday?
- Are there co-workers with whom you only have a relationship during the workday?
- Are there other individuals who are *co-workers* during the workday and also *friends* beyond the workday?
- Are there individuals in the workplace who have been assigned to evaluate, monitor, and supervise your work performance?
- Are there individuals in the workplace who have been assigned to teach you how to perform new and updated work skills?
- Are there individuals who advocate for you either formally (e.g., union representatives) or informally (e.g., friends)?

These various types of interactions provide not only a means to translate necessary task- and work-related procedures but also an opportunity for developing important friendships and relationships among co-workers. For many individuals, friendships that are made at work also become an important part of their social life outside of the workplace. For others, however, the people with whom they work are strictly "co-workers," and social relationships are held at a distance from those of the workplace. The important distinction is the issue of choice and the opportunity for individuals to selectively engage in social relationships both at work and in the community. The social and relational aspects of working are both benefits of employment and focal points in facilitating employment and delivering those supports necessary to maintain employment. Hagner and Dileo (1993) summarized this important point as follows:

> This can be summed up by thinking of supported employment not as supporting employees with a severe disability, but as supporting relationships between and among employees and employers. Working together means being a member of a social group, giving and receiving support, and being included in the culture of a workplace. In practice, most job coaches and other employment specialists have . . . developed techniques for facilitating the natural processes of relationship formation and admission to the culture. (pp. 44–45)

To move productively and effectively within the business world, human services personnel often must adjust their thinking and their actions. These adjustments are necessary in response to juggling and addressing the business and rehabilitation factors that may ultimately affect the success of employment for individuals with severe disabilities (Galloway, 1982; Mcloughlin et al., 1987; Simmons & Flexer, 1992). Human services personnel who may be conversant in the skills necessary to identify an individual's rehabilitation needs also must be able to interpret those needs in relation to necessary supports. This ensures a compatible match between the individual and the workplace and clearly communicates to potential employers the issues in a way that enhances worksite decision making. As has been noted, many of the individuals who are responsible for employment facilitation may have a working knowledge of rehabilitation principles but a limited knowledge of the daily principles and operations of the business world (Defazio & Flexer, 1983; Simmons & Flexer, 1992). The effective blending of business and rehabilitation concerns is perhaps one of the most critically important skills that employment personnel can possess.

We analyze the social and interpersonal aspects of the workplace from two differing perspectives: 1) the viewpoint of employers and 2) the viewpoint of co-workers. In each of these areas, implications are identified relative to the activities involved in planning and facilitating ongoing supports and services.

THE VIEWPOINT OF EMPLOYERS

The term *employer* refers to the individual or group of individuals within a company who assumes responsibility for hiring decisions. In many local businesses (e.g., restaurant, retail store, manufacturing company), employment decisions may be made by the person who actually owns the company. Even if they do not make those decisions directly, there generally is some awareness or indirect involvement in this process. These individuals are likely to have a long-term commitment to the business and to remain as part of the daily operations for an extended period of time. In some ways, their decision to hire a particular applicant (including an individual with disabilities) involves a decision to invite that individual into an important part of their life—their business. In this context, the employer–employee relationship often can take on added significance. Nisbet and Callahan (1987a) described the potential implications of business size as related to the employment of individuals with severe disabilities:

> The size of a business or operation may be important. Generally, small businesses where bureaucratic mechanisms are minimal may be preferable over large, potentially impersonal enterprises because of the ability to negotiate directly and easily with management. While large businesses are not necessarily unwilling to provide flexible opportunities and work schedules, more time may be required to develop individualized opportunities. (p. 185)

In larger businesses, this issue of familiarity with disabilities can likewise have an impact on the process of employment. A study by Levy, Jessop, Rimmerman, and Levy (1992) surveyed the chief executive officers of the Fortune 500 industrials and the Fortune 500 service corporations. The median number of employees in the corporations represented in this sample was 7,500. Respondents were asked a series of questions intended to assess attitudes and practices regarding the employment of individuals with severe disabilities. Results indicated that the employers who were the most favorable toward employing individuals with disabilities were those who had previous experiences with individuals with disabilities and who described those experiences in positive terms.

For the person who owns a business or for the individual who has the responsibility of making employment decisions in a large corporation, the issue remains "doing what is best for the company." Rhodes, Ramsing, and Bellamy (1988) concluded that the decision to employ an individual with disabilities often boils down to a matter of cost–benefit analysis. In this analysis, the reasons an employer should strongly consider employing an individual with disabilities include the following: 1) the benefits that derive from having "good" employees, 2) improved community relations, 3) enrichment of the company's culture, 4) a potential edge in a labor-short economy, 5) some minimal impact on business taxes, and 6) improved possibilities for responding to governmental regulations.

Most employment specialists probably have their own personal preferences about the advantages of small versus large businesses and their potential for employment opportunities. Despite the differing needs of large employers and small, privately owned business, one theme shines through: the importance and value of *personal involvement* by those responsible for employment decisions within the employing organization.

Implications for Planning

Employer contacts are an important and necessary aspect of planning for employment. Discussions regarding the "business angle" on the development of employment opportunities for individuals with severe disabilities historically have had a primary focus on issues related to making initial contacts with employers; the use of business cards, brochures, and other marketing tools; methods of communicating effectively with employers; negotiation strategies; and strategies for "closing the deal" (Culver, Spencer, & Gliner, 1990; Galloway, 1982; Hagner & Dileo, 1993; Mcloughlin et al., 1987; Nietupski, Verstegen, & Hamre-Nietupski, 1992). These are important strategies for job development personnel. These tools repeatedly have been shown to be effective in the facilitation of employment opportunities. Another factor that should be addressed and assessed during the job development phase is the nature of the relationship between the employer and the prospective employee. The degree to which the employer and co-workers can build a "connection" with the new employee can greatly affect the success of the employment process.

During the process of facilitating employment for David, a young man with disabilities, the owner of a local restaurant was approached about the availability of a job for a dishwasher and cook's assistant. During initial conversations, the restaurant owner was somewhat reserved and seemed resistant to the idea. Later, however, she agreed to "give him a try" but stipulated that the restaurant trained its own employees. Based on his performance during the training period, she would make a decision about formalizing his employment.

David began to work in the restaurant. The manager provided him with training on operating the dishwasher. David responded favorably to the training provided by the employer. In addition, David's regular attendance pattern, his promptness and work efficiency, and his positive attitude all contributed to his initial success as an employee. Over time, David and the restaurant owner established a friendship that proved to be an important aspect of his employment. As time passed, David's work responsibilities were expanded to include the tasks involved in being a "cook's assistant." David was happy at his new job, and the restaurant owner was pleased to have him as an employee.

The job developer was later told by the employer that one of the reasons she hired David was his sincere desire to be a dishwasher. In her experience, many people took the dishwashing job in her restaurant until they were able to find another job or because they could not find another job. David truly wanted to be a dishwasher. This commitment, in her words, "touched her heart." David also was able to put this desire to be a dishwasher into action as he gave his all to meet the demands of the job and to please his new employer.

David's story points out an interesting and important consideration in the job development process. Although one of the major roles of job development personnel is to influence the decision making of employers, there also is an implicit requirement that the job developer maintain a loyal allegiance to the needs and preferences of the individuals whom they are representing. Armed with the knowledge and understanding of the dreams and goals held by the person with disabilities that he or she represents, the job developer can knowingly and confidently seek out employment opportunities that match those dreams and goals. Discussions with an employer about available jobs can be effectively matched and compared with the needs of the individual. This approach is vastly different from those used in earlier times when the goal was merely to find an employer who would agree to hire an individual with disabilities—with little or no preference given to the types of work experiences that were sought by the individual.

Implications for Providing Supports and Services

After the employer has decided to provide a job opportunity for the individual with disabilities, issues related to the nature of available supports and services become paramount. Although these issues may have been discussed during the process of job development, they take on a new level of importance when the new employee actually reports for his or her first day of work.

It is critically important for employment specialists to maintain an awareness of these issues during their day-to-day contact with individuals in the workplace. Basic assumptions in the application of natural ways and natural means include the following:

- In the worksite you will observe many different activities, task routines, cultural rituals, and interpersonal ceremonies.
- Generally speaking, things are the way they are for a number of reasons.
- The reasons for these routines, rituals, procedures, or ceremonies may not be logical, sensible, reasonable, or productive.
- As an employment specialist, it is not within your realm of responsibility to modify or eliminate any of these observed routines, rituals, procedures, or ceremonies.
- It is your responsibility to move and maneuver within that culture in a manner that promotes the success of the individual with disabilities whom you are representing and promoting.
- These tasks of representing and promoting should be carried out in as inconspicuous, natural, subtle, and innocuous a manner as possible.

If these assumptions are continually reinforced and remembered by employment specialists, then it will be relatively easy to promote the supported employment experience of individuals with severe disabilities. One easy way to remember this is to place the role of the employment specialist into its most basic perspective: The primary role of the employment specialist is to arrange supports for the individual with disabilities in such a way as to promote a long-term employment experience without the need for continued outside support and intervention from a human services source. If this can be accomplished, then the employee and the employment specialist both can boast a feeling of pride and accomplishment in their chosen careers. Also important, the employer can feel great pride in making a wise decision to hire an individual with severe disabilities and to view this individual as a welcome and valued member of the workplace.

THE VIEWPOINT OF CO-WORKERS

Issues surrounding the attitudes and perceptions of co-workers regarding the employment of individuals with severe disabilities have been a frequent topic of research and investigation. Studies that focus on interactions in the workplace do serve a purpose. These studies illustrate that individuals with severe disabilities typically do not undergo an isolated or solitary work experience. This is a validation of a primary purpose for supported employment. Hagner (1992) observed that many of the available studies of supported employment have a pronounced focus on the quantity and quality of interactions that occur between individuals with severe disabilities and their co-workers. He also warned that a capability for counting social interactions does not automatically translate into a good understanding of the workplace culture. Hagner's observations regarding the complexity of the work culture also deserve credence by employment specialists as they attempt to observe and evaluate the natural ways and means of the workplace.

Acknowledging the limitation identified by Hagner (1992), there are several findings from research and practice regarding the nature of social interactions between supported employees and their co-workers that have implications for the facilitation of employment opportunities. As a starting point, it is important to acknowledge that for individuals with severe disabilities, the likelihood of interactions with people without disabilities is greatly enhanced through participation in supported employment (Nisbet & Callahan, 1987a; Rogan, Hagner, & Murphy, 1993). This finding should come as no surprise. Within the life experience of most adults, the workplace serves as a major arena for social interactions, friendships, and relationships. Nisbet and Hagner (1988) cited the work of Henderson and Argyle (1985), for example, who analyzed the frequency of social interactions among co-workers during the course of a workday. Their findings revealed that during an average workday, employees spend between 35% and 90% of their time interacting with co-workers in various ways including "joking, teasing, helping with work, chatting casually, discussing work, having coffee or meals, discussing personal life, asking or giving advice, and teaching or demonstrating work tasks" (Nisbet & Hagner, 1988, p. 262). This finding emphasizes that the workplace is more than a means to earn a living—it is also an environment rich in opportunities for socialization and relationship building.

Even within the context of an environment that has a predominant theme of social interactions, is there a differing pattern of social contact between individuals with severe disabilities and their co-workers? Rusch, Hughes, Johnson, and Minch (1991) observed several types of interactions that occur between supported employees and their co-workers. These interactions included association, evaluation, training, data collection, and friendship. Their findings indicate that the level of disability experienced by the supported employee has an impact on the frequency and type of interactions that occur in the work setting. Interactions between individuals with severe disabilities and their co-workers tend to have more emphasis on task completion than on socialization (Parent, Kregel, Metzler, & Twardzik, 1992; Rusch, Johnson, & Hughes, 1990; Shafer, Rice, Metzler, & Haring, 1989).

Implications for Planning

During the process of employment planning, employment specialists continually observe and record information about the workplace culture. During this time of observation, it is critically important for employment specialists to take note of social aspects of the workplace that compose the overall culture of the workplace. These social aspects include social customs, stories and roles, language and symbolism, social activities, work space, power and influence, style of leadership, tone of interactions, gathering places, celebrations, and company image (Hagner & Dileo, 1993). (For a further discussion of these issues, see Chapter 9.)

As planning proceeds, observations can focus on the overall social climate of the workplace. Several key questions can help the employment specialist anticipate the degree to which social interactions and relationships are part of the overall culture of the workplace:

- Do employees engage in spontaneous interactions with one another during the workday?
- Does the social climate seem to promote acceptance of individual differences?
- Do management personnel model positive regard for the needs of their employees?
- Does the company sponsor activities and events that promote socialization among its employees?
- Is there an informal social "pecking order" among the employees?
- Who are the most socially influential employees? What are the personal characteristics that may have contributed to this status?
- Do the employees demonstrate any interest in your work as an employment specialist?
- What kinds of questions do they ask about the individual whom you are representing?

A great deal of information can be gained through informal conversations with employees and management personnel in the hallway, in the lunchroom, or around a coffee pot. Although these questions can provide some insights into the social milieu of the workplace, any potential findings should only be viewed as areas for further investigation and consideration. At the same time, there may be obvious "red flags" sighted during these initial visits to the workplace that may be an indication that this particular worksite is not the best choice for the individual being represented.

Implications for Providing Supports and Services

The role of supported employment personnel has been completely reconceptualized and revitalized through a greatly enhanced emphasis on naturally occurring supports within the workplace (Hagner, Rogan, & Murphy, 1992; Rogan et al.,1993). Previous models of supported employment (e.g., enclave, one-to-one job coach, mobile work crew) provided new opportunities for individuals with severe disabilities to work in the community but also virtually ignored the elements of socialization, friendships, and the natural ways and means of the work environment. Brown et al. (1991) have called for a total rejection of any supported employment models or approaches that, by their very nature, inhibit opportunities to be fully included in the social environment of the workplace.

As supported employment practices have become more sensitive to the personal needs, dreams, and visions of the employee, there has been a corresponding increase in the significance given to the opportunities for socialization and naturally occurring supports that are provided to employees. In this context, there often is a need to facilitate social interactions in the workplace (Fabian, Edelman, & Leedy, 1993). Unfortunately, as employment specialists attempt to facilitate connections between the supported employee and his or her co-workers, they may inadvertently inhibit social interactions, informal supports, and friendships (Brown et al., 1991; Hagner, 1992). If socialization is to be one of the primary benefits of supported employment, then the specialist must seek to promote this priority with full awareness and consideration of the role that supports play in this process. Nisbet and Hagner (1988) observed the following:

> Start with an examination of the social interactions and supports characteristic of natural work environments, prior to considering habilitation techniques. Then support system interventions can be designed to build upon and augment the natural processes and interaction within community businesses rather than replace or short-circuit them. Support models that extend from an examination of natural support models are likely to avoid many of the difficulties of the job coach model. (p. 261)

Nisbet and Hagner (1988) proposed alternatives to the traditional supported employment models that tended to isolate the employee from the culture of the workplace:

1. *Job coach*—job coach trains and then fades
2. *Mentor*—job coach trains and supervision is transferred to mentor
3. *Training consultant*—job coach trains with co-workers
4. *Job sharing*—job coach identifies, trains, and assists individual to share a job with supported employee
5. *Attendant*—attendant trains and assists with consultation from job coach

These models provide a more balanced and inclusive approach for entry into the workplace. Interestingly, since 1988, the term "job coach" has become less popular in favor of terms such as "employment specialist" and "employment consultant," which connote a role that is more parallel than direct in relation to the supported employee.

Rogan et al. (1993) suggested several strategies that can be used by the employment specialist as a means of enhancing the use of naturally occurring supports and the degree of involvement demonstrated by other workers: 1) establish personal connections between the supported employee and his or her co-workers, 2) strongly consider the match between employee preferences and the "worksite social climate" when considering potential employment opportunities, 3) collaborate with employees of the worksite in developing adaptations and modifications, and 4) facilitate the ongoing involvement and support of co-workers.

Bill's personal history in the human services system contained many episodes of challenging behavioral outbursts, which included acts of physical aggression, verbal threats, and the destruction of property. At the same time, those who knew him well often commented on his ability to be helpful, kind, and personable. This paradox was confusing and challenging to those responsible for locating employment opportunities for Bill. It generally was believed that Bill would be most successful in a job that was not stressful or anxiety provoking, that provided some opportunities to casually interact with a variety of people, and that included a specific and strictly defined set of work tasks.

An opportunity was found for Bill to work in a donut shop. Bill would report to work in late afternoon, do some cleanup work, wait on the very few customers who would come in at that time of the day, and lock the doors at closing time. Bill would be alone at the donut shop for his entire work shift with the exception of customers who would come in to buy a donut or drink a cup of coffee. Many of the human services professionals who were involved in considering this option for Bill had some serious concerns about his ability to complete these assigned responsibilities in a safe and predictable manner. There also was concern about the possibility of behavior difficulties and liabilities that these episodes may present for Bill, the employer, and the human services agency. The final decision, however, was "take the risk" and provide the support necessary for Bill to take this new job at the donut shop.

An employment specialist was assigned to assist Bill. During the first few days on the job, one of the other donut shop employees voluntarily extended her shift to help Bill learn the routines and tasks of his new job. As each day passed, she began to play a more active role in this process. Interestingly, no one asked her to become involved—she simply had an interest and took the initiative necessary to assist Bill. During his second week of work, Bill became somewhat upset with his employment specialist. He began to raise his voice, stomp around the donut shop, and make derogatory and threatening comments (in the absence of any customers). In retrospect, this situation appeared to be the result of Bill's perceptions about the presence of the employment specialist, his desire to be more independent of human services supports, and the availability of assistance from an actual employee of the donut shop. Despite this behavior difficulty, a decision was made, in cooperation with the employer, to continue Bill's employment. Finally, one day, the co-worker who had taken an interest in assisting Bill made a culminating comment to the employment specialist: "You can leave now." The employment specialist took this "hint" that Bill was in good hands . . . and left the donut shop. Bill continued on with his assigned tasks.

What are we beginning to learn from this and other experiences related to the full utilization of naturally occurring supports *and* to promoting maximized social opportunities for supported employees? The following is a beginning list of our revelations:

- We seem to be learning over and over again (or forgetting over and over again) the tremendous natural resource that is available in co-workers and friends from the workplace.
- The naturally occurring supports of the workplace must always be our starting point—to begin with the assumption that the human services machinery (of which we have become so fond) can solve all of the challenges of a work setting dooms our efforts to failure.
- Each new employment opportunity presents new and unusual challenges.
- We must remember that we always should and will have a great deal to learn about how to effectively facilitate employment.

A FINAL THOUGHT

When planning for the employment of individuals with severe disabilities, it is critical to give consideration to the human side of the enterprise. A strict focus on the "mechanics" of the process (e.g., job duties, tasks to be performed, wages, benefits, working hours, personnel policies) will provide a distorted and myopic view of the total work experience. Much of what any of us do in a work environment necessarily involves and revolves around social interactions with our co-workers, our supervisors, and some form of customer or consumer. The degree to which these social and "human" factors will affect the employment success of an individual with severe disabilities cannot be understated. Take the time and effort necessary to become aware of the social milieu of the workplace. It may make all the difference in determining the ultimate success of the employment experience.

II

Planning for Employment

The history of facilitating employment opportunities largely has been centered around training as the key ingredient in determining the success or failure of a "job placement" (Callahan, 1986; Hagner & Dileo, 1993; Mcloughlin, Garner, & Callahan, 1987; Nisbet & Hagner, 1988). This approach implies that individuals with disabilities and the degree to which they are able to obtain memberships within work cultures largely are dependent on the training skills of their employment specialist. This position, perhaps unwittingly, minimizes the potential contributions that people with disabilities can make in a workplace (e.g., as workers, as co-workers, as friends) and maximizes the extent to which training and skill acquisition are the overriding issues in obtaining and maintaining employment. Available data indicate that skills are only a small part of the total picture when discussing employment (Greenspan & Shoultz, 1981; Hanley-Maxwell, Rusch, Chadsey-Rusch, & Renzaglia, 1986).

Clearly, training (or, more precise, systematic instruction) is a critical part of employment facilitation. What we are beginning to realize, however, is that there are an infinite number of other strategies that can be used to strengthen an individual's compatibility with the work environment, including the use of supports that occur naturally in the work setting (e.g., employees assisting one another, in-house training programs available to all personnel, friendships that include assisting one another in various ways while on the job). The challenges that lie ahead for employment personnel are 1) becoming skilled in analyzing work environments in regard to the availability of potentially useful and naturally occurring supports, 2) maintaining a constant awareness of the needs and desires of the individual for whom they are facilitating employment, and 3) making skillful and accurate decisions regarding the relative value of naturally occurring supports and the implementation of more traditional systematic instruction procedures.

Section II addresses several issues surrounding the identification and use of supports to promote community for individuals with severe disabilities. In

Chapter 6, the Seven-Phase Sequence, an approach for balancing natural supports and individual needs in the process of facilitating employment, is reviewed and analyzed. This approach to planning and providing acknowledges the importance of the workplace culture but also accepts that many individuals with severe disabilities may require support in the form of systematic instruction as a means of acquiring required worksite competencies.

Chapter 7 details the Vocational Profile as a planning tool designed to assist individuals with severe disabilities, their families and friends, and human services professionals as they collaborate to generate specific employment outcomes. As part of the planning process, the Vocational Profile can be used to link the individual with ensuing job development efforts and to the actual job tasks identified by potential employers; to paint an accurate picture of the individual's life and relationships; and to counteract the potential impact of negative evaluations, reputations, and perceptions that might exist concerning the individual.

Chapter 8 provides an overview of job development strategies and issues from a vantage point that values and respects the desires, goals, and dreams of individuals with severe disabilities. Finally, Chapter 9 summarizes a plan for Job Analysis that focuses on both work task/routine requirements and the supports that may be available in the work environment. By gaining a thorough understanding of the demands and supports of the workplace, we are much more likely to experience success in facilitating employment outcomes for individuals with severe disabilities.

The Seven-Phase Sequence

 **6**

I want to be seen in my simple, natural, ordinary fashion, without straining or artifice, for it is myself that I portray. . . .

M.E. de Montaigne, 1580

The information in this chapter is pivotal to implementing virtually every strategy in this book. Individualized planning must consider all of the relationships and connections available to applicants. This allows job developers to identify potential employers who not only match personal preferences but who also might be willing to provide naturally existing supports. *Job development efforts must successfully communicate to employers the redefined role of human services supports as additive and supportive to natural procedures rather than as an artificial substitute.* In this context, job analysis becomes a cultural interpretation of a work setting rather than a human services–referenced training plan. Finally, jobsite facilitation is fundamentally changed by the Seven-Phase Sequence by reconceptualizing the role of outside supports. It may be helpful for the practitioner to return to this chapter as the subsequent information is read to "ground" him- or herself in the direction provided by the sequence. In this way, the value of the concept can be fully implemented to ensure that individual needs *and* the features of naturalness are balanced.

Successful facilitation of employment for people with disabilities requires balancing two perspectives that are often at odds in community workplaces—the general decisions made by employers regarding the support that is routinely given to their employees and the specific needs of the individual workers. Traditionally, the human services field has assumed that the needs of workers with disabilities, especially employees with severe disabilities, could not be adequately met by employers (Hagner & Dileo, 1993; Nisbet & Callahan, 1987a; Nisbet & Hagner, 1988). Most training and facilitation strategies, therefore, have evolved from a human services perspective rather than from more naturally defined sources. Since the early 1990s, however, employment facilitators have begun recognizing the possible contributions of employers when they are included fully in supported employment. Perhaps more apparent are the limiting effects on integration and full participation when employers are excluded from this process.

The involvement of employers in the facilitation of supported employment has been labeled as "natural supports" (Hagner, Rogan, & Murphy, 1992). Natural supports have been suggested as one solution to the need to provide "consistent and ongoing training and follow-along services" (Nisbet & Hagner, 1988, p. 263) in work settings. This concept has experienced such universal acceptance that the U.S. Congress has suggested the use of natural supports as a source of extended services in its deliberations on the Rehabilitation Act Amendments of 1992 (PL 102-569) (Senate Report 103-357).

The involvement of employers in the support of people with disabilities has created its own set of challenges and pitfalls for providers of supported employment services. Questions abound concerning how best to start implementation including

- Is there a need for "purity" of natural supports?
- Is it acceptable to pay natural supporters?
- How do we identify whether a certain employer will have sufficient capacity and desire to support an employee with a disability?
- What will happen to supported employees if natural supports are not sufficient for success?

This chapter provides direction for employment facilitators to use in addressing these difficult issues.

WORKPLACE FORCES: EMPLOYEE NEEDS AND NATURAL FEATURES

Every employee experiences two great forces that tend to pull in different directions—the individual life needs, which are unique to each person, and the natural features of the work culture in which he or she is working. These forces must be kept in reasonable balance if employees are to view their employment experience as successful and personally rewarding (see Figure 6.1).

In our Western capitalist society, employees generally are expected to begin their jobs by acclimating to the existing demands and conditions of the workplace. Later, through negotiations, relationships, and seniority, employees often begin to make more personalized arrangements that better address their unique individual needs (e.g., varied work schedules, differences in work assignments, opportunities to redefine job descriptions, sharing of certain responsibilities with co-workers). In this situation, the *initial* balance is slanted strongly in the direction of naturalness. We all learn, for example, to expect and accept this important fact from our parents, older siblings, relatives, or friends. A clear message often is conveyed to novice employees: "Find out how the boss wants the job done and what is expected, and just do it." Later,

Employee Needs

Natural Features

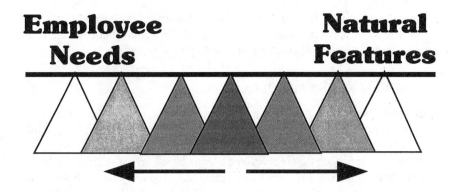

Figure 6.1. Workplace forces: Employee needs versus natural features.

as employees have "time in" on the job, the possibility exists that the balance will shift in favor of opportunities for their reasonable, individual needs to be met. It also helps if the individual needs that an employee has are naturally met in the features of the work culture. This factor, of course, is of significant concern in job development for supported employment. Hagner and Dileo (1993) provided the following examples of these individualized arrangements in employment:

- The employee who returns from maternity or paternity leave to work only 4 days per week
- The employee who is averse to learning word processing and is allowed to continue using a typist for written products
- The employee who receives permission to leave early on Tuesdays to take a college course (p. 118)

These forces provide a useful template from which supported employment can be analyzed. Traditionally, supported employment providers have tended to negotiate a "support relationship" that begins employment with a greater emphasis on individual needs than is natural for most employees (Nisbet & Callahan, 1987a; Nisbet & Hagner, 1988). The employer often is told, for example, that because of the severity of the applicant's disability, it is necessary for a human services professional (i.e., "employment specialist," "job coach," "employment facilitator") to initially teach the person, to make necessary adaptations and modifications, and to generally provide all direct supports. Later, through the use of fading procedures, the supported employee is expected to function successfully in relation to the natural features of support.

Even though this approach to employment facilitation results in significantly more attention to the individual needs of people with severe disabilities, it casts the supported employee as "different" from other employees. It also neglects the potential success of the natural features of support that are available to other new employees. Most important, this "backward" approach releases the employer from ownership of solutions that evolve and that relate to the impact of the supported employee's disability. This "locks in" the need for continuing outside supports by human services agencies.

THE SEVEN-PHASE SEQUENCE

There must be a solution to the paradox created by the need to initiate and maintain employment in a manner that is as naturally referenced as possible while acknowledging the extensive support needs of people with severe disabilities. The approach that is recommended is based on a modification of the Seven-Phase Sequence for training originally developed by Gold (1980b) and revised for natural work environments by Callahan (1991b) to help answer these questions (see Figure 6.2). This sequence represents a conceptual model designed to balance the natural capacity of community workplaces and the individual needs of employees. The evolution of Gold's original model has proceeded from a narrow training focus in the 1970s through a broadened, naturally referenced focus in the 1980s and has culminated in a culturally referenced approach based on the natural features of supports in the 1990s (Callahan, 1986, 1992; Gold, 1980a).

The first four phases of the Seven-Phase Sequence clearly articulate a strong preference for using natural processes to assist supported employees as they learn and maintain their jobs. This strategy and the accompanying job analysis activities that are performed require the employment specialist to carefully examine and utilize all of the features of "natural capacity" that exist in a workplace to assist each employee to learn and perform his or her job.

The back-up phases of the sequence (i.e., Phases Five through Seven) are designed to provide whatever additional assistance may be necessary, in a manner that is as natural as possible, to teach the job in those cases in which natural procedures have been shown to be insufficient. Employment specialists are faced with the need to provide creative and effective strategies that supplement the natural supports available on a jobsite. In some cases it may even be necessary for the employment specialist to completely take over the instructional responsibility for an employee. It is important to note, however, that under the auspices of a traditional "job coach" model, this process of taking over instructional responsibility was a *starting point* in the facilitation of employment (Bellamy et al., 1988; Mcloughlin et al., 1987; Rusch, Chadsey-Rusch, & Johnson, 1991). In the Seven-Phase Sequence, these activities become a backup to the natural ways and means of the workplace culture.

This new perspective results in a new role for employment specialists and raises difficult questions regarding technical assistance and staff competence:

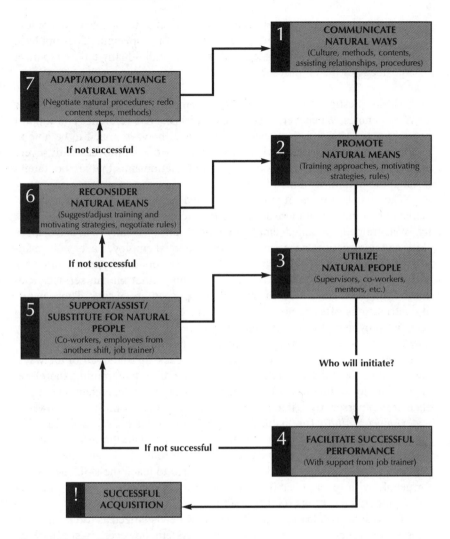

Figure 6.2. The Seven-Phase Sequence.

- How can an employment specialist effectively implement systematic instructional procedures if this individual does not have a solid understanding of the task requirements and procedures?
- How can a new employee with disabilities take full advantage of the naturally occurring supports in the workplace?
- How can an employment specialist offer creative solutions if he or she does not know powerful instructional techniques?

- How can an employment specialist expect to effectively teach an employee who finds it extremely difficult to learn if the specialist does not have knowledge of effective strategies that can be individually tailored to meet the needs of the employee?

These questions create a paradox for employment specialists and their service agencies. Whenever feasible, specialists need to reference and support natural procedures and relationships. They also, however, need to be able to go beyond natural capacity, when necessary, to offer employees with severe disabilities access to the necessary skills and relationships that are not taught through the natural features of support.

The first key to resolving this dilemma requires the employment specialist to recognize that there are limits to natural supports and natural capacity. Well-trained, seasoned employment specialists usually will have those skills and perspectives necessary to meet individual employee needs in a manner that is more technically effective than those found in typical employees and supervisors. There are, however, many things that human services specialists can never do as well as "natural" people can on jobsites. Those natural contributions often relate to the most critically important aspects of success. Employment specialists must, therefore, recognize that although they may need to possess a range of skills to ensure the success of an employee, those skills are always viewed as a secondary, back-up role to all of the ways, means, and people that are natural to the jobsite. Effective training, therefore, operates under an umbrella of guiding principles and is dependent on the balance of two perspectives that are often at odds: generic validity and power.

Generic validity (or "naturalness") refers to the degree to which a training approach can utilize, approximate, or accommodate the teaching strategies used in any given community setting. *Power* refers to the amount of intervention, assistance, effort, and creativity needed to teach the skills necessary for people with severe disabilities to successfully participate in community-based, integrated settings (Gold, 1980b).

These concepts, in their purest form, may be visualized as forces that pull in opposing directions. An effective training system, however, must offer *both* options to trainers (i.e., employment specialists). The relative degree of generic validity or power to be utilized during training is an individualized decision to be made by the trainer. The rule of thumb for the approach to training suggested here is for the trainer to initiate instruction that is as generically valid as possible but backed up with sufficient power to successfully teach the task.

Approaches to systematic instruction that do not recognize both of these perspectives can result in real problems for learners. If generic validity is the sole consideration, then employees who need more instructional power to learn tasks than is typically available in the setting might be underemployed or even excluded from the setting. If instructional power is arbitrarily used from the beginning of employment, then it will be difficult, if not impossible, for natural people in the setting (e.g., co-workers, supervisors) to assume responsibility for teaching and supporting the employee at that same level of intensity. The employment specialist will become permanently attached to the employee with a disability and to the employer in a dependency relationship. The Seven-Phase Sequence resolves these issues in a manner that encourages natural means to be used initially and for increasingly powerful procedures to be implemented as a reserve or backup in situations in which individuals need more than what the setting is able to provide.

The Seven-Phase Sequence provides a clear course for providing instruction and support using the natural ways, means, and people available to any new employee. It is important to remember, however, that this is not a lock-step model. The specialist must carefully identify the features of naturalness by using the first three steps of the Seven-Phase Sequence. Unless there is compelling evidence otherwise, the specialist should proceed to support, not substitute for, the natural processes of the jobsite for initial instruction and orientation (Hagner & Dileo, 1993; Hagner, Rogan, et al., 1992; Nisbet & Callahan, 1987a; Nisbet & Hagner, 1988).

USING THE SEVEN-PHASE SEQUENCE

Implementing the plans and decisions made through using the Seven-Phase Sequence is the first step in a process that is critically important to the success of supported employment. This process involves supporting the direct facilitation of training by natural supporters or providing direct training of the supported employee by the facilitator, as appropriate. The decisions of *who* will provide the initial assistance, *how* the job will be taught, and *how* the job will be performed are covered in Phases One, Two, and Three of the sequence.

This implementation begins on the first day of employment for the supported employee (or possibly during a negotiated orientation period) and continues until all of the necessary job routines have been learned by the employee. In addition, the facilitator must ensure that the employee is made aware of the nuances and subtleties of the workplace culture (Hagner & Dileo, 1993).

The Natural Phases

The first three phases of the Seven-Phase Sequence provide all of the information necessary for the facilitator to consider the features of naturalness that might be used to provide support and direction while assisting the employee to successfully perform the job. These phases require facilitators to perform a "cultural analysis" of each setting in which a supported employee will work. Phase Four is the point at which facilitation, support, and training strategies are implemented within the workplace. This phase is implemented in accordance with the information gleaned during Phases One through Three.

It is critical that the individual responsible for employment facilitation maintain a sense of wonder and discovery in all workplaces, no matter how familiar they may seem. In this way, every work setting can be appreciated in relation to its unique features of support and naturalness.

Phase One: Communicate Natural Ways   Phase One references the *natural ways* in which jobs are performed in work settings. Natural ways include nuances of the workplace culture, methods of performance for targeted job tasks, step-by-step procedures, the manner in which workers interact, the managerial style of the setting, and all other natural features that describe the unique characteristics of performance and behavior desired by the employer.

This phase is crucial because it provides the information necessary for the new employee to effectively "fit in" to the ongoing flow of the workplace. Employees who perform their jobs in a manner similar to others not only are more likely to be accepted as "one of the gang" but also make it easier for supervisors and co-workers to provide assistance and troubleshoot problems. Following are suggestions and guidelines for employment facilitators during Phase One:

- The initial phase of the Seven-Phase Sequence is accomplished during *job development* and *job analysis.*
- Identify the unique features of the *culture* of the work setting.
- Get a clear image of the *ways* in which people perform their jobs, how they interact with each other, the style of management, and the relationships between co-workers and supervisors.
- Carefully observe the *specific tasks* that will comprise the supported employee's job.
- If the required task(s) are to be performed in a reasonable time, then ask permission to *perform* the various tasks.
- Identify written *policies* and *rules* that describe the official "company line" for appropriate employee behavior.
- Notice all subtle, unwritten rules of the setting.
- Convey the message that *co-workers* and *supervisors* are the "experts" and that the job facilitator is there to learn and to assist only as necessary.

Phase Two: Promote Natural Means   Phase Two requires facilitators to examine the *natural means* used by employers to communicate the natural ways desired for employee performance and behavior. This concept concentrates primarily on the teaching strategies, if any, used by employers to introduce new employees to their jobs and to support them when they need assistance and upgrading. Training procedures certainly will vary among worksites in any community. A troubling aspect of this phase is the possibility, even the likelihood, that the means used to teach and support employees will vary from person to person in the worksite and that these approaches may be unstructured and ineffective.

Perhaps the most effective way to assess the natural means of a jobsite is to first ask the employer to describe those procedures used to communicate the natural ways desired for employee performance and behavior. Second, if possible, observe teaching activities that are naturally performed by employees in the setting. Finally, and most important, ask to be taught how to perform the job tasks by the people who would naturally assist the jobs to be performed by the new employee. This approach will provide the employment specialist with a valid perspective from which to make decisions later in the sequence.

As noted previously, experienced facilitators will probably conclude that their skills in the use of systematic instruction are far more effective than those observed in the natural setting. It should not be assumed, however, that those natural procedures will be insufficient to teach successful performance to the supported employee. The Seven-Phase Sequence contains a strong bias for providing the natural means of the workplace with the chance to be effective. It can even be argued that it is reasonable to accept the reduced levels of performance that may result from natural features of supports rather than those potentially achievable through powerful training procedures from the employment facilitator. The Seven-Phase Sequence attempts to keep such situations from becoming "either/or" decisions. The back-up phases discussed later will provide greater levels of assistance for those occasions when naturally occurring procedures have been shown to be insufficient. Following are suggestions for employment facilitators for completing Phase Two of the Seven-Phase Sequence:

- Observe and, as appropriate, experience the *natural means* that the employment settings use to introduce and maintain the natural ways identified in Phase One.
- Observe *training interactions among employees,* especially between new employees and the people responsible for teaching them their jobs.
- Ask the employer to describe *the manner in which employees receive training and support,* and review any written materials and procedures.
- When appropriate, request that the employer provide you with *training on the tasks to be performed by the supported employee.*
- Look for *informal assistance* provided by co-workers to others in the setting.
- Ask the employer and others in the setting about the *flexibility* that is offered to employees and what the *conditions* are for this kind of consideration.
- Compare the *strategies observed* with the anticipated training needs of the supported employee.

Phase Three: Utilize Natural People   In Phase Three of the sequence, the facilitator identifies and enlists the *natural people* who typically support new employees with performing their jobs. This is the first phase of the *cultural analysis* of the activity traditionally referred to as job analysis. This activity is possibly the most novel aspect of natural supports for traditional providers of supported employment services. In the past, job developers often promised employers that job trainers would provide "all of the assistance necessary for successful performance." In that way, the employer was required to make no investments in the initial training and support of the employee. This practice resulted in the isolation of supported employees within the context of their own work settings. The job coach often acted as an interpreter for all of the information, rules, policies, and activities of the workplace for the supported employee. This role placed the job coach between the employer and the employee. That approach also did not account for the fact that many employers wanted to train new employees themselves rather than rely on assistance from an "outside" source.

The Seven-Phase Sequence asks employment facilitators to get to know all of the different people who are responsible for providing assistance or who may be willing to provide assistance to new employees. There is also a need to enlist those people to provide training and support for the new employee. Following are suggestions for employment facilitators for recruiting and involving natural people:

- Identify the *personnel* who are typically responsible for teaching new employees how to perform the job to be performed by the supported employee.
- Even though some businesses may have specific personnel to provide training and orientation, often it is necessary to observe or ask the employer directly in order to *identify the co-workers or supervisors* who offer this service.
- Assume that the supported employee will receive the *same initial orientation and training* support offered to all other new employees.
- Try to *form relationships* with support personnel as early as possible during job analysis.
- Answer direct questions concerning the supported employee's disabilities in a positive manner and in terms that describe the *impact of disability.* Avoid disability labels.
- If specific support personnel are not available, *recruit* co-workers or supervisors who seem interested in your job analysis and who are most willing to provide you with assistance.

Phase Four: Facilitate Successful Performance   Phase Four of the sequence involves providing initial and ongoing assistance to the supported employee. All of the information gained during the first three phases and the job analysis are considered in implementing this phase. Facilitators must now determine the degree of naturalness that will be used during initial training. It is strongly suggested that unless there are clear indications to the contrary, preference should be given to using natural procedures.

If the facilitator has decided to follow the sequence and to engage natural supporters to initiate instruction, then it is necessary to plan a strategy for observing training and for providing suggestions and technical assistance. Implementing this phase requires the facilitator to be physically present at the jobsite during this initial period. Depending on the factors determined during the first three phases of the sequence and the job analysis, the facilitator may choose a range of approaches varying from a discreet observation point to proximity to the employee.

Plans also must be made to offer feedback and suggestions to the natural supporter. Depending on the needs of the employee and the capacity of the employer, the appropriate strategy for feedback will vary—as will positioning of the facilitator. It may be necessary to offer almost immediate feedback in some instances; in others hourly intervals or even longer may be appropriate. When significant problems arise, the facilitator should implement the back-up phases of the sequence for more individualized attention for the supported employee.

There might be several situations in which a facilitator would consider less natural procedures during implementation of Phase Four. Often the roles of the job developer and the employment facilitator are performed by different people. The job developer may indicate to the employer that the employment facilitator will perform all of the initial instruction of the supported employee. In this case, the facilitator often finds it necessary to initiate training, involving the natural supporters as much as possible, then fade to them as training allows. It is therefore critical that job development reflects the values for natural supports embedded in the Seven-Phase Sequence.

There also may be instances relating to the specific impact of an employee's disability in which the facilitator may feel that it is necessary to model effective techniques for the natural supporters. There might also be situations that are so fragile in relation to the employer's low expectation of success or of the employee's or the family's low expectations that the facilitator might feel that a period of greater instructional control is called for than is available from natural procedures.

Finally, job stations and jobsites may require modifications to ensure accessibility and productivity for employees with physical disabilities. These modifications often are best made before an employee begins work. The employment facilitator, however, should include the employer in the solutions to these needs rather than independently assume this responsibility. Following are suggestions for employment facilitators for facilitating successful performance in Phase Four:

- After completing the job analysis, decide *who will facilitate* Phase Four.
- *Assume* that the *natural personnel* identified in Phase Three will facilitate Phase Four.
- Phase Four requires, initially at least, the *presence of the job facilitator* close enough to the job that assistance can be offered when necessary.
- Negotiate an *unobtrusive observation* position in the work setting.
- In some cases, it may be helpful to develop a *facilitation plan* with the employer to cover varying support needs during the initial stages of employment.
- A facilitation plan may include *natural co-workers or supervisors* who typically teach the assigned tasks, *co-workers from other shifts* paid overtime for support, and the *job facilitator.*
- *Build the support capacity* of the employer whenever possible; do not simply substitute for the employer in providing direct support.

The Back-Up Phases

It is important to realize that regardless of who provides the initial training of the supported employee—it is likely that adjustments to the features of naturalness identified in Phases One, Two, and Three will be necessary. The facilitator, therefore, should not depend on initial strategies and decisions to be sufficient in facilitating successful employment. During the early days of employment, facilitators must constantly monitor the performance of the supported employee. If initial strategies are not successful, then the back-up phases of the Seven-Phase Sequence must be implemented.

Possibly the most significant contribution of the Seven-Phase Sequence is its role as a safety net. Rather than blame acquisition problems on the employee or the employer, the sequence asks employment facilitators to consider increasingly powerful strategies to achieve successful performance. Phases Five, Six, and Seven represent a logical closed loop of decisions that encourage the facilitator to remain positively focused until the employee successfully learns the job.

Another feature of the Seven-Phase Sequence is its ability to balance naturalness and the needs of individual employees. The initial three phases are naturally derived, and the last three phases allow for more powerful, individualized strategies. Facilitators must be careful, however, not to switch immediately and completely from natural to individualized approaches. The Seven-Phase Sequence provides for a fluid, constant analysis of the ways, means, and people involved in assisting supported employees. It is important that if facilitators depart from natural strategies that it is done in a measured manner by using small, incremental changes from more natural procedures.

Phase Five: Support/Assist/Substitute for Natural People   Phase Five involves supporting or possibly substituting for the natural people who are responsible for teaching job tasks. The facilitator *must* be present on the jobsite to successfully make this and many other back-up decisions. There are a range of ways in which the natural people on a jobsite can be supported:

- *Demonstrate* a more powerful technique.
- *Negotiate* a time for discussion and feedback with the natural supporter.
- *Offer* training information formally or informally.
- *Shadow* the natural supporter and offer ongoing feedback.
- *Substitute* for natural people by negotiating for a different co-worker or trainer to provide assistance.
- *Use* personal assistance providers, volunteers, parents, or other family members who might be appropriate substitutes for natural supporters. (Of course, the most likely substitute is the employment facilitator.)

These strategies represent only a few of the many ways in which natural people can be supported. The Seven-Phase Sequence allows for direct training by the employment facilitator, but other approaches should be considered first. At this stage of the sequence, the employment facilitator is required to make a series of judgments regarding the degree to which the feature's naturalness must be altered in order to ensure the likelihood of employee success.

Phase Six: Reconsider Natural Means The decisions made during Phase Six involve a reconsideration of the natural means used by employers to teach and motivate employees to perform their jobs. This is another point in the sequence in which the employment facilitator's knowledge of the subtleties that comprise the work environment become critically important. It is likely that many workplaces will not have a single approach to teaching and motivating but rather a hodgepodge of approaches individually determined by each co-worker and supervisor. Facilitators must be careful not to generalize too much in this area. The teaching style of one co-worker may differ significantly from another and further yet from a supervisor. In these cases, it is important to consider the various strategies that seem to be working and who uses them. It may be necessary to offer specific suggestions to specific natural supporters—each different from the other—in order to achieve successful performance.

Following are possible considerations for employment facilitators in implementing Phase Six:

- *Review* any written materials and procedures to determine any back-up procedures that may have been overlooked or not used.
- *Reanalyze* the environment to locate any forms of informal assistance that have not been used and that could be provided by co-workers or others in the setting.
- *Rethink* the strategies being used to meet the learning and employment needs of the supported employee. Seek input and guidance from other employment facilitators or members of the planning team.

Phase Seven: Adapt/Modify/Change Natural Ways   Phase Seven decisions involve adapting, modifying, or negotiating for flexibility in the natural ways that workplaces operate. Natural ways include task methods, step-by-step procedures, rules, customs, and the overall culture of the work setting. These decisions are considered last because they often are the most consistent and unchanging features of workplaces. It is necessary in some instances, however, to negotiate for changes in this area even before the employee begins employment. For example, if the natural way to get paper for a copier in an office is to reach up into the storage cabinet to retrieve the paper, a modification would be immediately necessary for an employee who uses a wheelchair and has limited reach.

Following are possible considerations for employment facilitators in implementing Phase Seven:

- *Alter* the specific tasks that will comprise the supported employee's job (i.e., add or delete specific tasks or components of tasks).
- *Arrange* for specifically negotiated alterations in the time requirements for performing each task.
- *Encourage* co-workers and supervisors to assist in taking a fresh look at the strategies and procedures being used to complete the assigned tasks.

Suggestions for Implementing the Back-Up Phases

Because the back-up phases of the Seven-Phase Sequence provide facilitators the opportunity to meet the individual needs of employees with disabilities in a more powerful manner than that available through natural features of support, it is important that the degree of power to be used is carefully considered. It does not make sense to swing from total naturalness to complete individualization the first time a problem occurs. Therefore, a measured problem-solving approach that references naturalness as much as possible is best. Naturalness should exert a tug on individualized solutions to worksite problems much as gravity constrains a jump. We often have barriers to overcome, but the effects of gravity must be considered in our strategies. Following are suggestions for employment facilitators to assist in implementing the back-up phases:

- Modifications, changes, or direct facilitation should first be addressed to the features of work settings that *change the most.*
- Each change from "natural procedures" should proceed from *least intrusive to more intrusive* or from *most natural to less natural.*
- Invite the *employer* to solve problems *first* before offering suggestions.
- Treat the employer as the "*apparent customer*" and the *expert* in relation to the workplace.
- "*Naturalness*" should always exert a pull on all decisions made to modify the ways, means, or people of a work setting.

- Even though the suggested sequence of this approach *usually is the most effective* way to proceed, it is not necessary to take each of the back-up phases in turn.
- Remember, *embracing natural supports does not mean relinquishing our role* as facilitators and "experts" in the area of disabilities.

A FINAL THOUGHT

The facilitation of employment requires a constant awareness that there are limits to natural supports and natural capacity. At the same time, it is important to resist the temptation to charge into the workplace and assume the role of a training expert and overwhelm the situation with instructional technology and sophisticated data-collection procedures. The balancing act described in this chapter requires that the employment facilitator develop a sensitivity to the climate of the workplace, a collection of strategies for actively involving the employee within that setting, and a genuine respect for the needs and preferences of the individual.

The Vocational Profile
Building a Foundation for Skills and Supports

7

Storytellers and listeners benefit from stories in different ways. Each of us comes to a story—and away from it—with different experiences. Each of us focuses on different details. I don't even expect your story to be absolutely accurate historically because I understand that you, the storyteller, have selected those parts of your story that mean the most to you, that move you the most.

T. Chappell, 1993, p. 70

Planning is a critical aspect of securing responsive and appropriate vocational and career outcomes for people with severe disabilities. Any planning activities must be grounded and supported by a solid value base. Planning also must be organized in a manner that ensures a comprehensive approach to collecting relevant information; opportunities for understanding the individual's personal history; an articulation of the individual's dreams and vision for the future; and a creative, flexible approach to securing and allocating resources. Finally, planning must be viewed as more than an administrative process; planning must always be viewed as a dynamic outcome-based process.

The Vocational Profile is an information process—a guide that suggests questions to ask in order to discover information about an applicant. In addition, the time spent with the applicant and the subsequent relationship that is formed provide a facilitator with knowledge and insights into the life experiences of the applicant and provide direction for employment. This approach differs from traditional assessments in that it does not measure anything, and it supports utilizing involvement and interaction with the applicant in natural settings rather than in contrived evaluation settings. More important, it provides a complete picture of an applicant rather than focusing attention on one or two skill areas. A specific job can then be identified that is consistent with the person's entire life, not merely with an instance of performance.

The Vocational Profile is a planning tool designed to assist individuals with severe disabilities, their families and friends, and human services professionals as they collaborate to generate specific employment outcomes. As part of the planning process, the Vocational Profile can be used to accomplish the following outcomes:

- To link the individual with ensuing job development efforts and to the actual job tasks identified by potential employers
- To paint an accurate picture of the individual's life and relationships
- To counteract the potential impact of negative evaluations, reputations, and perceptions that might exist concerning the individual
- To welcome and empower others, especially those closest to the individual, into the development of life and employment outcomes
- To develop relationships and connections with potential sources of support and mentorship in the community
- To assist with the transition from the individual's current life circumstance to the life of an employee
- To facilitate an individualized job for the person with a disability that reflects personal preferences, employment goals, gifts, and talents

THE ROLE OF EVALUATION:
TRADITIONAL USES AND EMERGING PRACTICES

Supported employment has caused a stir of excitement in the field of human services. This approach validates that employment is possible for those individuals who were formerly considered "too disabled" to benefit from traditional vocational rehabilitation services. Despite the intended purpose of supported employment, access to these programs has, for many years, remained somewhat restricted and dependent on the results of a formal, standardized evaluation (Callahan & Mast, 1994; Gaylord-Ross, 1986; Gaylord-Ross & Browder, 1991; Gaylord-Ross, Forte, Storey, Gaylord-Ross, & Jameson, 1987; Mcloughlin, Garner, & Callahan, 1987; Smull & Bellamy, 1991).

Most supported employment funding has been channeled through state rehabilitation agencies. These agencies typically require a vocational evaluation as a means of determining eligibility for any of their services. People who meet the established criteria are considered eligible for services. Those who do not meet the established criteria are excluded from receiving services or referred to another service provider, typically for day or sheltered activities. Frequently, the same eligibility criteria established for rehabilitation services are used to establish eligibility for supported employment services (Mast & Callahan, 1994).

Traditional assessment procedures often include educational, vocational, and psychological test batteries and rating scales, work samples, and situa-

tional assessments. The intended purpose of these evaluation activities is to
verify the vocational "potential" of applicants by answering the yes/no question of employability. There is a limited probability that these types of assessments (i.e., standardized, norm-referenced) can predict the likelihood of an individual's success in employment or an individual's potential to benefit from systematic instruction. In keeping with the trends established in recent legislation and policy development, it is more productive to assume that all individuals with severe disabilities can be trained and supported in a manner that facilitates employment in the community (Gaylord-Ross, 1986; Rogan & Hagner, 1990). The key variable in this endeavor, however, is the availability of an appropriate blend of supports, services, and values.

Changes in the regulations that govern the implementation of supported employment services reflect a reduced emphasis on traditional evaluation activities. The Rehabilitation Act Amendments of 1992 (PL 102-569) indicate that the need for an evaluation that documents rehabilitation "potential" has been replaced by a "presumption of ability" (Button, 1992). These amendments cast an entirely different light on the evaluation process and the determination of eligibility for supported employment:

> It shall be presumed that an individual can benefit in terms of an employment outcome from Vocational Rehabilitation Services—unless the designated state unit can demonstrate by clear and convincing evidence that such individual is incapable of benefiting from Vocational Rehabilitation Services in terms of an employment outcome. (Section 123[c][4][A]) (emphasis added)

By valuing people with disabilities and assuming that they can contribute through the use of systematic instruction, technology, and effective matches, the starting point of vocational services is moving away from evaluating and toward discovery—discovery of who people really are behind the veil of disability and of what they want and what they might be able to contribute to employers. This shift in emphasis can have a dramatic impact on the employment opportunities available to individuals with severe disabilities. It is also important, however, that human services professionals adjust their thinking to include this presumption of employability within the planning processes that guide supported employment (Mcloughlin et al., 1987).

The Vocational Profile differs from traditional assessment procedures in several ways:

1. It identifies information about the individual that reflects his or her history and experience in community and with the human services system. Evaluation procedures result in the production of current data but only provide an extremely narrow perspective on an individual's life experiences, gifts, and abilities. Choosing a particular job for a person should be based on information obtained from the person's entire life and not from one instance of performance.

2. It frees the applicant from the competition inherent in taking standardized or norm-referenced tests as proof of his or her employability. Readiness to begin work is assumed for all applicants.

3. It is used only as a guide for matching an individual with an appropriate job. It is not intended to exclude an individual from the opportunity to work (Callahan, 1991b).

4. It seeks to have *ecological validity* rather than *predictive validity*. It is more important that a match between an applicant and an employment location make sense in relation to an individual's life situation rather than attempt to predict success. Because of their reliance on competition, predictive measures consistently forecast employment failure for people with severe disabilities (Brown et al., 1986; Nisbet & Callahan, 1987b).

5. It communicates a belief that a person's skills, experiences, available supports, preferences, needs, and living situation cannot be best captured on a standardized checklist or diagnostic report. A format composed of open-ended categories allows each person's life experiences to be described in a unique manner (Ohio Safeguards, 1990a, 1990b).

6. It empowers and involves applicants and their families and friends rather than excludes them. Natural, common sense approaches to employment are given priority over strategies that rely solely on professional judgment and service.

Rogan and Hagner (1990) captured the importance of clarifying and limiting the role of traditional vocational evaluation procedures, as well as generating alternative methods for gathering employment-related information, as follows:

> Whenever any evaluation is performed, the all-important first step is to determine what question is being asked and for what purpose information is being gathered. Within a supported employment context, the question is not "Which people belong in community settings?" Nor is it correct to ask, "In which of a series of continuum options should this person be placed?" . . . The appropriate questions are, "In which community settings is this person likely to be successful?", "What adaptations are required?" and "What support services should be provided?" The purpose of vocational evaluation is to provide a structured approach for obtaining answers to these questions. We have argued that more than mere tinkering and repackaging is required if vocational evaluation is to serve the needs of supported employment programs . . . with the basic belief that people with severe disabilities can be successfully employed if placed in individually appropriate settings and provided training and ongoing support. (p. 50)

VOCATIONAL PROFILE DEVELOPMENT: A PROCESS, NOT A FORM

It is critically important that individuals responsible for facilitating the completion of the Vocational Profile remember that the *process* is always more important than the *product*. The development of a Vocational Profile must be a collaborative process involving the individual with disabilities, his or her family and friends, and other individuals who are or may be involved in the facilitation of employment outcomes. For an employment specialist to "fill out" a Vocational Profile without full advantage of the rich perspectives that can be obtained from these other sources defeats many of the central purposes of this process.

Who should gather the information on the applicant? Because the relationship between the information discovered in completing a profile and identifying a good job match are directly related, the most appropriate person to target is the person who will be representing the applicant for a job. This often is an employment specialist. It should also be noted that family members, friends, and others can play a role in compiling the profile. Ideally, however, the person developing the job should be the person gathering the information.

Painting the Picture

It is important to realize that a profile actually is a picture of the individual painted in words. The process is somewhat like completing a paint-by-number picture. The categories of the profile are like the different numbered colors. If you paint with quick broad strokes—say, by combining all of the shades of green together—then a rough outline emerges. If time is taken to fill in each space with richness and care, then a life-like portrait results. It is exactly the same with the profile. The comprehensive array of categories included in the profile provides the subtle tones necessary to fully describe an applicant with a significant disability.

The types of information that are in the Vocational Profile include the following:

- *Identification information*—name, date of birth, Social Security number, address, telephone number, marital status, current occupational status
- *Residential/domestic information*—family/extended family; names, ages, and relationships of individuals living in the same home or residence; residential history; family support available; description of typical routines; friends and social group(s); description and location of neighborhood; services near home; transportation availability; general types of employment near home; specific employers near home
- *Educational information*—history and general performance, vocational programming/performance, community functioning programming/performance, recreation/leisure programming/performance
- *Work experience information*—informal work performed at home, formal chores performed at home, informal jobs performed for others, sheltered employment, paid work

- *Summary of present levels of performance*—domestic, community functioning skills, recreation/leisure skills, academic skills, motor/mobility skills, sensory skills, communication skills, social interaction skills, physical/health-related skills and information, vocational skills
- *Learning and performance characteristics*—which environmental conditions that the applicant likes best, which instructional strategies seem to work best, degree of support typically required for learning and participating in community activities, which environments/strategies should be avoided
- *Preferences*—type of work that the applicant wants to do, the kind of work that the applicant/family always wished could be obtained, type of work that the parent/guardian believes is appropriate, what activities the applicant most enjoys doing, observations of the kinds of work that the applicant likes to do best
- *Connections*—friends of family; potential employment sites in neighborhood; business/employer contacts for leads through applicant, family, and friends
- *Flexibility/accommodations that may be required in workplace*—potential need for accessibility assistance, rehabilitation technology, and/or personal care assistance; habits, routines, idiosyncrasies; physical/health restrictions; behavior challenges; degree and type of negotiation with employers likely to be required

Blank and completed Vocational Profiles are included in Appendix A and Appendix B, respectively, for reader reference and use.

Gathering Information for the Profile

The process of gathering information and completing the Vocational Profile should include the following activities (Mast & Callahan, 1994):

- Conducting the initial meeting with the applicant
- Completing the Neighborhood Inventory
- Observing the applicant
- Seeking other sources of information
- Completing a technology assessment (if necessary)
- Compiling the information
- Conducting the profile meeting

The relationship among these various components of the information-gathering phase are graphically delineated in Figure 7.1

The Initial Meeting with the Applicant

Our experience has been that most applicants who are referred to supported employment programs come equipped with a 3-inch-thick file folder. The folder often is full of tests and inventories that quantify and label the

Figure 7.1.   Preparation process for the Vocational Profile.

individual's performance levels and describe the perceived barriers to employment. The folder also often contains a litany of the reasons why the individual should be considered "unemployable." This information should only be used as background material and for understanding the individual's personal history. Although it is necessary to consider this information, we strongly suggest that these materials not be reviewed until *after* getting to know the individual on a personal basis through numerous contacts and conversations.

The development of the Vocational Profile begins with an introductory meeting among the applicant, the employment specialist, and any other person who the applicant might feel is appropriate. The purposes of this meeting are to establish rapport and to begin a relationship with the applicant. This is also an opportune time to obtain some preliminary information about the individual's current life situation, to identify some preliminary areas for future exploration and discussion, to set times for other interviews and personal observations, and to obtain any necessary information releases.

In order not to be "just another human services person who will be trying to find employment," it is best to hold the initial meeting in a setting that is both comfortable and familiar to the person with disabilities. Sitting across a table or desk from someone is not conducive to establishing rapport. By meeting in a community setting familiar to the individual—ideally the person's home—the baggage associated with authority is left behind, and the applicant is encouraged to feel that he or she is driving the process. After initially meeting the applicant, it often is necessary to conduct a follow-up meeting with family members, neighbors, and friends to gather additional information from their unique perspectives. (See Chapter 4 for suggested strategies for involving families in this process.)

The Neighborhood Inventory

The Vocational Profile is intended to direct the employment specialist to an appropriate job for the applicant based on the applicant's needs, preferences, and skills. The job also must make sense in relation to where the applicant lives. If we look at the criteria that most of us put into place when finding employment, proximity to home or easy access to transportation often is high on the list. Why should it be any different for people with severe disabilities? Because of the difficulties of transporting people with severe disabilities, getting to and from a job becomes a major factor in determining whether a job is appropriate. If the transportation issue is not resolved before a job begins, then it may impede the success of the individual's employment experience. For this reason, it is recommended that we treat the applicant's home as the "center" for all future job development considerations.

The Neighborhood Inventory asks the employment specialist to identify the businesses in the applicant's neighborhood. Driving or walking around the neighborhood will give the employment specialist a good idea of whether there are appropriate places to pursue for job development, whether public transportation is available, and whether businesses are accessible.

Observing the Applicant

Traditional assessments attempt to measure the abilities of an applicant by utilizing a standardized format. Such evaluation provides a narrow "either/ or," black-and-white description of the individual and his or her perceived abilities. The profile, conversely, asks the employment specialist to observe the applicant performing routine, everyday tasks in his or her home and in community environments. This provides positive, realistic data about the abilities of the applicant, provides details, and allows the employment specialist to see the applicant interacting with situations and people in realistic settings.

We strongly recommend accompanying the applicant to events in the community. These outings provide good observational data and an opportunity to interact on a more casual and personal level. The employment specialist can observe how the applicant uses natural supports and cues to do what he or she wants to do and go where he or she wants to go. It also provides the opportunity to observe novel and unanticipated situations and to see how well they are handled.

Other Sources of Information

Speaking personally with applicants and observing them in various settings often provide the best sources of information. It is often necessary, however, to delve more deeply to complete the picture of the prospective applicant. File sources include agency records, school records, and psychological and vocational assessments. Talking with direct services staff, counselors, and teachers who are familiar with the individual also is important. This information will provide a history of the applicant and should be considered after compiling the personal interview and observation data.

Information also can be obtained from roommates, friends, family members, caregivers, and neighbors. These people provide a different perspective of the applicant than can be gained from the applicant him- or herself or from human services personnel. Frequently, friends and acquaintances see the unique attributes and interests of the applicant in a completely different light than family or staff. In all cases, it is important to advise the applicant of the sources of information that will be used during the formulation of this part of the profile.

In summary, the use of interviews and other informal information-gathering strategies provide the employment specialist with important insights regarding concerns such as transportation, Social Security, Medicare, hours, wages, and the potential need for ongoing supports. Putting all of these pieces together into the profile will provide a picture of the applicant that will help the employment specialist find an appropriate employment setting for the applicant. It is helpful to think of the quality of the information to be gathered as an investment: The more time and effort you put in, the more quality information you will get.

Technology Needs Assessment

Technology often plays a critical role in the successful development of employment for individuals with severe disabilities (Callahan, 1991a; Garner & Campbell, 1987). It is important, therefore, for employment specialists to understand and appreciate the importance of technology in facilitating employment opportunities. This includes a general awareness of various assistive devices and adaptations but also extends to an understanding of the degree to which technology can be integrated into the workplace (e.g., employer flexibility in regard to altering the workplace, awareness of the need to use the least intrusive strategy).

Many times, assistive technology needs are evident before a job is developed and an applicant goes to work. This is particularly true when the applicant experiences needs in positioning or mobility. It is important to discover the applicant's potential needs in these areas. The method of positioning required by an individual with physical disabilities often plays a critical role in employment and, to a large extent, dictates the types of jobs that *can* be developed (Sowers & Powers, 1991). The applicant should always be advised of any potential positioning or mobility adaptations that may be necessary and should feel comfortable with those changes before beginning employment. If these changes include a different wheelchair or other method of mobility (e.g., scooter, different type of crutches or walker, cane), then training should begin immediately as a means of increasing the applicant's comfort and awareness of this new mode of mobility.

Another common area of concern related to the use of technology involves individuals who have problems producing or understanding verbal language. These people typically will need to rely heavily on adaptive devices to communicate their ideas, feelings, and needs. There are many sophisticated communication devices on the market. The challenge becomes locating a communication device that is functional, affordable, portable, durable, and user friendly. In addition, it is often necessary to customize the communication content of the device to the needs and vocabulary of the workplace. Once again, this is an area in which technical supports and consultation can be gained from a variety of individuals and professional disciplines.

The same general principles also apply to other areas in which technology may be necessary to facilitate employment. If necessary, appropriate assessments should be completed so that training can be facilitated as soon as possible. These explorations and assessments often can provide answers to the following types of questions:

- Will the applicant need an adaptation to reach the buttons on the elevator or to facilitate feeding him- or herself during lunch?
- Does the applicant need adaptations in order to button his or her own shirt or coat, to open doors, to hold a telephone, or to get a drink of water?

- What method of transportation is needed or available to assist this individual as he or she travels to and from work?

The applicant, the employment specialist, and those closest to the applicant frequently are the best people to make observations and suggestions about technology needs. Many times, occupational and physical therapists will have excellent insights into the potential needs of the applicant in the workplace. They also may have very specific views and suggestions on the use of adaptations. Other professional rehabilitation technologists (e.g., rehabilitation engineer) also may be asked to perform an evaluation of the applicant for assistive needs. As a general rule, it is important to remember that "simpler is often better" when making final decisions about the types of technology to use in the workplace.

After the job is developed and the applicant is on the job, technology needs should be reevaluated. A follow-up assessment of the jobsite and job tasks provides for those subtle nuances that may have been overlooked during the initial appraisal of technology needs. This process also provides the employee with an opportunity to comment on the comfort, usability, and functionality of specific adaptations.

Compiling the Information

After completing the information-gathering phase, it is possible to begin the process of compiling and organizing the information that will be included in the Vocational Profile. This process should result in the development of an ecologically validated, positive picture of an applicant's entire life. In addition, this process should direct the employment specialist to develop a job that is appropriate to the needs, goals, and lifestyle plans of the applicant.

When compiling the information that will comprise the Vocational Profile, it is critical to use positive language, complete sentences, and descriptive narrative to the greatest extent possible. The applicant should not be described in sweeping terms and generalizations; rather, specific points or conclusions should be illustrated by specific examples. When the profile form is completed, the applicant or someone of his or her choosing should be given the opportunity to review the final product and offer suggestions for additions, deletions, or modifications. It is important that the information is correct and not just a reflection of the writer's opinion. Compiling profile data is an ongoing process, and any new information should be added as developments and changes occur in the life of the individual. In the case of disagreements between different sources of information, favor the more optimistic view. If both seem to be valid, then simply place each perspective in the profile.

Other considerations in compiling the Vocational Profile should include the following:

1. Fill out the Vocational Profile form using positive language that protects the dignity and value of the individual (i.e., refrain from using labels or categories, resist the opportunity to use professionalized language to describe behaviors). Because the purpose of the profile is to provide an ecologically valid picture of the applicant, all information should relate to facilitating successful living and working opportunities for the person who is the focus of the profile.
2. Any significant physical or intellectual disabilities or challenging behaviors should be referenced to the specific instances that they were problematic. The person of concern should not be described in sweeping generalizations such as "self-injurious" or "aggressive." Always cite specific contexts and examples.
3. Make every attempt to involve the applicant and his or her parents or representatives in every aspect of finding employment. Ask for referrals, ideas, and support from the family.
4. Frame the entire process from the applicant's perspective rather than from an agency perspective.
5. The entire profile activity usually takes approximately 16–24 hours to complete and is usually accomplished in 2–3 weeks. Resist the temptation to take short cuts.

THE PROFILE MEETING

The profile meeting is the culmination of the entire process and is the tool that will ultimately lead to a job match. If the profile is the "picture," then the profile meeting is the "plan." The purpose of this meeting is to clearly define an "ideal" employment situation based on the available information gathered from the Vocational Profile. This information is then used to direct job development personnel as they seek a compatible match between the employment needs of the individual and employers in the community.

Before describing the activities that comprise the profile meeting, the reader should give consideration to a distinction between the actual *Vocational Profile* document and the *profile meeting*. The Vocational Profile provides a picture of the individual who is the focus of the employment process. As stated previously, the profile is similar to a paint-by-number picture. By gathering varied but important bits of information about the individual, we begin to fill in the blanks left by traditional sources of information (e.g., clinical records, labels given to the individual, the results of standardized testing); we begin to visualize the nature of the person's life, experiences, dreams and desires, and gifts and talents. The result is a summary of the individual's gifts, strengths, talents, preferences, and aspirations. In this way, we can begin to understand and appreciate the unique contributions that the applicant can make to a work setting—and how the employment experience will, in turn, enrich his or her life experience.

By contrast, the profile meeting is the point at which the information contained in the Vocational Profile is used to *begin* the planning process and to identify potential employment locations and outcomes. In planning for the profile meeting, the following matters should be considered (Mast & Callahan, 1994):

1. Decide early whose perspective can "trump" others. Typically, the applicant's wishes trump all others. Immediate family is next, followed by the employment specialist, friends, and other paid human services personnel.

2. Identify, with the applicant's assistance, who should be invited to attend the profile meeting. Consider all of the people involved with the applicant—friends, family, the mail carrier, the bus driver, vocational rehabilitation counselor, and any other individuals identified by the applicant. It is critically important that the *majority* of the people attending be family, friends, and other *nonpaid* people rather than staff members who are paid to interact with the applicant in some type of professional capacity.

3. Discuss the profile meeting with the applicant, and set a convenient time. Provide whatever assistance the applicant might need to contact these people. A letter should be mailed at least 1 week in advance to prospective participants stating the purpose of the meeting and providing each invited person with a completed profile to read before the meeting. The sole purpose of this meeting is to identify employment possibilities. Employability for the applicant is already assumed. Now it is time to identify the position(s) that will be pursued and explored. Peripheral issues, especially those related to assumptions about employability, benefits, transportation, or "readiness," should be discussed at another time. The profile meeting should focus only on identifying employment possibilities and employment sites.

4. Hold the meeting in a room large enough for everyone to be comfortable. If the applicant is willing, then hold the meeting in his or her home. This continues to reinforce the message that the applicant is "in charge" of this process and holds the primary ownership for the derived outcomes. It also is important to remember that this meeting has a very focused and serious goal of employment and needs to be conducted from that standpoint.

5. The meeting typically should be facilitated by the person who has completed the profile process and will be doing the job development with direction and guidance from the applicant. This allows the facilitator to keep the meeting focused on generating a high-quality job match.

6. Use a flipchart or blackboard to record information visually for the group.

7. Introduce everyone, and review the goals and guidelines for the meeting: a) employment is the goal, b) the focus will be on employment possibilities, and c) other issues will be discussed at another time. Example:

   "It will take the input of everyone here to assist in locating the best employment situation. We want to look at possibilities, not talk about impossibilities or limitations. We want to focus on identifying employers; nonemployment concerns can be dealt with at another time. This meeting is primarily directed toward identifying a job for _____."

8. Ask the applicant to describe his or her ideal job. Write on the flipchart the key information that is given. Define the ideal job in terms of the applicant's preferences, contributions, and conditions. Open this discussion to others in the room, realizing that the definitions by the applicant are the guidelines for the job and that discussion should expand or enhance those criteria. Example:

   Conditions: in a bright warm environment; want to work alone but have people around; sitting job; within easy distance from home; can use public "call-a-ride"; part time; mornings or morning to early afternoon; little or no telephone work; repetitive work; work station near the accessible bathroom

   Preferences: use of the computer or microfiche; in a medical setting or office building; in a music store but no customer contact; at radio or TV station where music is played; "I don't want to work for..."

   Contributions: good attendance, gets along with everyone, is attentive to detail, knows every musical group since the seventies, WANTS TO WORK

   Remove this page from the flipchart and hang it in a place where it is easily visible. Refer to it often. Clarify or revise this information as the meeting proceeds. Encourage meeting participants to assist in synthesizing this information.

9. Once the job characteristics are identified and defined, begin to identify the types of employment situations in the designated geographical area that meet those identified criteria. Also list these types of employment situations on the flipchart. Begin with just three or four job types. (Always make attempts to ensure that all of the participants are engaged and involved in the discussions and activity of the profile meeting.) Example:

   a. Data entry
   b. Transcribing files
   c. Insurance
   d. Stock person at record store

10. When the job types have been identified, specifically identify employers in the area who utilize those types of jobs. Be specific, naming businesses in the area. Be sure that all of these businesses meet the key information identified in the applicant's ideal job description. Example:
Data entry:
a. Memorial Medical Center
b. SIU School of Medicine
c. Horace Mann Insurance Company
d. Franklin Life Insurance Company
e. Family Medicine Clinic
f. Lens Lab
g. Department of Public Aid
h. Tower Records
Stock person:
a. Tower Records
b. Sam Goody
c. Music Land
d. Coconuts
e. Best Buy
f. Smith's Old Records
g. Municipal Library
h. WQAP radio station
Give the applicant a chance to eliminate any of the listings that he or she does not want to pursue. Expand the categories if necessary to facilitate the planning process and the identification of possibilities. Example:
What about looking for stocking jobs in places other than record stores, say at the hospital, at video stores, or in department stores? Identify specific employers from each of those businesses.

11. Ask if anyone in the room has a contact in that place, a name, or a friend who knows someone there. The more specific the information that is available, the easier it is to make a good contact. Example:
"Who knows someone at Memorial?"
"I have a friend who works in the X-ray department that might be of help."
"Will you contact your friend?"
"Yes."
"Will you contact them within the next week?"
"Yes."
Write down on the flipchart the name of the person who will make the contact and when he or she agreed to make the contact.

12. A critical step in this process is for the applicant to identify which of the employment locations are preferences and which should be contacted in priority order (i.e., first, second, and last).

13. Record the information from the meeting on the profile meeting form (Appendix A), a three-part form that includes 1) characteristics of an ideal job, 2) the types of jobs in which these components are found, and 3) specific employers who may have these types of jobs.
14. When the meeting is over, transcribe the outcomes, and mail a copy to all of the participants.
15. Begin making contact with identified employers from the developed list.
16. Talk to the applicant during the time that contacts are being made with employers. Keep the applicant a central and vital part of the process.

A FINAL THOUGHT

This process results in a clear list of prospects for the job developer to use in beginning the job development phase, prospects that are specific to the applicant. The applicant must continue to be involved in each step beyond this point. It will be the applicant's job! Now the work of the employment specialist turns to the process of job development. This activity is undertaken in response to the information gathered and recorded on the Vocational Profile. We are yet one step closer to securing the employment opportunity that meets the individualized needs of the applicant.

Individualized Job Development

 **8**

*I am an invisible man. . . . I am a man of substance, of flesh and bone,
fiber and liquids—and I might even be said to possess a mind. I am invisible, understand, simply because people refuse to see me.*

Prologue to The Invisible Man, *R. Ellison, 1952*

This chapter is designed to update and expand the perspectives presented by the authors in their 1987 text on employing people with disabilities, *Getting Employed, Staying Employed* (McLoughlin, Garner, & Callahan, 1987). Although much has changed since the period that marked the beginnings of supported employment, the strategies that were described relating to a systematic marketing approach to employers have not. The essence of the Job Development section of that book continues to represent our best ideas on managing a prospecting list, making employer contacts, holding initial meetings, and conducting employer negotiations. In other words, the structure of job development remains basically the same.

What has changed since the mid-1980s relates more to the starting point, the touchstone, from which job development begins. In the 1980s, the realities and needs of the labor market, defined by employers, described the basis from which human services job developers sought employment opportunities for people with severe disabilities. This approach attempted to match the requirements of employers, typically represented by a job description of an available job opening, with the skills of any one of a number of people with disabilities. At that time, we were much more interested in following what we presumed was the "way everyone else got a job" than we were in ensuring that all people, even those with the most severe disabilities, had an opportunity to become employed.

Problems, however, were lurking in relation to this strategy. In its deliberations on the reauthorization of the Rehabilitation Act Amendments of 1992 (PL 102-569), the congressional subcommittee in the U.S. Senate on Disability Policy lamented

> that creaming (serving those individuals with the most mild disabilities) is occurring. . . . This is particularly disconcerting in light of the fact that the supported employment program was established to serve individuals with severe disabili-

ties for whom competitive employment has not traditionally occurred. (Senate Report 102–357)

The changes presented in this chapter reference a shift toward the individual—the applicant with a severe disability—as the starting point for job development rather than the labor market. In order to accomplish this shift, job developers will need to accommodate a number of behavior changes. If they do not, then creaming of those people with the most skills and flexibility into employment will continue to occur. This creaming will occur at the expense of those people whom the Rehabilitation Act Amendments are intended to assist—people with the most severe disabilities. The following issues and strategies are covered in this chapter to assist in the shift toward individualized job development:

- The difference between labor market and individualized job development
- The use of a "contribution" versus "job description" basis for job development
- A reconsideration of the factors that comprise the basis of an employer–employee relationship
- Carved jobs, created jobs, and negotiated jobs—tools for individualization
- The increased importance of using personal contacts and relationships in job development
- Using the profile meeting as the blueprint for job development
- Explaining and negotiating naturally referenced supports using the Seven-Phase Sequence
- The overarching importance of job development in ensuring the benefits of employment to people with severe disabilities

The literature on job development in the period since the origins of supported employment affirms the importance of these issues. Hagner and Dileo (1993) asserted that job development should always be referenced to individuals and that personal contacts predominate the key factors for success. Fabian, Luecking, and Tilson (1995) devoted an entire text to the critical importance of job development. Murphy and Rogan (1994) suggested that job development should be driven by who the applicants are rather than solely by labor market considerations. Experienced practitioners and researchers in Virginia (Moon, Inge, Wehman, Brooke, & Barcus, 1990) clearly stated the need for creating positions in companies and that the supports necessary for success may require us to reconsider traditionally held ideas of employment.

LABOR MARKET VERSUS INDIVIDUALIZED JOB DEVELOPMENT

Human services traditionally have based their supported employment assistance to people with disabilities on the perceived necessity of assessing the skills of the people who are to be represented, so as to know the "features of one's product line." The extension of this sales analogy then led job developers to survey the labor market to determine its needs. The needs of the labor market traditionally have been defined by the requirements that employers have described for any jobs that may be or that will soon be open. Another fundamental practice has been the general representation of a group (or caseload) of people who want to become employed. By representing a group rather than specific individuals, job developers seemed to be better able to meet the needs of employers, their apparent customers.

The effects of implementing this approach have been both successful and subtly problematic. The success has been evident: There have been more than 100,000 people employed in supported employment since 1986 (Wehman & Kregel, 1995). Something must be working when a strategy produces results of this magnitude. Of course, there is no way to know how many of these people were represented with a labor market approach, but it is likely that most were. This is evident from the similarity between this strategy and the approaches implied in the description of supported employment found in federal statutes and regulations. The congressional charge of creaming is only one of many that have been sounded in the early 1990s that warns of underlying problems with this approach (Hagner & Dileo, 1993; Murphy & Rogan, 1994; Wehman & Kregel, 1995).

To understand the limitations imposed by a labor market strategy for job development, it is helpful to trace the experiences of an applicant with severe disabilities.

A young man named Juan wants to work. To qualify for rehabilitation services, his state continues to use a protocol of standardized assessments, work samples, and situational assessments to determine his vocational goals. Because Juan has cerebral palsy, moderate cognitive disability, and a host of adaptive issues in his life, he performs very poorly on the assessments. Because the Rehabilitation Act Amendments of 1992 (PL 102-569) requires that applicants generally should be considered feasible for employment, Juan is approved for services and is represented by a traditional supported employment agency that uses a labor market approach to job development. He is one of approximately 25 people who is assigned to a job developer at the agency. The job developer reviews Juan's evaluation and meets with him to discuss his employment goals and needs. Juan simply wants to work.

The job developer maintains contacts with employers throughout the community. At this time, in Juan's geographic locality, service industry employment related to the travel industry is the hot area for potential employment. A job development call is made to a local car rental agency, and the developer finds that there is an opening for a car cleanup attendant. A detailed job description is provided, which describes all of the duties, prerequisites, and general expectations of the job.

The employer asks whether the people whom the developer represents can perform this job. The first problem of the labor market strategy arises with the job developer's answer. It is clear that all of the applicants will not be able to perform the entire job but that some will. What typically occurs at this point is a seemingly natural reordering of the applicant pool, based on legitimate, unbiased labor market needs. The applicants who have the skills will move to the top, and those who do not will move to the bottom of the list for consideration.

Even this unfortunate circumstance can easily be explained by the logic of the labor market approach. Several deserving people with disabilities got a chance for a job, and, if this was a successful experience, then one of them actually secured a job. As for those who applied and were not chosen, as well as those who were not even considered, this represents a natural lesson in life. Juan is urged to "hang in there." His chance will come.

The logic in asking people like Juan to wait is based on the notion that if a job developer calls on enough companies, some of them will eventually match the skills of all of the applicants represented. But this simply does not seem to be happening. People with the most severe disabilities remain in seg-regated services or unemployed, as job developers have recruited more skilled applicants to meet the needs of employers as detailed by job descriptions (Callahan, 1991b).

The fatal flaw to this approach is that for many people with the most severe disabilities, their chance is never going to come as long as they have to compete against others with more skills and against the standard of job descriptions. In fact, a functional definition for people with the most severe disabilities is that they do not tend to win in competition with others and that there is not likely to be an existing job that they can perform in its entirety.

To overcome this limitation, job developers who represent people with severe disabilities must change their focus (Fabian et al., 1995). Applicants must receive individualized representation so that the unique skills that they possess can be described and promoted in relation to the employer's needs rather than in competition with the skills of other applicants. To accomplish this, developers will need to use a process like the Vocational Profile strategy (presented in Chapter 7) to obtain an accurate picture of the applicant, which is used as the basis for the profile meeting (also presented in Chapter 7).

Individualized job development differs from labor market strategies in that the developer represents only one applicant at a time. In this way, com-petition with other applicants is removed, the skills and potential contributions of the applicant can be fully described, and the possibility is opened for negotiating a personalized job description for the targeted applicant. The following sections in this chapter discuss issues that must be addressed when using this approach.

Reasonable questions remain to be answered relating to labor market versus individualized approaches. Are the needs of the labor market no longer important? Should supported employment agencies stop using labor market strategies? Is it possible for a person with a severe disability to perform an existing job? What happens if an employer contacts the agency with a job or if a job simply "falls into our lap"?

The first general response to these questions is that we must reasonably consider any employment possibility, for there will always be valid exceptions to general intentions. Individualized representation does not in any way diminish the validity of labor market needs. It simply offers another way for employers to consider their needs than based solely on their job descriptions (see the section Contribution versus Job Description Basis for Employment).

Let's be clear—labor market job development works. This approach, however, simply does not work very well for people with severe disabilities. In addition, most people would rather have job representation efforts reflect *who they are individually* instead of a group of people. It is also entirely possible, through the use of careful matching and technology accommodations, that some people with the most severe disabilities will be able to perform the requirements of existing jobs. Experience has shown, however, that many will not and that these people will have to wait a long time for just the right combination of duties and technology to come along.

Finally, if employers initiate contact or if individualized approaches generate an unexpected job not connected to an applicant, we do not recommend that such jobs be arbitrarily turned down. But we do recommend caution. When unsolicited jobs are offered, care must be taken to trace the employment needs back to the skills, conditions, preferences, and potential contributions of your applicants. Remember, because the job was offered by an employer, it will probably be defined by a job description and will not likely meet the needs of applicants with more severe disabilities. As a last resort, if the job does not fit any applicants in your agency, then offer the opening to a local rehabilitation counselor or to other agencies that represent people with less significant disabilities. In this way, organizations that represent people with the most severe disabilities can be viewed as part of the overall community effort to find jobs for people who need them.

CONTRIBUTION VERSUS
JOB DESCRIPTION BASIS FOR EMPLOYMENT

Job descriptions are so important in the business community that the framers of the Americans with Disabilities Act (ADA) of 1990 (PL 101-336) used them as a benchmark to determine whether discrimination existed in hiring, accommodating, or terminating employees with disabilities; however, the ADA has had an unintended and potentially negative effect on people with the most severe disabilities: In an effort to ensure that their companies offer a "level playing field" for applicants with disabilities, many employers have taken a fresh look at their job descriptions, which has resulted in more concrete descriptions of the performance and productivity requirements of the various jobs that employers offer. This clarification is occurring for all of the right reasons—clear, measurable job requirements allow applicants with disabilities to know exactly what is expected for the job, and they allow employers to ensure a bias-free hiring process—but many people with severe disabilities cannot fulfill all of the responsibilities of a general, albeit concrete, job description. This situation relates to the impact of disability on job performance of the tasks to be performed and can exist even when reasonable accommodation is available. Even though the applicant often has much to contribute to work settings, general job descriptions typically contain duties that simply are not possible for the applicant to perform.

According to the opinion of the United Cerebral Palsy Associations' Governmental Activities Office (Button, 1992), the ADA *does not* require employers to amend their basic job responsibilities to accommodate applicants with disabilities. Rather, they are required to offer reasonable accommodation to allow applicants to perform *already-existing* jobs.

A solution to this dilemma is for job developers to focus their efforts on the specific contributions that applicants with severe disabilities can make to employers. This is accomplished in two parts: 1) by getting to know applicants sufficiently well during the planning process that potential contributions will emerge and 2) by asking employers to consider whether they have unmet needs in their workplaces. This approach allows applicants with severe disabilities to make a genuine contribution to employers with an individually negotiated job description, without having to perform all of the tasks of a general job description. Characteristics and suggestions for negotiated job descriptions are addressed later in this chapter.

Even though employers are not required to negotiate carved-out job descriptions for applicants with disabilities, their willingness would certainly be an indication of an employer's good-faith efforts to comply with the ADA. In this way, the value of a negotiated outcome can be used to show compliance with a concept described in statute. Employers across the country are accepting this approach to job development and seem to easily see the opportunities that it offers their businesses (Callahan & Mast, 1994).

Contribution-based job development requires developers to describe the features that relate to the applicant's potential contributions to an employer and to ask whether the employer has specific needs that match this listing. Care has to be taken not to begin employer contacts with the indication that a job opening is sought. By presenting the contributions that the applicant can make to the setting, employers have the opportunity to view hiring people with severe disabilities in terms of a net gain to their companies rather than as something that must be sacrificed or compromised (e.g., salary, possible modifications of previously designed job descriptions and task assignments). Of course, every employer will not need the specific skills offered by the applicant, and others will not be willing to negotiate the basic responsibilities of their jobs. Many employers, however, will need the skills offered and will respond positively to this concept. In many ways, this mirrors the challenges presented to traditional job developers in that persistence and hard work remain necessary components of finding jobs.

THE ESSENTIAL CHARACTERISTICS
OF AN EMPLOYMENT RELATIONSHIP

The issue of employment for people with the most severe disabilities and the innovative approaches that often are necessary to achieve success force us to examine a topic that is seldom discussed in the human services field—the essential characteristics of an employment relationship between an employer and an employee. Perhaps it is because so many of us have always worked as adults, often for years, that we feel this relationship is clearly understood.

On the face of the issue, employment comprises an arrangement in which an employee provides stipulated time and effort to an employer in return for pay. In this definition, time, effort, and pay can vary in countless ways. But there are confounding issues to consider. For instance, a pure capitalist might argue that an employment relationship must be based on employees producing more monetary outcomes for employers than they receive in pay. In fact, this arrangement closely resembles the payment schemes of many sheltered workshops and work activity centers. But few human services and rehabilitation professionals work under this kind of relationship. And what about support? Does an employment relationship exist if an employee receives support beyond that offered to most other employees? If some support is permissible, then can that support be open ended? If an assisting person has to perform parts of a job for an employee with disabilities to be successful, is that employment? What if the support person costs more than the employee earns and produces? Should supported employees be paid based only on the value of what they produce? How small of a contribution can comprise a job?

The answers to these questions often evoke heated debate among employment professionals. Defining the employment relationship might be a bit like the difficulty that the U.S. Supreme Court had in defining "pornography." It was difficult to define, but everyone seemed to be able to know it when they saw it. The differences among the various perspectives in the rehabilitation field seem to fall into two broad categories: 1) those who believe that jobs should meet strict characteristics of an ideal employment relation-ship and 2) those who urge flexibility to the very limits of an employment relationship.

Paradoxically, a combination of both perspectives probably offers the best route. Our culture acknowledges unwritten features of an ideal employ-ment relationship, even though few of us actually have that relationship with our employers. The value of having an ideal is that we feel that we are a part of something bigger than just our jobs. When there is uncertainty or unfair-ness, we can relate to each other more easily and solve problems with the help of many others. Job developers, therefore, should strive to meet that cultural-ly ambiguous ideal in each job that they develop. It is equally important, how-ever, to have sufficient flexibility to meet the challenges and preferences of people with the most severe disabilities. With the ideal relationship clearly in mind, job developers must be able to consider any possibility. Ultimately, the best individuals to determine whether a job is indeed a job are the employer and the supported employee. Human services professionals may disagree about the definition of a controversial job, but if an employer feels that a need is being met and is willing to pay a fair wage, then whatever the characteris-tics, it is probably a job. An example of a dilemma around the characteristics of employment occurred with Laura, a young woman who had just finished her school eligibility.

Laura's mother contacted a local vocational rehabilitation counselor in an effort to open a case for her daughter. Laura was evaluated by a contracted vocational assessment center and was found to have "significant impairments in many areas of adaptive behavior." It was clear before the evaluation that Laura truly was a person with the most severe, multiple disabilities. The results of the testing caused the counselor and others to wonder whether employment was feasible for Laura. In an unusual decision, the counselor decided to support Laura for rehabilitation services and opened a case on her. In planning meetings held with Laura's mother, the counselor had an unex-pected stipulation that had to be met by those who were attempting to find Laura a job. The counselor stated that his professional colleagues had to see that Laura had a "real job"—not some approximation. We asked what was meant by the term "real job." It was difficult for the counselor to define the characteristics of a "real job." Pay was a necessary condition, but not suffi-cient. Intensive support was permitted, but "too much" support would tip the scale toward being unacceptable. The issue was finally narrowed down to the notion of autonomy. Was Laura making decisions regarding job performance, or were these decisions being made by the individual who was providing on-the-job support? If the supporter was making the response decisions, then, the counselor believed, there would be no "real job."

In a situational assessment completed in an amusement park, Laura was to press a digital counter, which was connected to a large touch switch mounted on her wheelchair tray, as people filed through the line. After several months of performance, the counselor determined that Laura was not making the decision to hit the switch as a customer came through the line. This meant, in his opinion, that Laura was not performing a real job, even if the employer was willing to pay Laura for her time and effort. Later, Laura's mother had an idea concerning a nonwork task at church. She negotiated with the local priest for Laura to pass out the Sunday church bulletins before mass. With her mother assisting, Laura offered a bulletin to parishioners as they came into church. Laura's mother asks all of us a simple question: "If we could find Laura a job like this for pay, say at the visitor's center at a nearby park, would that be a job?" Even with all of the valid issues that swirl around this problem, somehow the answer must be "yes" if people with severe disabilities are to have the opportunity to be employed.

DEVELOPING INDIVIDUALIZED JOBS

The lack of large-scale success in employing people with severe disabilities (Wehman & Kregel, 1995) has led to the development of strategies that bypass two of the toughest barriers to employment for these people—competition from other applicants and general job descriptions. It is gradually becoming clear that the issue is not that people with severe disabilities do not have much to contribute to employers. They do. When they are required to compete against other applicants or against an arbitrary standard, however, the impact of their disabilities forces a comparison that often calls their potential for contribution into question. This has been a hard lesson for human services representatives to learn. There is nothing more culturally fitting than competition against one's peers to get a chance to fulfill an employer's expectations for a job. Along with the weight of federal law (the ADA and the Rehabilitation Act of 1973 [PL 93-112]), we have employed business-based sales strategies, advanced technology, systematic instruction, and natural support capacity to level the playing field so that a fair, head-to-head competition would result in access to employment for people with severe disabilities. It is clear to most observers of these efforts that success remains a hope rather than a reality. Is it possible that there is a flaw in the fundamental principle of competition in relation to securing jobs? In some instances, there is a flaw in the process.

First, it seems that many people without disabilities, whenever possible, would go to great lengths to avoid a "cattle call" competition for a job. We would prefer to use personal connections to avoid this approach to securing a job. In addition, it has become more common for people to negotiate a niche for themselves in a business rather than to simply accept a job slot. This has become necessary in many instances as a result of the downsizing practices of numerous large companies in the United States. These observations seem to suggest that competition against other applicants or an arbitrary standard might not be as common as we have thought.

Second, the impact of severe disability is a significant factor in the lives of the people we represent. This impact does not fit well with competition. As much as we might like for it to be different, winning is not guaranteed even with the assisting forces of personal determination, federal law, accommodations, and all of the other strategies that we can muster. In fact, competition is only the arbitrary proving ground that employers use to get what they really want—contribution to their company. If this is true, we can plan to bypass competition so that we can present the critically important information to employers of how the applicant being represented can contribute to the needs of the company. There are three effective strategies that can be used: 1) carved jobs, 2) negotiated jobs, and 3) created jobs.

Carved Jobs

Carved jobs result from efforts by the job developer to remove certain aspects of a general job description to meet the specific contributions of an applicant with severe disabilities. This approach requires the job developer to individually represent an applicant who has participated in a person-centered planning process that resulted in a clear picture of the applicant's potential contributions and realistic conditions that may restrict performance in certain work areas. The initial contact by the job developer typically references the general job descriptions of available job openings. After carefully reviewing the requirements for the job, the developer can negotiate the removal of certain problematic aspects, possibly balanced by adding other duties, in an effort to carve or tailor an individualized job description for the applicant.

What does an employer gain from this arrangement? Many employers are looking for ways to hire people with disabilities, and this strategy offers them an acceptable alternative. Also, by trading or shifting duties among job descriptions, it is possible that the employer will experience no net loss by carving or tailoring job duties. If successful, the job developer has assisted the applicant to avoid the competition with other applicants and the restrictions of the general job description; however, this strategy should be used only when a general job description does not fit a particular applicant or when an applicant cannot perform an existing description. The weakness of this approach is the possibility that employers will feel that they are giving up an aspect of a job for an employee. Even if they agree initially, this lingering feeling may result in later problems for the supported employee.

A carved job might be developed in a situation in which a job developer is representing a person who wants to work in a warehouse. A job development call to a plumbing supply house identifies an opening for a warehouse helper position. The position is described by the following duties:

1. Unload trucks using hand trucks and pallet jacks.
2. Retrieve stock and bring it to the front desk.
3. Clean the general warehouse area.
4. Rearrange stock using a forklift.
5. Hold a commercial driver's license.
6. Accompany the lead warehouseman to make jobsite deliveries.

After considering the responsibilities in relation to the applicant's skills and contributions, the job developer informs the employer that the person represented will likely do an excellent job on duties 1, 2, 3, and 6 but that numbers 4 and 5 present a problem based on the applicant's disability. After discussing with the employer the importance of duties 4 and 5, it is discovered that duty 4 is a favorite job of another employee. The employer shifts a cleanup duty from the other warehouse helper to the supported employee and approves an exception on duty 5. In this way, a carved job description, which meets the needs of both the employer and applicant, has been accomplished.

Negotiated Jobs

Negotiated jobs originate directly from the individualized planning process that precedes job development. This strategy uses the potential contributions of the applicant as the basis for a job that meets the needs of an employer for job duties that currently exist but for which there is not an existing job description. In this way, the issue of competition, as well as whether a job opening is available, can be bypassed.

A negotiated job is based on a more fundamental concept in a business than the duties listed on a job description—employers' needs. If a match can be discovered and negotiated between the contributions of an applicant with the most severe disabilities and the needs of employers, then a fully personalized job can result. Standards will remain, but the standards will no longer be general; rather, they will relate directly to the employee's best features. Job developers must begin negotiations by probing for employer needs in the areas described by the applicant's potential contributions. To accomplish this, developers must also avoid initiating negotiations that reference the availability of job openings. The basis of this strategy is a compatibility of needs and contributions, not job openings and job descriptions. An example of a negotiated job occurred with a young man named Ling.

Ling is able to use his wheelchair to deliver goods. He also has an excellent memory and is well-liked by others in most relationships. Based on these factors and a number of other potential contributions that were identified during the Vocational Profile process, a job call was made to a large office complex in his area. The job developer explained to the administrator that Ling had previously demonstrated his ability to reliably and accurately deliver goods during his school experience. The employer was asked whether a need existed in the office complex for someone to transport materials. The employer responded that a specific need existed for someone to deliver computer printouts from the computer department to each of 36 departments throughout the facility. A personalized job description was negotiated for Ling, and he began his job. At the time of publication, Ling has been working for 3 years, and several other duties have been added to his job description.

Created Jobs

Created jobs are jobs that did not previously exist in the workplace but that were negotiated to meet the needs of employers. The creativity of people with disabilities, their parents, and job developers is used to identify heretofore unrecognized possibilities in a work setting, which can be performed by the applicants. As with carved jobs and negotiated jobs, the basis for the potential contributions comes from a person-centered planning process such as the Vocational Profile. There also is, however, a marketing research aspect to this approach. It is necessary for someone, usually the job developer, to identify a potential need in a company that can be met by the applicant. If a close relationship exists between the job developer and the company, then the employer also may be willing to consider new ways in which an applicant's contributions may meet business needs. This approach has been shown to be particularly effective for employing people with severe or multiple disabilities (Sowers & Powers, 1991). It also can result in the development of a small business, managed by the individual, with assistance from the employment specialist.

An example of a created job occurred in a large office building in Los Angeles. An insurance company that employed nearly 100 people received hundreds of fax transmissions each day. The traditional practice called for the mailroom clerk to place the faxes in employee mailboxes, where they would be picked up at lunch or breaktime. This practice had generated many complaints from employees to the office manager. They requested a more efficient handling of faxes, but a solution was not easily addressed because of the work load of the mailroom clerk. Coincidentally, a job development call was made by a local supported employment agency to the company. A man with severe cerebral palsy who used a power wheelchair for mobility was interested in delivering goods in an office setting. A job was created that required the man to pick up faxes from the mail clerk and deliver them to the appropriate offices. He also was able to return material to the mail clerk to be faxed or mailed. Even though the man could not handle papers, employees were willing to remove and place items in his chairside bins. This created job represents an addition to the work setting that meets a need not previously addressed.

PERSONAL CONTACT AND RELATIONSHIPS

A factor of underlying importance to the successful shift from labor market driven to individualized strategies is the use of personal contacts and relationships to connect the applicant to potential employers. Job developers have known for years that referrals and personal contacts will ease the way into a company and may provide the extra push needed to have an employer carefully consider a presentation (Mcloughlin, Garner, & Callahan, 1987). A relationship between the employer and the applicant or job developer now is considered virtually a necessary ingredient for successfully negotiating individualized jobs for people with severe disabilities. This relationship need not be based on friendship, kinship, or other direct relations. It is important, however, for job developers to be able to establish a connection that allows an employer to think outside of his or her traditional frame of reference. The Vocational Profile process offers an excellent opportunity to discover or establish possible connections to be used in job development.

There are two perspectives from which to explore the availability of connections: 1) the applicant and the applicant's family and 2) the job developer and the agency. A person-centered planning process can easily identify potential connectors for jobs and, by welcoming family members into the job development effort, can recruit assistance from relatives, family friends, business contacts, and neighbors. In this way, the applicant and his or her family can be active participants in the process rather than just spectators. The roles that family members can play also may vary. Some parents are willing to initiate or participate directly in making employer contacts whereas others may be willing to suggest names of friends and associates.

Job developers have prided themselves on their singular ability to find jobs for challenging people in all economic times. Because of a focus on business rather than on programs, the role often has been separate from the balance of a human services agency's staff. This separation has led to isolation, with the job developer functioning as the sole lightning rod for the delays and problems associated with applicants getting jobs. We are learning that this solitary approach will not work when developing individualized jobs for people with severe disabilities. The responsibility is simply too great and the tasks too varied for one person to handle alone. If the process used to find jobs encourages others to participate, however, then job developers can attract assistance from throughout the agency and beyond to share the load.

We suggest that the profile process and the results of the profile meeting be shared with other staff members, administrators, board members, and the job developer's personal circle of friends and associates. By reaching out, connections that were not known to exist can be discovered. The development of potential jobs and ideas needs to be owned by *every* member of the agency. In some areas, even the agency's business advisory board is given an update on the results of profile meetings so that members can assist job developers with the connections necessary to make successful contacts.

NEGOTIATING NATURALLY REFERENCED SUPPORT STRATEGIES

In order to fully realize all of the benefits of an individualized job, developers also need to change their presentation concerning the manner in which the new employee will receive support on the job. Traditionally, job developers have used the promise of full job coach support to sway employers toward hiring supported employees. As discussed in Chapter 6, this promise has too often resulted in separation rather than acceptance, discomfort rather than relationships. The Seven-Phase Sequence should become the conceptual framework for the developer to explain supported employment to prospective employers.

One employment specialist made the following observations regarding the process of naturally referenced support strategies:

> The way we provide support is to spend time in your company learning the way you do things here. After we do this, you will be provided with a copy of our plan. On the first day of work, we want the applicant to receive the same training which you give any new employee. Our analysis will help ensure that the jobs are performed the way you want. Whomever you usually assign to orient and train new employees for this job should be assigned to our applicant. We will be right there with you in case there are any problems. Our job is to provide all the assistance you will need to make sure our applicant is successful. We stand ready to substitute for the job trainer, when necessary, to offer suggestions for strategies to improve training and performance and to suggest adaptations and modifications that may improve performance. Use us as a resource.

This kind of presentation to employers redefines the traditional role of the "job coach" as a replacement for all employer responsibilities. Job developers who have tried this approach have found that employers see this as much more natural and logical than the former relationship. Those employers who have had traditional job coaches or who have heard the presentation of those support relationships will need a plausible explanation for the change. Try to frame the shift in terms of employer outcomes rather than as a new human services concept. Another observation made by an employment specialist captured the differences found in the relationship with the employer and the employee:

> We found that under the old approach we were getting in the way between employers and their own employees. This was not a positive outcome. In this more logical approach, we are still there to offer all the assistance needed; we simply want to offer that help to you, the employer. If you need us to fill in or to take on support that goes beyond your capacity, we will be ready to do so. We feel that in this way we can help build the ability to deal with unanticipated problems within your company.

Because of this shift, job developers and employment specialists need to be on the same page conceptually. If job developers sell the traditional approach, and facilitators attempt to use a naturally referenced support strategy, then there will be confusion and trouble. Coordination between these roles is critically important to the success of this approach.

A FINAL THOUGHT

Over the years, many analyses have been conducted on the state of supported employment and the solutions to the problems that have been identified (Nisbet & Hagner, 1988; Wehman & Kregel, 1995). There is a troubling aspect, however, to most perspectives on this approach to employment—job development is rarely referenced as an issue or focus for solutions. We feel that this is a significant oversight. Job development explores the "no man's land" between the separate lives led by people with disabilities and the mainstream of community work life. Without success in this one area, all of the discussion on person-centered plans, naturally referenced supports, teaching strategies, behavioral interventions, and myriad other value-based human services is moot. It is critical that human services agencies recommit to job development as a fundamental outcome for quality service. Nothing less than finding jobs that meet the individualized conditions, preferences, and contributions for all of the applicants that we represent will be acceptable. We must commit to that goal and ensure that our efforts and our resources match our rhetoric.

Job Analysis

A Tool for Assessing
and Utilizing the Culture of Workplaces
to Support Employees with Disabilities

9

Our life is frittered away by detail. . . . Simplify, simplify.

H.D. Thoreau, 1854

During the formative stages of a technology for employment training, the process of job analysis was primarily directed toward identifying the skill sequences necessary for an individual to perform specific work tasks (Bellamy, Peterson, & Close, 1975; Gold, 1972, 1976; Hunter & Bellamy, 1976). The focus was almost exclusively on the minutiae of task performance *and* an assumption that any learning that might occur in relation to those skill sequences could only be facilitated by a highly trained professional. Little interest was shown in the cultural milieu of the workplace. Although there was an awareness of the value of integrated employment, any emphasis on social relationships or interactions with other employees largely was incidental. The primary goal was to ensure that the individual with disabilities could perform the assigned tasks at a rate and level of quality that would allow continued employment.

Job analysis in supported employment is a strategy designed to assist employment specialists to 1) recognize the natural ways, means, and people used by the employer to typically perform and teach the job; 2) organize the information to be performed by the supported employee; and 3) develop a plan for balancing the natural features of support in the jobsite with the needs of the employee by using the Seven-Phase Sequence.

The activities involved in job analysis are undertaken *after* the employer has given approval for employment to proceed but *before* the applicant with disabilities begins to work. Although job analysis occurs after the employment decision has been made, it is important that the job developer reference the features of job analysis during negotiations with the employer. In addition, the

127

employment specialist should always view the job analysis as a "work in progress" and continue to make refinements and revisions after the job has begun.

There has been some discussion and debate as to whether it is best to have the job analysis performed by an employment specialist provided by a human services agency or to use existing job analysts available in the workplace. It has been suggested that the presence of an outside support person interferes with the natural processes that are used by companies to plan for employee supports (Nisbet & Hagner, 1988). The employment specialist's role continues to be a critical feature of supported employment. The employment specialist must be able to make decisions using the Seven-Phase Sequence that balance the needs of the employee with the natural support features of the setting. Effectively making these decisions requires an awareness of all of the conditions of the work culture and a full understanding of the job expectations held by the employer.

One important reason that the employment specialist's role remains critical to successful employment facilitation is the continuing belief that many people with severe disabilities will require supports beyond those typically offered by employers in order to be successfully employed. At this time, the funding and responsibility for providing these supports rests primarily with human services agencies. The use of natural supports does not imply that human services supports are bad but that they can best be used in a role that encourages and enhances the natural supports available to *all* employees. It is vital, therefore, that the employment specialist be aware of all of the conditions and expectations of employment for supported employees. In this regard, the information contained in a job analysis can be of great value.

The usefulness of this approach to job analysis depends on the employment specialist following a "chain of logic" throughout the process, which results in the maximum use of natural conditions and supports while meeting the individual needs of the supported employee. The sequence of activities suggested here can be divided into three major categories:

1. Steps performed during job development and before a jobsite visit
2. Steps performed on site designed to learn and organize the task for decision making
3. Steps that enhance the likelihood that the employee will "fit in" in the work setting

THE RELEVANCE OF A JOB ANALYSIS

The relevance of these considerations is that each has an impact on the role and use of natural supports and teaching of skills. Core routines are naturally repeated often during the workday. Therefore, these tasks might be more quickly learned, but they will likely require more time in direct supervision, because of the repetitive performance, in order to ensure successful acquisition of the task. Episodic and job-related tasks often are more difficult to teach because of the time delay between cycles, but natural co-workers or supervisors need not tie up significant time for support due to the occasional nature of the tasks. Cultural rules and mores are best taught by those natural to the setting, but employment specialists must ensure that the supported employee understands the importance of these conditions, which often are subtle and not directly taught. (See Chapter 10 for a thorough discussion of these various types of job tasks.)

Perhaps even more important is the opportunity provided by the job analysis to study and analyze the various work cultures in which people with disabilities will be employed. There is no more opportune time to observe the ways, means, and people natural to an employment site than during the period between acceptance by the employer and the date that work begins.

Finally, job analysis allows the employment specialist to clearly imprint the manner in which tasks are typically performed in the setting. This critical aspect of training often is overlooked even by those natural to workplaces. The employment specialist can bring this clear standard of performance to the training and supports offered to the supported employee. Without this perspective, it is likely that the performance of many people with disabilities will continue to reflect human services rather than natural conditions.

A TASK ANALYSIS FOR JOB ANALYSIS

The activities that compose a job analysis as described in the following section are based on the assumptions that 1) a well-matched job has been developed for the supported employee; and 2) the employer has agreed, at least to some degree, to the provision of natural supports as suggested by the Seven-Phase Sequence. Steps 1–5 relate to these considerations. Job developers also must effectively negotiate for a set of potentially achievable tasks that will compose the employee's personally tailored job description. This final fitting of the applicant to the job expectations allows the employment specialist to anticipate any accommodations that must be made in advance by the employer. It is suggested that initial negotiations for technology, accessibility, and workstation redesign be based on the belief that the accommodations are in keeping with the Americans with Disabilities Act (ADA) of 1990 (PL 101-336) and Section 504 of the Rehabilitation Act and its subsequent amendments. If there are other, more questionable, conditions that might become problematic, then the job developer or employment specialist should wait and use the Seven-Phase Sequence to resolve any problems.

The steps involving the observation and performance (i.e., steps 6–12) are included so that the employment specialist can gain an accurate mental picture of all of the responsibilities of the job. It is from these pictures and the subsequent content steps that flow from them that the employment specialist will make decisions on the implementation of the Seven-Phase Sequence for initial training of the supported employee.

The final set of steps (i.e., steps 13–16) involve getting a feel for the natural procedures, relationships, politics, and other subtle features of the culture of the setting so that the supported employee can be as successful as possible during the early days of employment. The employment specialist must try to get to know who can and cannot be counted on to provide assistance, who needs to be avoided, and whom the employee must please in order to stay employed.

THE JOB ANALYSIS PROCESS

1. *Conduct* a Vocational Profile or other individualized planning process to determine applicant needs and desires. (See Chapter 7 for a further discussion of this process.)
2. *Target* job responsibilities in relation to the applicant's conditions, preferences, and contributions (from the profile meeting).
3. *Assess* the culture of the workplace. At this stage, the employment specialist should examine the potential for natural supports and the capacity of the setting to support all employees. This information often is gained through informal observation and discussions with employees and supervisors. It is important for the employment specialist to follow any "hunches" that he or she may have regarding potential sources of trouble or difficulty that may affect the employee's possibility for success. At this point, it is important for the employment specialist to be aware of how the environment "feels" as a potential worksite for the applicant.
4. Through tours and site visits, *"capture"* all components and requirements of the job in large chunks of information using the Job Analysis Form (Appendix C). This merely provides an overview of the potentially required job tasks and routines and serves as a source for later refinement, observation, and investigation.
5. *Consider* all information about the job in relation to the person(s) targeted for the job. If the "fit" seems right, then go on to step 6. If not, then develop another job, or target another prospective employee. The decision not to accept a worksite as appropriate for the identified needs of the applicant should not be considered as a "failure" to develop a job for the individual. Early decisions to look elsewhere for the right employee–workplace match could save many hours of frustration and difficulty.
6. *Visit* the jobsite to begin a detailed Job Analysis for the tasks/routines identified in step 4. Advise the employer that you will be taking notes on this aspect of the job analysis process. Do not expect your memory

to carry you through this analysis process. There are many details to remember—details that may become critically important during the facilitation of supports or learning on the part of the employee. To aid your recall of the situation, draw diagrams and write out narrative comments in enough detail that they will be meaningful at a later date.

7. *Observe* the way in which current employees perform the various routines. This particular skill is one that employment specialists develop as they gain experience in varied types of work locations. Once again, it is helpful to look for opportunities to talk with the actual workers to gain their "inside" perspective on the required work routines. Following are examples of the types of questions that could be asked:
   - What are the most important components of this task or routine?
   - Which aspects of the job are most troublesome?
   - Where is accuracy an absolute must?
   - Are there any subtleties of the task or routine that an outside observer might not notice?

8. Based on the analysis, *determine* who will be the initial trainer, and *decide* on the need for detailed job analysis and inventories for the various tasks/routines of the job. Some tasks may be deemed especially important by the employer; others may correspond to an identified limited skill of the prospective employee. Employment specialists may have direct input in the most *critical* routines and may work less directly with co-workers and supervisors in less critical and more infrequently performed routines.

9. *Perform* the routines that are the most critical for success until you have a "feel" for the job. Have someone at the jobsite *teach you* the routines. It is one thing to observe a job being performed; it is quite another to actually experience the feel of performing the job. This experience, combined with your personal knowledge of the applicant, will provide great insight on the advisability of this particular job as an appropriate location for employment. Notice the procedures, cues, amount of supervision provided, and complexity of the routines. Also take note of how you are feeling as you perform the work routines. For example,
   - Which aspects feel awkward or difficult?
   - Which parts of the work might be the easiest to learn?
   - Is stamina or strength an issue when performing the required routines?

10. *Write* task analyses and inventories for the tasks/routines that you feel will require the most support and assistance. Write the steps of the analyses and inventories to reflect the needs of a *typical employee* of the company. Consideration for the methods chosen for the various tasks/routines should reflect first the natural methods used in the company and second, if necessary, the particular needs of the employee.

11. *Get approval from the employer* on the methods chosen for the tasks/routines to be trained and any modifications or adaptations that you feel are necessary to begin employment. Once again, communicating these issues to the employer in advance may save later embarrassment for you and difficulties for the employee.

12. *Identify* procedures, including natural cues and consequences, in the work routines of the employee. For example, the natural cue to take a break might be that the clock shows 10:00 A.M., and the consequence of not responding to the natural cue is that you miss your break. In another company, the natural cue for break may be a buzzer and everyone leaving his or her work station, and the consequence of not responding may be that the supervisor comes by and says, "It's time for a break." These are the subtleties that can make all the difference in ensuring that the employee becomes part of the workplace social environment.

13. Based on step 10 and your knowledge of the needs and skills of the employee, *consider* potential training strategies, motivating strategies, possible adaptations, and opportunities for job restructuring and partial participation with other workers that may be necessary in the back-up phases of the Seven-Phase Sequence. Also, develop data sheets to reflect the number of steps that you expect that the employee will actually need in order to perform the critical tasks. The data sheets should be based on the steps identified in the analyses and routines developed in step 9.

14. *Meet* and get to know other co-workers and supervisors in the setting. Try to remember names of employees so that you can facilitate introductions when the employee starts work. If this is a difficult task for you, then write down this information for later reference and review. People like to know that someone else remembered their name. This can be a great means of encouraging further interactions and increased levels of cooperation.

15. *Ask about and observe* company policies, acceptable dress codes, orientation procedures, and other components of the company's culture. Quite often, the "cultural" aspects of a workplace are only captured through careful visual observations and by listening to the comments of the supervisory personnel and the employees. It is also recommended that the employment specialist validate any perceptions regarding the workplace culture before taking actions that could jeopardize success for the applicant.

16. *Set* a start date, *communicate* with the employee and his or her family, and *begin facilitation*.

The actual performance of the job analysis by the employment specialist requires a visit to the jobsite of at least half a day but ideally 1 or 2 days. Generally speaking, the more time invested, the more useful the job analysis becomes in facilitating successful performance and enhancing natural supports. Mcloughlin, Garner, and Callahan (1987) offered the following practical suggestions for enhancing the likelihood of success during the job analysis process:

- Dress in the same manner as the other employees—not the supervisors.
- Come on the shift at the same time as the other employees, and leave only at a logical break time, such as lunch.
- Answer questions honestly, although not necessarily in complete detail. Remember the need to respect the new worker's privacy. Stress the concept that the new worker will produce at the quality level expected of others. Do not use labels.
- Ask questions of co-workers, and show interest in their opinions.
- Take notes but not at the expense of doing the job you are supposed to do.
- If you wish to observe someone, ask for their permission, tell them what you want to do, and show them your analysis or inventory of their work.
- Do not be too familiar with supervisors or the employer while in the work area.
- If in doubt, do not sit down on the job.
- Wear comfortable shoes and, if requested, wear the uniform or other specialized clothing common to the site.
- Write down *everything* of importance. (p. 135)

TO WRITE OR NOT TO WRITE:
SHOULD JOB ANALYSIS BE A *FORM*-ALIZED PROCESS?

It is valid to consider whether it is necessary to "write up" the findings of the job analysis process described in the previous section. There has been discussion in recent years as to whether a job analysis should be conducted by a human services facilitator (Callahan & Mast, 1994). The simple question is, "Why not rely exclusively on natural features of employee support?" Responses to this reasonable question are that a job analysis need not interfere with or replace any natural feature of support and that a written job analysis stands as the blueprint for the human services supporter's role in facilitating job success for people with disabilities and, as such, represents a necessary document of accountability for supported employees, families, employers, and funding sources. (A Job Analysis form is included in Appendix C, which can be used by the employment specialist to summarize the findings of the job analysis.)

The employment specialist will identify the natural ways in which the employer wants the job performed, the natural means used to teach and maintain the job, and the natural people who are responsible for training new employees. The job analysis form also requires the employment specialist to examine relationships among employees, physical requirements of the job, cultural aspects of the setting, and other factors related to successful job performance. For employees who will need jobsite modifications and technology, the employment specialist will need to conduct an accessibility survey and will attempt to identify for the employer any reasonable accommodations that might be covered under the ADA and Section 504 of the Rehabilitation Act.

Finally, the employment specialist must consider how to best proceed with the use of natural supports in relation to the direct support and training available by the employment specialist. This may involve providing information to designated co-workers and supervisors, modeling good training techniques, or simply answering concerns and questions by the person(s) responsible for supporting the new employee.

USING THE SEVEN-PHASE SEQUENCE
FOR DECISION MAKING DURING JOB ANALYSIS

The Seven-Phase Sequence provides a useful road map for employment specialists to use in identifying critical aspects of the workplace—the ways, means, and people that comprise each site's unique culture. The strategies described in this chapter provide the framework for gathering this information and preparing the foundation for an applicant's first days of employment; however, this process often will raise more questions than it answers. Employment specialists will need to consider when to bring up potential problems and whether to proactively suggest solutions or to wait for employers to provide answers. The traditional role assumed by supported employment personnel has been to identify every conceivable problem in advance and to suggest possible solutions to the employer at the time that the problems are identified. Experience has taught us that if employment specialists identify and solve *all* of the problems that arise during supported employment, then employers will learn to rely, indeed depend, on us for that role. This dependency drives a wedge between employers and their supported employees. The solution requires employment specialists to carefully consider each jobsite problem, potential or actual, as an opportunity to welcome employers to begin owning the impact of their employee's disability.

It must be recognized that this charge represents a considerable challenge for human services employment specialists. We have assumed that it is the role of effective human services to identify and solve any problem associated with the work performance of people with disabilities. Indeed, from a bottom-line perspective, it is still our responsibility. Supported employment must continue to provide the "safety net" so essential for maintaining employment for people with severe disabilities; however, we must begin to change our practices to ensure that supports do not lead to dependency—either on the part of the employer or the supported employee.

The use of the Seven-Phase Sequence, as implemented during job analysis, raises numerous situations that require employment specialists to consider the balance between employer ownership of the solutions and the degree of human services input.

Scenario

The following scenario of an actual supported employment relationship exemplifies the issues that must be addressed and possible solutions.

Maria is a 28-year-old woman with cerebral palsy, has a mental health label of severe depression, and has been described as having a mild to moderate cognitive disability. She has worked in a work activity center since leaving high school at age 21. She lives at home with her mother and younger sister. Maria uses a wheelchair for mobility. She can handle paper products with both hands, although she must use care not to wrinkle individual sheets. Her speech is affected by her cerebral palsy in that she requires that others listen carefully when she speaks. Maria is able to handle most of her toileting needs independently, but she does require assistance unsnapping and unzipping her slacks, pulling down her slacks and underpants, and then readjusting her garments after using the toilet.

A negotiated job eventually was developed for Maria in a medium-size legal services office in her community. The job entailed performing the photocopying duties formerly assigned to the mailroom clerk named Jacob. A new combined position was created for Jacob that encompassed the remaining duties of his former job with new responsibilities of a vacant receptionist position. When the office manager was asked about the training and support offered to new employees in that setting, the employment specialist was told that, when available, the person who previously performed the duties would offer as much as 2 weeks of training to the new employee.

The employment specialist scheduled a job analysis to begin a week before Maria's first day of employment. During the 2-day job analysis (4 hours each day), the employment specialist observed Jacob's performance and received training from him on operating the copy machine. The following issues were identified:

1. At the center, Maria used a wooden platform to reach an appropriate operating level for the copy machine. This office does not have a platform that would allow Maria to reach the top of the copier and the controls.
2. When Jacob added paper to the supply tray, the employment specialist noted that he moved a rolling step stool in front of the copier, stepped up on the top step, and removed two reams of paper from a cabinet above the copier. Maria would not be able to reach the paper from her wheelchair.
3. When Jacob began teaching the employment specialist to perform the job, his teaching style involved a constant barrage of verbal instructions

followed by a question: "Do you see what I mean?" If Jacob used this style with Maria, it was feared that Maria would simply indicate that she understood, even if she did not. Maria seems to learn more effectively through gestures and short verbal directions.

4. At 10 A.M., Jacob's beeper sounded, and he abruptly left the area saying that the daily court documents courier had arrived. The employment specialist was unsure whether Jacob realized that Maria might need supervision or training during that time.

5. Maria had given permission for the employment specialist to provide to the employer a nondiagnostic, label-free description of the impact of her mental health issues. The employer had expressed a personal understanding of mental health difficulties through the experiences of a family member; however, both Maria and the employment specialist felt that it was important for at least one co-worker to be aware of some of the indicators that Maria exhibits when she cycles into a problematic phase of her condition.

6. During the break, the employment specialist went into the women's restroom to check out accessibility. The toilet stall door looked to be narrow and, upon measuring the door with a 6-foot steel tape that she carried with her, the employment specialist found that the 28-inch-wide door was 2 inches narrower than Maria's wheelchair axle width of 30 inches.

7. Inside the stall, the employment specialist found sufficient room for a wheelchair and grab bars that Maria could use to stand up and to pivot around so that she would be in position to use the toilet; however, it was clear that Maria would still need assistance to handle her garments before and after using the toilet.

8. During both days of the job analysis, the employment specialist had lunch with some of the other employees of the office in a breakroom provided for that purpose. Several of the workers indicated that they have lunch there at the same time that Maria would, every day. The employment specialist remembered from Maria's profile that her mother stated that Maria was most particular about her lunches. She preferred a sandwich each day with a prepackaged cupcake and a soda. Maria's mother further indicated that Maria needed assistance opening both the cupcake and the soda.

These problems represent only a fraction of the scores of situations that arise during the job analysis and subsequent job facilitation of supported employees. Traditional practice indicates that the employment specialist should bring up problems as they are identified and should proactively suggest solutions to the employer. The Seven-Phase Sequence, however, directs employment specialists to consider ways to increase ownership by the employer *and* solve the problem at the same time.

Solution Strategies

In reference to the eight problem areas listed for Maria, it is certainly possible to re/solve some of the issues during job development negotiations. Whenever possible, however, employment specialists should consider waiting to address problems until later in an effort to build a relationship around sharing solutions. Other problems will simply not be known during job development. Although there are a number of ways to accomplish employer ownership, employment specialists should consider which of the following strategies is best suited for each problem:

A. Bring up the problem as soon as it is identified, and suggest possible solutions to the employer.
B. Bring up the problem as soon as it is identified, and wait for or encourage the employer to suggest a solution.
C. Wait until the problem occurs during performance on the job, and suggest possible solutions to the employer.
D. Wait until the problem occurs during performance on the job, and wait or encourage the employer to suggest a solution.

These alternatives encompass most of the options available to employment specialists for resolving jobsite issues. There is an additional category that attempts to build the supported employee into the ownership formula. We fully support any and all efforts that will effectively result in supported employees' assuming responsibility for solutions relating to the impact of their disabilities. It is important to recognize that the solutions called for can come from, directly or indirectly, the supported employee; however, many employees, with or without disabilities, attempt to resolve workplace problems and are faced with the need for further assistance or advocacy. This scenario addresses the "buck stops here" position, which most employment specialists find themselves in at one time or another on virtually every supported employment jobsite.

It is fair to say that reasonable and experienced employment specialists might disagree on the best strategy for resolving problems and building ownership. As long as the decision has been carefully thought out in relation to the unique situation in each jobsite for each employee, the different strategies may be equally effective in solving each problem. In the scenario presented previously, the following decisions were made by the employment specialist. We suggest that you reread the problems identified, and make your own decisions for each one.

Problem 1: The platform for Maria's wheelchair
Solution: Strategy B
   The employment specialist decided to bring up the problem during job analysis because if she had waited until the first day of work, then Maria

would not have been able to reach the photocopier. She chose B rather than A because she felt that if the employer could easily solve the problem, then it would be better than having an outside agency do so. The employment specialist also knew that she had a back-up solution ready in case the employer could not think of a way to solve the problem.

Problem 2: The paper in the overhead cabinet
Solution: Strategy D
The employment specialist believed that this was a problem that could be easily solved by the employer. She also realized that even if the solution were more complex than it seemed, then Jacob could perform her job, with assistance in this area. By allowing some problems to be solved by the employer during performance, employment specialists can start to build confidence and ownership by the employer.

Problem 3: Too much verbal instruction during training
Solution: Strategy C
The employment specialist decided that, based on her experience, Jacob might change his training style when he met Maria and realize that he needed to slow down. Conversely, Jacob might have disagreed that his style would create problems for Maria. It is often better to address specific problems than general predictions. The employment specialist chose C rather than D because the relationship between verbal information overload and learning often is complex even to those who have studied systematic instruction procedures. The employment specialist used nonthreatening humor to connect with both Maria and Jacob in suggesting potential solutions.

Problem 4: Jacob's leaving to pick up the court document delivery
Solution: Strategy A
This one was tricky for the employment specialist. When Jacob left her with the copier on the first day, the employment specialist considered each strategy in turn. For employer ownership, she wanted to try B or D. It seemed clear, however, that Jacob's abrupt departure indicated either that he felt that a novice employee did not need supervision or that the employment specialist would simply step in for assistance. The employment specialist chose this problem as an opening to explain to Jacob, before Maria arrived for work, the role of the employment specialist as approved by the employer. In this way, it would be possible to wait until Maria's performance on other, similar problems.

Problem 5: Indicators of Maria's behavior related to her mental illness
Solution: Strategy C
The employment specialist sought Maria's input as well as her mother's in making the decision to wait until the problem occurred during perfor-

mance. Maria did not want her co-workers to be edgy with anticipation surrounding her illness. She did wish, however, for the employment specialist to model and suggest ways of interacting with her that would result in both assistance for her and a continued good relationship after the episode of difficulty had passed.

Problem 6: The narrow toilet stall door
Solution: Strategy B

As with Problem 1, the employment specialist knew that the toilet stall door needed to be widened before Maria started work; therefore, she would choose either A or B. Because issues surrounding accessibility are some of the most sensitive concerns of employers as a result of the ADA, the employment specialist carefully approached the office manager to raise the problem. The employer seemed caught off guard because the company had been told by a contractor that the entire restroom was accessible for all wheelchairs. The employer indicated that he would immediately call the contractor for a solution.

Problem 7: Maria's need for assistance in the bathroom
Solution: Strategy A

Because using the toilet is an inherently personal issue and because it is unlikely that there would be any "natural ways" for the employer to fall back on to consider a solution, the employment specialist, with Maria's approval, brought up the problem during job analysis and suggested a solution. The agency had access to funds for time-limited personal assistance services for newly employed individuals. The plan was to use the funds until Maria became known to co-workers and her employer. The assistance of a co-worker was negotiated after about 4 months. Maria pays for the service and claims an Impairment-Related Work Expense (IRWE) from the Social Security Administration to recoup her expenses.

Problem 8: Assistance at lunch and break
Solution: Strategy D

Maria's employment specialist recognized the friendly, informal atmosphere in the office breakroom. She felt that any of the co-workers would be glad to assist Maria if she asked in a polite manner. Before the first day of work, the employment specialist and Maria practiced asking for assistance and thanking the person for help received.

These decisions represent a new role for employment specialists in that not only do they recognize the necessity of solving problems for a supported employee, but also each one tries to assist in the transfer of ownership of the impact of the employee's disability from human services to employers.

ACCOMMODATING THE CULTURE OF THE WORKPLACE

Accommodating the culture of the workplace deals with the behavioral expectations that an employer has for the employees and the degree of flexibility that is allowed in a workplace. Trainers often make the assumption that all employers have the same expectations and will allow only a small degree of difference in their companies. The fact is that worksites differ widely in the way in which they view employee behavior. In some work settings, it is fine to sit when a worker has completed a certain amount of work; in others, the worker may be fired for sitting. Some employers expect workers to deal with personal differences away from work, whereas others tolerate occasional spats among workers. It is in this category, particularly, that effective job matches are made. The job analysis provides facilitators with time for exploring and clarifying the culture of work settings. This "cultural analysis" is possibly the most compelling reason to spend time in workplaces prior to the initial day of employment for the supported employee. Work cultures often are subtle and complex. Job analysis provides an opportunity to observe work cultures without the distraction of job facilitation required after an employee's first day of work. Of course, a cultural analysis is not completed during the job analysis visits. Facilitators must be constantly receptive to the information that unfolds during the employee's time on the job. If jobsite developers more closely considered this category of skills, then many more people with severe disabilities could be employed. Even people with significant "excessive behaviors" can be matched to particular job settings by creative and committed job developers and trainers.

In an analysis of the many factors that can be included under the rubric of "workplace culture," Hagner and Dileo (1993) identified the following ingredients:

- *Social customs*—informal "rules" that guide interactions, what goes on in the breakroom
- *Stories and roles*—making memories together about the many remarkable and unexpected things that can happen at work. These can be told over and over and always get a laugh.
- *Language and symbolism*—the "in" ways and slang terms used to describe various activities and situations that occur
- *Social activities*—get-togethers, hang outs, times to kick back and enjoy one another
- *Workspace*—the places where things are kept, the sanctity of another person's workspace or personal/work-related possessions
- *Power and influence*—who exerts the greatest influence over the workplace, either formally or informally; who is good to know
- *Style of leadership*—how the manager or supervisor interacts with his or her employees

- *Tone of interactions*—discriminating between serious and joking comments/directions
- *Gathering places*—places at work where people gather to chat, where people meet after work to socialize
- *Celebrations*—birthdays, holidays, promotions, retirements, or for no reason at all
- *Company image*—representing the employer in a positive light, manner of dress, and appearance

Employment specialists often will treat cultural issues such as these as tasks to be learned. In those cases, it is necessary to get a clear "picture" of the appropriate natural method of performance and to then consider a content task analysis based on that method. In situations in which it is not feasible to teach appropriate cultural behavior, it may be necessary to more closely consider the match of the company's culture to the needs of the employee. For instance, a man who came from a family culture that did not emphasize the importance of daily bathing was employed in a restaurant as a dishwasher. He wanted to be a dishwasher, but he was not able to deal with the restaurant's need for personal hygiene. After months of intrusive assistance involving supports around bathing, a new job was developed with a friend of the family who is a house painter. The man was excited because he loved to paint. The match was also an effective way to deal with the issues raised by the cultural incompatibility in the restaurant because the culture of the painting job did not have personal hygiene as a value.

SUMMARIZING THE OBSERVATIONS AND INFORMATION GAINED FROM COMPONENTS OF THE JOB ANALYSIS

The components of the Job Analysis can be summarized in written form as a reference tool for the employment specialist and as a means of communicating with the employer relative to identified sources of support. Job Analysis forms (one blank form and one completed form) have been included in Appendix C and Appendix D, respectively, for reader reference. The factors that are included in the written Job Analysis are

- *Identifying information*—name, worksite, address, telephone number, worksite supervisor, date the job is to begin, employment specialist
- *Tasks and routines*—core work routines, job-related routines, episodic work routines, important cultural aspects
- *The way in which the job tasks are typically performed*—the method(s) used by employees to perform assigned tasks, step-by-step procedures, physical demands, sensory/communication demands, academic demands, general strength/endurance requirements, pace of work, potentially dangerous components of the job, critically important components of the job, established learning curve or probationary period for the job, special

clothing or uniform requirements, tools to be used, equipment to be operated, materials to be handled, special terms used at the worksite, and a description of environmental conditions of the worksite

- *Description of the company's orientation procedures*—company's typical procedures and any identified adaptations or additions that may be necessary to meet the needs of the employee
- *Description of the company's procedures for initially training and supporting new employees*—including a request to be trained on at least one of the tasks that will be expected of the new employee
- *Description of specific strategies used by the employer*—identification of the individuals who typically provide new employees with training, availability of company trainers assigned to employee, availability of co-workers/supervisors as trainers, a description of strategies used by the employer, important rules stressed by the employer and co-workers, unwritten rules unique to the setting, potential for use of adaptations and modifications in the worksite, and the willingness of co-workers/supervisors to provide support and assistance
- *Culture of the workplace*—the employer's concern for quality, the employer's concern/need for productivity, flexibility/rigidity observed
- *Personnel: managers, supervisors*—names and titles
- *Employer social groups and nonwork activities*
- *Leaders and potential allies among co-workers and supervisors*
- *Job description*—schedule, days per week, chronology of typical work days
- *Description of job tasks*—name of task, how often task is performed, content steps/skills

A FINAL THOUGHT

Job analysis provides an excellent opportunity for employment specialists to understand the culture of the setting and to prepare for problems that may arise during natural supports. There remains a need for employment specialists to enter into workplaces *before* a supported employee begins work. The time spent on job analysis must identify and reference features of naturalness, as well as the individual needs of the applicant. Time spent on the process of job analysis may save many hours and headaches as the process of employment moves into the actual provision of supports and services in the work setting.

III

Systematic Instruction in the Workplace

In the mid-1970s, any discussions regarding the employment of individuals with severe disabilities were automatically linked with a review of procedures for training (e.g., task analysis, training strategies, behavior modification, reinforcers, data collection). Whether an individual with disabilities was sucessfully "placed" in the community was considered to be a reflection on the quality of the training provided by human services personnel. The emergence of "natural supports" drastically reduced the frequency of discussions regarding training or instruction. Although the outcome remained the same (i.e., employment), the measure of "success" was then changed to reflect an emphasis on the degrees of naturalness that were used to achieve a successful employment experience. An outside observer may be tempted to assume that natural supports are the "answer" to the supported employment question: What is the most effective approach to ensuring that all individuals with disabilities have the opportunity to work in community settings?

There is no simple or universal answer to this question. If "person-centered planning" and "individualized planning" are to remain an ingredient in the delineation of valued outcomes for people with severe disabilities, then we must be prepared to use a variety of strategies, approaches, and procedures that are as diverse as the group of individuals for whom the planning process is undertaken.

Throughout this text we have stressed the need to blend and combine the features of "natural supports" with the features of "systematic instruction." In Section III, we turn our attention to systematic instruction as a *necessary* tool for implementing supported employment. Chapter 10 provides a strategy for organizing and integrating the information gained through the Job Analysis and Vocational Profile into a plan of action for providing systematic instruction and naturally referenced supports in the workplace. It also provides a means for documenting the degree to which the process of systematic instruction has achieved the desired goal: the acquisition and demonstration of required skills and competencies.

Chapter 11 describes various guidelines and strategies for communicating the information "to be learned" in the process of facilitating community employment (e.g., formats for presenting information, when to offer information to the employee, how much assistance should be provided, what kinds of assistance should be provided, where to best teach the task) and includes strategies for motivating and reinforcing the learner within the context of a natural work environment. We conclude this text with Chapter 12, a mixed bag of practical tips regarding this process in our movement toward full employment opportunities for all individuals with severe disabilities.

Strategies for Organizing
Information and Collecting Data

10

Order and simplification are the first steps toward the mastery of a subject—the actual enemy is the unknown.

T. Mann, 1924

The challenge of any instructional approach to be used in facilitating community-based, integrated opportunities for people with severe disabilities is that the approach must be effective for each individual and must be compatible with the setting in which it is being used. The intervention strategies must be governed by a set of values that guide the trainer in knowing what to do and what not to do, how much is too much, and when to and when not to. In addition, adequate data must be collected on all training interactions to ensure maximum success of the employee with disabilities. This chapter focuses on strategies that will help the facilitator visualize, categorize, and capture in writing all of the components necessary for successful participation in the work setting.

ORGANIZING INFORMATION

Method, content task analysis, and types of job tasks are used to provide the system for organizing the information to be trained. Keep in mind that every strategy used in teaching must be compatible with an understanding of the rights, humanity, and dignity of the person being taught. *Any* discrepancy between values and strategies is *always* decided in favor of values. This provides the protection and oversight that are so necessary but often missing in human services' rush to accomplish its goals. It is the facilitator's responsibility to help resolve any job-related issue from a value perspective.

Method

All workplaces comprise a multitude of job tasks that, taken as a whole, describe the type of business activity performed in that organization. These job tasks also describe and distinguish the roles of the various employees of the setting. Because the survival of a business organization often depends on the manner in which job tasks are performed, companies typically prefer, even mandate, that job tasks be carried out in a consistent, prescribed manner.

Traditionally, the rehabilitation field has viewed the individual rather than the natural features of the setting as the starting point for considering how job tasks should be performed (Gold, 1980b). This tendency undoubtedly was strengthened by the Americans with Disabilities Act (ADA) of 1990 (PL 101-336), which requires employers to offer reasonable accommodation on job tasks to employees with disabilities. We strongly support the ADA and reasonable accommodation. If the Seven-Phase Sequence is followed, however, natural ways of performing tasks are considered and attempted before changes are made, except in circumstances in which the need for a change is overwhelmingly evident in advance. The natural ways in which job tasks are typically performed on jobsites provide a logical starting point for employees with disabilities to begin their jobs.

From a systematic instruction perspective, *method* is the concept that relates to how tasks are performed. Method involves two issues critical to effective training: 1) how a task/routine is typically performed in a natural setting and 2) the trainer's conceptual standard of "correctness."

Method is the mental picture that a trainer carries of the task with which the performance of the learner is compared. The best way to determine the methods to be used for teaching on a job is to observe the way current employees typically perform the tasks of concern. In some settings, there will be a number of different methods used. In other companies, tasks will be performed with tightly managed consistency, with close attention to the smallest details of performance. Close observation by the employment specialist during the job analysis activity and, later, during employee support enables the picture of correct performance to be imprinted for use as a standard. If during Phase Four of the Seven-Phase Sequence it is determined that the natural method of the task presents an insurmountable problem for the employee, then the method can be either modified or changed completely.

The Importance of Method   Because the method of a task will be the standard of performance by which the natural people of a setting or the employment specialist, as appropriate, will gauge the performance of the employee, it stands as a fundamentally important concept. A common mistake that most employment specialists in natural settings make is viewing outcome or product of a task as the standard for correct performance. For instance, when a restaurant manager is teaching a busperson to clean tables, the manager often is more interested in whether a table is clean than in how the table was cleaned. The attention in this case is on the *outcome* rather than on the *process*. This "cut to the chase" approach to instruction is efficient, but it often creates problems for employees with disabilities, who may require a significant number of correct performances of the task in order to truly learn the task.

Method, therefore, is a systematic training concept that can be imported into natural settings and can provide a focus for all of the component steps of a job task. Because methods occur in real time, they can be rather elusive. The best way to "capture" the method of a job task is to think of your brain as a videotape on which the video camera of your eyes will imprint a "movie" of the task. Of course, because your brain is not a videotape, it often requires a significant amount of observation to get a clear picture that can be replayed by the facilitator, paused, and fast-forwarded throughout the method. Once this has been accomplished, the method becomes a resource for a job trainer, natural or otherwise, to instantly assess the performance of the employee.

Without the concept of method, the manner in which an employee performs a task might vary each time. This variance likely will create a number of problems:

- The task will take longer to learn for most people (Gold, 1976).
- It will take the employee longer to perform the task.
- It is likely that the task will be performed differently than the natural method.
- It will be more difficult to solve any problems related to performance.
- The variation might cause the employer to focus solely on the outcome of performance. This is not favorable to people who can learn to perform correctly if consistency is ensured.

It has been our experience that many natural people in employment settings perform their job tasks in a consistent manner but that they do not seem to realize that they are doing so. In other words, they do not see the critical importance of their own actions, especially in relation to teaching others how to perform job tasks. The need for consistency is a concept that employment specialists can bring to natural work settings through the Seven-Phase Sequence. It must start with the employment specialist, usually during job analysis, getting an accurate picture of the methods of each of the job tasks to be performed by the employee with a disability. If the employment specialist does not have a clear picture of the method, then it will be impossible to identify problems related to method when the employee begins work.

Modifying the Method   If it becomes necessary to change the method of a job task, then the first consideration should be to modify the method in a manner that changes the natural procedures as little as possible. For example, an employee in an envelope factory was having difficulty maintaining the count as she fabricated a stack of 20 boxes before moving to another stack of 20. Visual height cues placed on the finished goods pallet were suggested by the employment specialist as an indicator for "20 boxes." This did not provide sufficient information for the employee. A punch counter, strapped to the leg of the box machine, provided the employee with the consistency needed by the company for this job. A step was added to the method that required the employee to punch the counter after each box was built. She then changed stacks when the counter indicated 20, 40, 60, and so forth. This modification only changed one step of the method and, therefore, represented an ideal initial strategy.

Occasionally, it will be necessary to completely change the method if it is shown that the employee is not capable of performing even a modified version of the natural method. Experienced employers and employment specialists often can conceive completely different ways to perform a task. The search for alternative methods is a skill that stems from remembering that many routine tasks have a variety of alternative methods. For example, there are a number of methods for washing a car. One method is to drive the car to an automatic carwash and enter the tracks provided for the car. Another method is to go to a self-service carwash, get out, and wash the car with the spray wand. Still another way is to get a hose, sponge, soap, and bucket and wash the car by hand. Also, within each of these methods are alternative methods that might be used. An example of how a method can be completely changed on a job task for an employee with a disability follows.

An employer became concerned that an usher with cerebral palsy would not be able to keep up with ticket collections for summer blockbuster movies. The natural method called for the usher to accept tickets from customers, tear the tickets in half, return the stubs to the customers, and place the remaining stubs through a slot in a receptacle next to the usher's station. Because of the employee's cerebral palsy, the speed of the task was slower than needed for large summer crowds. The employer modified the method of the task by placing a placard on the ticket receptacle that read, "Please rip ticket at perforation and drop into slot." The change required customers to tear their own tickets and to place the stubs into the receptacle. This change resulted in the speed necessary to allow customers to get through the line quickly, while maintaining the need for security. The employee actually had more time to observe and interact with the customers.

When method changes are necessary, the Seven-Phase Sequence encourages facilitators to welcome employers into the effort to find solutions. This will require a behavior change for many facilitators who have traditionally rushed to offer various solutions so that employers would not be bothered; however, we have learned that this approach creates dependency and allows employers to avoid assuming ownership of the impact of an employee's disability. The Seven-Phase Sequence asks facilitators to consider ways to encourage employers to deal with the issues raised by the disabilities of their employees while providing back up and additional ideas when the employers' suggestions are not effective.

Two important factors to consider when modifying a method are 1) change the typically used, *natural* method the least amount possible; and 2) meet the *needs of the employee* learning the task. Ideally, the job developer has also identified job tasks with natural methods that can be performed by the learner.

Phrases that Can Be Used Instead of "Method"   When negotiating and discussing issues in natural work places, human services personnel should avoid using jargon associated with human services strategies (Hagner & Dileo, 1993). The best approach is to listen carefully during job analysis to the language used in the setting and try to find substitute words, whenever possible, rather than those used in this text; however, it is likely that many settings will not typically use any words that convey the meaning of a concept as "method" does. In that case, you might try, "The way you usually do the task," "The procedure that you use," or, "Show me each part of the process," as a substitute for the word "method."

Content Task Analysis

Content task analysis—breaking the method of a task into teachable component steps—has been a strategy available to trainers in business and in the human services field for years. In fact, content task analysis traditionally was viewed as the foundation or the starting point for any effective training. This focus led researchers and practitioners to concentrate on the minute aspects of a task and on the writing skills that were necessary to describe ever-smaller pieces of the method in a manner that would, it was hoped, convey an accurate image of the step. This attention to step-by-step detail was a good match for the motion and time studies required by law in sheltered workshops and work activity centers. Practical researchers (Bellamy, Peterson, & Close, 1975; Gold, 1972, 1976) suggested that content task analysis was a requisite for any effective training approach.

Because of the popularity of this strategy, content task analysis was considered by many to be an essential ingredient of quality supported employment services. As supported employment expanded in geometric proportions in the late 1980s, however, human services personnel recognized that most community businesses did not write content steps or any kind of step-by-step procedures for most of the tasks that supported employees were performing. This inevitably led to a tension between supported employment managers and researchers on one hand and employment specialists on the other. Individuals who are diretly involved in the actual worksite aspects of supported employment have always been reluctant to perform paperwork and data collection procedures that do not seem to be required by employers.

The problems associated with content task analysis, therefore, are as apparent as the tensions just described and as subtle as the uncomfortable and artificial images that any sophisticated approach can convey to the everyday people found in the workplace. For years, human services personnel undoubtedly have noticed the lack of fit between a detailed content task analysis and the real needs and natural procedures of the work setting. In the early days of employment support for people with severe disabilities, a Marc Gold & Associates job trainer related the following story:

> The job to be performed at Motorola involved the operation of a complex semiconductor testing machine. I spent 2 weeks on the job analysis and also wrote a detailed content task analysis on the operation of the machine. I noticed that when I was trained to perform the task the training supervisor presented about 15 steps—verbally, not in writing—as an explanation of the method of the job. In consideration of our employee with a disability, I wrote a content task analysis which involved 145 steps, each an accurately described component of the method. When I proudly presented my task analysis to the area supervisor as a tool to be used for further training and troubleshooting for our employee, she had an uncomfortable look on her face as she tried to make positive comments about the "thoroughness" of the analysis. Suddenly, she brightened and said, "This is exactly what the engineers have been asking for!" She immediately called two guys from Design and Engineering who looked at my analysis and exclaimed, "This is what we've been suggesting!" The supervisor gladly handed the document over to the engineers and asked them to study it a while. My content task analysis was never seen on the work floor again. (N. Rhoads, personal communication, 1983)

This experience surely represents countless situations in which the best human services intentions did not match the needs and realities of the natural work setting. We have been forced to question ourselves and the strategies that we had imported from artificial, simulated work settings. Probably no other human services concept has created more uncertainty than content task analysis in relation to the needs of people who find tasks difficult to learn.

A New Basis for Content Writing   The issues described have forced a reconsideration of the role played by content task analysis in the facilitation of supported employment. The Seven-Phase Sequence asks the employment specialist to examine and *follow the natural means* used by a company *to teach employees the natural ways* of the setting. In a business like Wendy's Hamburgers, therefore, the facilitator would encourage using the picture/task cards available to all employees in order to organize the information for teaching the job of "preparing and frying chicken fillets." Experience has shown, however, that many companies do not write step-by-step procedures for discrete job tasks. In those situations, employment specialists are advised to write a content task analysis on the steps of method *from the perspective of a typical employee of the setting*. This strategy is suggested for several reasons:

1. The reference point remains naturally focused, in keeping with the Seven-Phase Sequence.
2. Supervisors and other natural people will recognize the utility of the analysis because of the similarity to their perspectives.
3. It remains a good idea to write down the steps of the method for accountability, professional responsibility, and sharing.
4. Job tasks can always be broken down further in Phase Six of the Seven-Phase Sequence to meet the needs of employees who may need smaller steps in order to learn their jobs.
5. By waiting until Phase Six, facilitators avoid the need to break down all steps into smaller components. It is possible to focus only on those steps that are causing problems for the supported employee.

The Relationship of Content Task Analysis to Method   Content is simply the arbitrary number of steps into which a method is divided. It serves as a means to stop and capture the method much in the same way that a movie poster stops and captures a scene in a film. Perhaps an even more accurate analogy is that content steps are like the frames one sees when 16 mm projection film is held in front of a light source. What will later become real-time motion, when a projector light and motor interact with the film, is actually a lengthy series of frames much like small slides. Each frame has stopped the motion of the film, and each frame conceivably could be described as a "content step" of the movie. Of course, this would involve thousands of descriptions that would be distinguished from each other with the most subtle changes. This would represent, possibly, the most detailed content task analysis one could imagine.

If the film were taken of a job task, rather than of a movie concept, it would represent the method of the task when run on a projector. Rather than take each frame as a step, a facilitator would start with the first frame, sequentially, and include all of the frames that represent the first grouping of common actions. These frames taken together would become step 1 of the content task analysis. When considering the amount of action to be contained in any given content step, one must take into account the amount of information that can be utilized by a typical employee in the setting and when the action of the task changes (e.g., the difference between stuffing an envelope with a bill and sealing the envelope).

Method and content work together and, in virtually all cases, sequentially. Even though both concepts are important in the organization of the information to be trained, employment specialists must realize the role that each plays. *Method relates to the real time during which the task is being performed*. It is used as a standard by which a trainer can determine correctness.

Content is a strategy for managing the method. It stops the method and allows trainers to

- Give discrete information for achieving correct performance and consider alternative informing strategies for all of the different steps of the method
- Break the task into smaller, more teachable steps as required by the needs of various employees
- Collect data on the method in a way that would not be possible without a content task analysis

Writing Content Steps   Perhaps no aspect of systematic instruction in natural settings has created more tension and misunderstanding among employment specialists than the requirement to write detailed content task analyses on every job performed by supported employees. Gold (1980a) was merely one among many researchers and academics who strongly encouraged job trainers to write individualized, detailed task analyses for employees with disabilities on community jobs. One of the reasons for this attention was that traditionally it was believed that the correctness of each step (see the next section, Method and Content Considerations) was communicated and understood in the accurate written description of content steps. This perspective led to an inordinate amount of focus on the writing and analytical skills of job trainers rather than on teaching and communication skills. Systematic training often became the domain of articulate and educated staff members rather than an interaction between a person with information and another who needed that information.

As real business conditions began to influence human services strategies, method emerged as the more natural and comfortable concept to carry correctness. Because method is an image rather than a product of one's writing skills, "regular people" (i.e., non–human services) can be invited to use systematic instructional procedures. This shift also meant that the writing of content steps had to be reconsidered.

Human services personnel should write not only a general job analysis but also a content task analysis for each of the most critical tasks of the job. The difference now is that, initially, tasks should be broken into only as many steps as needed by an average employee of the setting. This change results in a "least amount" of effort and allows employment specialists to target only the most critical tasks for writing. If individual employees need smaller amounts of information than is available in natural steps, then the problem steps can be easily broken down on a data sheet (discussed later in this chapter). This approach to writing content steps will allow facilitators to share their task analyses with the employer and other natural people in the setting in a way that will connect the supported employee with the natural means useful for all employees.

Strategies for writing content steps vary among facilitators and the business in which they support employees with disabilities. If a company has already written step-by-step procedures for the job(s) to be performed, then it is not necessary to write additional content steps unless the supported employee experiences difficulty and needs smaller pieces of information in order to learn the task. If the particular job does not have written procedures, then try to model your content steps after the company's style. In cases in which no written procedures naturally exist on any of the tasks to be performed, facilitators are encouraged to write steps in a clear, complete style using language derived from the setting whenever possible. A well-written content step has a number of components. (Sample content task analyses are provided later in this chapter.)

It is more important for the trainer to "see," or conceptualize, the components (steps) of a task than it is to write each step in detail. The employment specialist should write out the steps of tasks that are important and that are expected to be difficult to train. This writing can be informal, and the steps should reflect the needs of an average person. Content steps serve to remind the employment specialist of the method rather than to accurately describe the method. Written content steps are not clear enough to communicate complex task performance. If there are to be multiple trainers for a task, then each trainer must "see" the same method in order to teach effectively.

The following is an example of a content step for replacing the toner packet in a copy machine:

4.   Insert the toner packet into the receptacle until it stops even with the front of the receptacle, and rotate the toner packet 180° to release toner.

Method and Content Considerations   There are a number of concepts related to the organization of training information using method and content. The first consideration is *correctness* and its "flip side" issue, *error.* Correctness occurs when an employee performs the steps of the method in a manner that results in a completed task that is acceptable to the employer. Note that this definition does not address how the task is performed, merely that the result is acceptable. This general view of correctness is common in many natural workplaces. Systematic instruction procedures, however, demand a more in-depth look into an employee's performance and require that distinctions be made between at least two categories of correctness: topographical and functional (Callahan, 1993; Ford & Mirenda, 1984).

Topographical correctness occurs when the steps of the method are performed as they are typically performed in the natural setting, as taught by the trainer, so that the task is completed with acceptable quality. *Functional correctness* occurs when a task is completed with acceptable quality but in a manner different from the method typically performed in the setting.

The degree to which an employee must adhere to topographical correctness or be allowed to use functional correctness is dependent on a number of factors, the most important of which relates to the balance between the demands of the work setting and the needs of the employee. For instance, if an employment specialist finds that a particular hotel wants its sheets folded so that the small hem around the edges is always folded inward with the edges lining exactly even, then it must be ensured that the employee understands this and folds the sheets in the correct manner. If the employee is unable to perform this step correctly with adequate training, then it is usually best to negotiate another task that can be learned. Other factors that influence the need for topographical correctness include the following:

- When safety issues are a concern such as in hand placement on a press machine. Functional correctness may inadvertently lead to an accident as the employee's hands are placed in various locations on the machine.
- When the productivity of the task is critically important. Often the topographically correct method is also the most efficient method.
- When the person teaching the task also performs the task using the same method. This will increase the comfortableness of natural people to teach supported employees.
- When teaching the task(s) that will be performed the most frequently during the workday. It just makes good sense to not encourage flexibility on the tasks that are performed the most often. Any problem related to functional correctness will be heightened.

Functional correctness is appropriate in a number of situations on the job. Facilitators must be careful, however, not to consider functional correctness as a starting point for teaching. When this happens, employees often take much longer to learn their jobs, and the quality of performance and safety considerations become problematic. Facilitators might consider allowing functional correctness in the following circumstances:

- On tasks that are inherently performed based on individual choice, such as the way one hangs coats and other personal items in a company locker
- On tasks that are performed only occasionally during the workday or week. The manner in which a task is performed is usually less important as the number of times it is performed decreases, unless there are safety or quality concerns.
- On tasks on which an aspect of the employee's disability hinders the performance of topographical correctness, such as the difficulty an employee with cerebral palsy may have operating a copy machine. Significant modifications to topographical correctness may be needed to accommodate the employee's disability.

An *error* in performance occurs whenever the employee does not perform the steps of the method in a topographically or functionally correct manner, and assistance is needed from the trainer for correctness. An employment specialist determines error by comparing the performance of the employee with the mental image of the method gained in job analysis. This view of error does not in any way imply that it is a negative concept. All employees will make errors during the acquisition of a task and even later, during performance. The important distinction that this approach to training makes is that employment specialists are encouraged to focus on the correction of errors made during the performance of the method rather than on simply the outcome or product of the job task. In this way, employees with disabilities can learn to perform their job tasks in ways that are as similar as possible to the typical methods used in the setting. This should enhance acceptance and comfort levels on the part of supervisors and co-workers as they relate to the supported employee.

It is necessary to determine when an employee has learned the job tasks that have been assigned by the employer. *Criterion* is the point in training at which the trainer believes that acquisition of the job task has taken place (Gold, 1980b). It is interesting to note that few natural work settings actually have an operational concept similar to criterion; however, it is critical to identify the point at which criterion performance can be assumed. Because there is not likely to be a natural standard for criterion, employment specialists usually will need to set criterion in a way that makes sense in relation to the demands of the job tasks and the work setting. Remember that no task will be performed correctly 100% of the time, day after day. Employment specialists must, therefore, set criterion as a reasonable percentage of perfect performance. The more complete the knowledge base about a work setting, the easier it will be to set a fair and effective criterion for job tasks.

Regardless of the number of cycles of performance that the facilitator chooses for criterion, it is necessary for the employee to perform *all* of the steps of the method, topographically correct (or functionally, as appropriate) without assistance from natural support or the employment specialist. This sets a high standard whether the target number for criterion is "3 of 4 cycles" of the task or "48 of 50 cycles."

A close cousin to criterion is *cycle constancy,* the topographically correct performance of all of the steps of the task, cycle after cycle (Gold, 1980b). This concept, borrowed from industrial time and motion technology, addresses a characteristic of tasks that have naturally repeating cycles. Gold (1980b) found that when a task is performed in a consistent manner, each time it naturally occurs, the time necessary to reach the level of criterion performance is lessened. In other words, cycle constancy offers "natural training power" on those tasks with naturally repeating cycles. This helps explain the observation noted by many job trainers that the basic job responsibilities are seldom problematic for employees with disabilities. Most often, it is episodic tasks and duties that create problems on the job.

The needs for attention to criterion and cycle constancy often operate together. Facilitators should set criterion high and closely monitor topographical correctness and cycle constancy when

- Safety is a concern
- Quality is an issue
- Productivity demands are high
- The task is a core routine (see p. 158)
- The cycle is short
- The cost of material and/or errors is high

The criterion can be lower, and functional correctness is appropriate when

- Safety is not an issue
- Training tasks have a variety of acceptable methods
- The task is episodic or job related (see pp. 158–160)

Content Steps   The content steps of job tasks vary in a number of important aspects. The following descriptions relate to various types of content steps. It should be noted that a given step might share a number of these characteristics. One distinction among the types of steps relates to the specificity of information contained within the step.

Discrete steps are steps of a task that involve *distinct or absolute action.* Correct action can be specified and easily evaluated. All other action is incorrect. An example of a discrete step would be "entering the price of a product in a cash register." These steps usually are more easily taught than steps requiring judgment.

Judgment steps are steps that involve a *range of correctness*—soft boundaries. The evaluation of correctness, therefore, often is subjective. An example of a judgment step would be "cleaning a table in an upscale restaurant." Judgment steps require *consistent practice* in order to be learned. Another perspective deals with the amount of information contained within a step and the impact on teaching and learning.

Natural steps are steps that contain the amount of *information typically needed by an average employee* of a work setting to learn the task. The facilitator often has to guess or estimate the amount of information in natural steps if no such determination has been made in the setting.

Teachable steps are steps that contain an *amount of information suitably matched to the needs of the learner.* Content steps can be continually broken down in Phase Six of the Seven-Phase Sequence to arrive at the ideal match for a given learner. Natural steps may or may not be teachable in their initially written form, depending on the needs of the employee.

A final distinction among steps involves the type of action required of the employee. Most natural steps of performance tasks can be divided into order, discrimination, and manipulation components that may be further broken down into teachable steps.

Order steps are steps that occur at the *beginning of each new action change* in the task. These steps relate to the sequence of the method. *Discrimination steps* require the *employee to distinguish the proper feature or cue* of the task for correct performance. *Manipulation steps* involve *physical interaction by the employee with a component* of the task in order to achieve correctness.

An example of each of these components occurs in the natural job task step "turn on the computer." In this step, there are actually three smaller, more teachable steps: 1) the order step of turning the computer on rather than inserting a disk, 2) the discrimination step of recognizing the on/off switch and its current position, and 3) the manipulation step of physically switching the computer to the "on" position. These steps are useful in Phase Six, when breaking a natural step into more teachable steps and, later, in training strategies, when considering the types of assists that may be effective in teaching the steps.

Natural Cues and Consequences   *Natural cues* are the existing features of any setting, task, or item that assist people to correctly perform the tasks or jobs of the setting. Some settings, such as airports and markets, provide a great deal of information in the form of signs and posters. Other settings, such as parks, have many fewer cues for visitors to use for correctness. Visitors may simply have to infer that the presence of swings and slides comprise a playground. A bank may use railings and signs to indicate the correct procedure for waiting for a teller. Some stores use large flashing signs to show that they are open. Large malls often provide an information booth for their customers.

In work settings, natural cues are important to trainers because they can be utilized to enhance the acquisition and maintenance of difficult-to-teach routines. All job tasks contain natural cues, but their use is much more critical on tasks with significant time delay between cycles of performance.

Virtually every component of a natural routine has a number of natural cues that can be referenced by the trainer to help teach and maintain the skill. It is critical that the trainer identify the most relevant or salient (Ford & Mirenda, 1984) natural cues and observe how the employee attends to those cues.

When a person performing a particular task fails to observe a natural cue, one of several *natural consequences* might occur: 1) the routine may be interrupted or, perhaps, terminated (*neutral* natural consequence); 2) the person may become injured, embarrassed, or frightened (*negative* natural consequence); or 3) the person may receive assistance or additional information (*assisting*). It is the responsibility of the trainer to ensure that the likelihood that a neutral natural consequence will occur is slight, that a negative natural consequence will occur is nonexistent, and that assisting will be used in teaching the targeted task. Additional perspectives on natural consequences for teaching are discussed in the following chapter. Natural cues and consequences should be identified by the trainer during the development of the inventory and utilized, as appropriate, during training.

Types of Job Tasks

Even though the concepts of method and content comprise the basis for organizing information for training on jobsites, distinctions among the types of jobs to be performed provide additional perspective for facilitators to consider before beginning instruction. This section presents the training issues associated with three types of job tasks—core routines, episodic routines, and job-related routines.

Core Routines Core routines are job tasks that have cycles that are repeating, without significant interruption between cycles. These tasks typically are those most frequently performed by the employee. The cycle of a task begins with the first step of a job sequence and ends with the step that precedes the initial step of the next sequence.

The importance of core routines lies in the natural instructional power available from the repeating cycles. Consistent cycles provide the facilitator with the opportunity to fine tune the employee's correctness simply by taking advantage of the opportunities for giving information each time the cycle is performed. In addition, Gold (1972) found that the practice effect available by correctly performing core routines in their natural cycles proved to significantly reduce the time to criterion for people with severe cognitive impairments. For most core routines, the facilitator will choose to directly observe the training of the employee and to be immediately available for assistance.

The following is a sample content task analysis for the core routine of operating a dishwasher in a restaurant:

1. Place rack on rinse table.
2. Load rack—large pans in rear, plates in front.
3. Rinse dishes with spray nozzle.
4. Check for stuck-on food, rinse again if necessary.
5. Make sure dishwasher is not running.
6. Raise door on dishwasher.
7. Slide rack into dishwasher, pushing clean rack out the other side.
8. Close door of dishwasher to begin wash cycle.
9. Move to sort table.
10. Remove similar items from rack and stack on table.
11. Place stacked items on appropriate shelves.
12. Continue steps 10 and 11 until all items are shelved.
13. Return rack to rinse table.

Episodic Routines Episodic routines are assigned job tasks that have cycles that occur infrequently—once or twice a shift or possibly even once a week—and are required by the employer as part of the job description. These routines often are more difficult to learn because of the time lapse between the cycles.

Because episodic routines lack the natural training power available from core routines' repeating cycles, facilitators must find other sources for additional instructional power as training problems arise. There are a number of strategies that a facilitator can use to offset the difficulty created as a result of the time delay between job cycles:

- Reference natural cues, and use assisting natural consequences.
- Pull the problem step out of the natural cycle or the task out of the natural flow of performance, and practice using repeating cycles.
- Negotiate assistance from others in the work setting for difficult components of the task.

Although these strategies can help facilitators gain instructional power, they may not be sufficient to teach tasks with significant time delay. In that case, the trainer must use a decision strategy (Ford & Mirenda, 1984) similar to the one suggested in the following chapter on informing strategies. If these approaches do not prove sufficient to teach the task, then facilitators may need to negotiate for partial assistance (Brown et al., 1984; Brown et al., 1987) from co-workers or supervisors in order to complete the problem step(s) of a task.

The following is a sample content task analysis for an episodic routine for cleaning up a work area in a restaurant:

1. Stop dishwashing duties at 10 minutes before end of shift.
2. Stack and store all clean items from stacking table.
3. Place all remaining dirty dishes in rinse sink.
4. Place all racks on shelf below rinse table.
5. Locate cleaning bucket, cloth, and cleaning solution.
6. Fill cleaning bucket with warm water.
7. Spray cleaning solution on rinse table.
8. Wipe table with damp cloth until clean.
9. Repeat steps 7 and 8, cleaning the dishwasher and the stacking table.
10. Empty cleaning bucket, rinse cloth, and return cleaning items to storage cabinet.

Job-Related Routines   Job-related routines are the skills and routines that are not part of the job but that are vital to successful performance. These routines may occur either on- or off-site and often are ignored by jobsite trainers. They are similar to episodic routines in that significant time delays often occur between cycles of performance. Poor performance of these routines is more likely to occur than on core routines. Examples of job-related routines might be "getting to work," "going to the bathroom," "taking a break," or "knowing when to stop work." Many workers with disabilities lose their jobs when assistance is not offered to facilitate acceptable performance.

The following is a content task analysis for getting ready to work in a restaurant:

1.   Get off of the bus in front of the restaurant.
2.   Walk to the employees' entrance.
3.   Enter door into foyer.
4.   Walk through kitchen area to employees' lounge.
5.   Locate and open personal locker.
6.   Take off coat and other items.
7.   Place all personal items in locker.
8.   Take apron from locker and put it on.
9.   Close and lock locker.
10. Go to lavatory and wash hands, comb hair, and check clothes.
11. Go to time clock to punch in to begin workday.

Although all of the strategies discussed thus far are critically important for facilitating the success of a supported employee in the workplace, they cannot work to their maximum potential unless employment specialists collect data on all training interactions.

DATA COLLECTION IN INTEGRATED WORK SETTINGS

The amount of data collected on supported employment jobs is a major factor affecting the employment satisfaction of human services facilitators (Agosta, 1994). Employment specialists have complained that there is an overload of paperwork required for every aspect of supported employment. As a result, the importance of data collection for the acquisition of tasks performed by the employee is often deemphasized or even ignored. It is, therefore, necessary to examine the traditional reasons for collecting data in light of the changes that are occurring in supporting employees in the workplace.

Trainers traditionally have been encouraged to take acquisition data for the purpose of making instructional decisions and to determine how the process of training is progressing (Gold, 1980b). As thousands of people with severe disabilities have had job opportunities in real work settings, however, it now seems that these two reasons relate more to research needs than to actual training needs. Most trainers simply do not use their data sheets for the purpose of decision making or for documenting the effectiveness of the instructional process. The progression of beliefs held by job trainers about data collection usually include the following:

*   "I have learned the method of the job tasks to be taught."
*   "I am available to the employee during the performance of the job."
*   "The status of training should be quite evident without consulting a data sheet."

Does this mean that collection of acquisition data is no longer needed? We think not. In fact, in some ways we would suggest that the importance of data collection has dramatically increased. With declining resources and expanded scrutiny of the rehabilitation field, data on task acquisition can substantiate and support our role in facilitating successful performance of work tasks by supported employees. In addition, there has never been a clear societal mandate from communities and employers to assist people with severe disabilities to find real jobs. We are, therefore, vulnerable to the issues created by inadequate instruction and skill acquisition by those supported employees for whom we have assumed some level of responsibility. The collection of acquisition data to the point of a specified performance criterion can provide a strong case that employment specialists have done their jobs to ensure the safest and highest-quality conditions for people with disabilities.

We now suggest that accountability is the number one reason to document the performance of supported employees. By tracing the progress of learning from the initial days of employment through criterion performance, employment specialists have powerful data to verify that tasks were learned, to offer encouragement to supported employees, to impress supervisors and company owners, and to meet most of the needs of human services agencies and their funding sources. This type of data also provides employment specialists with a valuable customer service tool. Supported employees and their families can see the progress made during the training process and the point at which the desired criterion was achieved.

Types of Data Collection

Data collection strategies must be tailored to meet the reasons for collecting the information in the first place. The primary reasons for collecting data during the acquisition phase of training are to verify criterion performance and to account for the training that was provided. If a human services agency is part of a research effort, then there may be additional reasons for data collection. There are two basic forms of data that address these primary reasons— coded data, which reference the steps of the task, and narrative data, which describe the performance and outcomes.

Coded Data Collection Strategies   When an employment specialist has completed the job analysis, the step-by-step procedures that describe the method of the job tasks are written, with the needs of a typical employee in mind. These steps also provide the framework for a data sheet, which the employment specialist can code with various indicators of performance and/or assistance. The exact steps of the content task analysis will become the steps of the data sheet. In this manner, the employment specialist can trace the performance of the supported employee from a perspective that is as natural and as brief as possible. The first decision to make when using a coded data sheet concerns the codes that will be used to describe the actions observed.

Traditionally, human services data collection procedures have taken on tasks that were broken into the smallest possible pieces of performance and involved coding systems that seemed to focus on every aspect of employee action except correctness. Data codes typically have referenced the assists that were provided by the trainer, the type of error made by the learner, and the degrees of correctness of the learner's performance. Often, codes referenced five, six, or more different considerations for error or assistance but only one code for correctness. One might wonder whether trainers really thought that the task would be learned by the employee. There are a number of subtle problems associated with traditional, research-based data collection procedures on supported employment jobs:

- A focus on trainer assists and employee errors shifts the attention away from the real goal of instruction—criterion performance by the employee.
- When numerous data codes are used, the employment specialist must mark every step of the data sheet in order to get an accurate picture. If a simplified, two-code strategy is used, then the employment specialist need only mark one code at any time. In this way, the employment specialist can choose to mark the code that is occurring the least.
- It is virtually impossible to keep step-by-step data, while teaching, when the data sheet describes a minutely written content task analysis and when using multiple data codes.
- No single instance of data is particularly important or even accurate. Employment specialists may miss or misinterpret employee action.
- Criterion comes from consistent performance over trials.

It is recommended that data collection using coded data sheets be simplified in a way to avoid these problems. First, employment specialists should focus on teaching the task to criterion rather than on the assist required or the errors of the employee. Second, using a two-code data system will simplify data collection and allow the employment specialist to make decisions regarding which code is likely to be needed the least. The codes to be used should reference 1) topographically correct performance of the steps of the method, without assistance from the trainer (most employment specialists use a plus or a checkmark for this code); or 2) anything other than item 1) (most use a minus for this code). Item 2) includes employee errors, functional correctness, trainer assistance of any sort, or performance of the step(s) by the trainer. This approach sets a high standard for teaching and employee performance. Third, we recommend that employment specialists implement a consistent strategy for data collection that does not require step-by-step marking of data codes on every cycle of task performance. This can be accomplished by using either a consistent recall strategy or a data probe. Finally, criterion performance, not individual data points, is the real payoff. Data collection procedures should focus more on establishing criterion than on providing minute information of errors and assists.

The Recall Strategy   When using the recall strategy, the employment specialist begins by estimating a period of time that can be remembered for accurate recall of employee performance. Typically, the shorter the cycle of the task, the shorter the interval between data collections and vice versa. Training is provided by the natural trainer or employment specialist, as appropriate. Begin the observation by focusing on steps performed topographically correct, without assistance from the trainer. Note the time, stop the performance briefly, and mark any pluses that may have occurred. It is not necessary to be completely accurate, although care should be taken to reflect the performance as carefully as possible. Resume training, again focusing on correctness. The initial interval for recall typically should be no longer than about 15 minutes. As performance improves, two changes can occur: 1) the focus could shift to marking errors or assists, as they are occurring less often than correct action; and 2) the interval for recall can increase to 30 minutes or more.

Data Probe   A data probe is similar to the recall strategy in that it frees the employment specialist from collecting data on every cycle of a task. The difference is that the employment specialist decides to focus on a given cycle in a consistent time interval. Rather than recall performance, one cycle represents all of the other cycles performed during the interval. If the employment specialist is directly providing instruction to the supported employee, then it is suggested that, at the end of the probe cycle, the employee is asked to wait a moment while the data sheet is filled out. If a natural trainer is teaching, then the employment specialist is free to follow each step as the action occurs. The time intervals selection should follow the same suggestions as for the recall strategy. The important thing to remember for either approach is that consistency is the key. Because these options allow employment specialists additional time to focus on teaching, it is critical that the time intervals be remembered for data collection. It is also important to take a moment and chart the number of cycles performed during the interval. If employment specialists do this, then they can use simple division to indicate the employee's production rate during acquisition. *Important note:* It is rarely necessary to use either a recall or data probe strategy for episodic or job-related tasks because of the singular nature of the job cycles. Employment specialists usually can chart the data either while or immediately after the task is performed.

Data Collection Strategies in Specific Circumstances

Data Collection When Training a Core Routine   Core routines typically are those most frequently performed by the employee. The following procedures should be used when collecting data on core routine performance:

1. Get to know the task to be trained.
2. Develop a content task analysis of the task.

3. Make initial data collection decisions regarding 1) the type of coding system that will be used and 2) whether a recall or probe strategy will be used.
4. Compile and *learn* the data sheet for the task.
5. Begin training the task, without taking data, for 15 minutes. During this time, keep in mind the steps or skills that can be performed without training assistance.
6. Stop training momentarily and chart data either from memory or from actual performance. Mark the steps that were performed without assistance.
7. Repeat steps 5 and 6.
8. Consider extending the data collection interval to 20–30 minutes. Once again, keep in mind the steps or skills that can be performed without training assistance.
9. Repeat steps 5 and 6.
10. Consider changing the focus to the steps requiring assistance and mark with a minus (–).
11. Repeat steps 5, 6, 8, and 10 until the learner reaches criterion.
12. After criterion has been reached, begin keeping narrative data on general performance, areas of difficulty, and productivity.

Addressing Problem Steps   During training and data collection, difficult steps of a task may require attention in Phase Six of the Seven-Phase Sequence—Reconsider Natural Means. Employment specialists often will find it necessary to break down a step into smaller pieces of action. If this is necessary, then the data sheet also must be changed to reflect the smaller steps. Table 10.1 describes the operation of a press machine in a factory and the breakdown of the problem step of removing papers from the press.

    This example shows the result of breaking step 3 into four smaller parts. The method of the task is unchanged, but the focus is now on smaller pieces of performance. The data sheet used by the employment specialists also would need to be adjusted to reflect the smaller steps.

Charting Criterion Performance   Even though the concept of criterion is not understood in most workplaces, it is one of the employment specialist's most important tools for ensuring the successful performance of supported employees. As discussed previously in this chapter, criterion is an assumption or indication, made by the trainer, that learning has taken place. Learning implies that the employee is able to perform the steps of the method, without assistance from the trainer, in the manner that the employer has prescribed. It also implies an assumption that the employee will continue to perform the task in this manner after criterion has been reached. The actual point at which criterion takes place is arbitrary—based on the trainer's best estimate that a certain consistency of performance indicates that the task is learned.

Table 10.1.   Operating a press machine

Original content task analysis	Modified content task analysis
1. Assume operating position.	1. Assume operating position.
2. Decide when sufficient number of papers are in bin—approximately 50 sheets.	2. Decide when sufficient number of papers are in bin—approximately 50 sheets.
3. Remove papers from bin.	**3. Place left hand under papers, palm up.**
	4. Raise right hand over papers, palm down.
	5. Watch for next sheet to exit press.
	6. When sheet hits stop, lift stack by moving left and right hands toward each other.
4. Turn with papers to stacking table.	7. Turn with papers to stacking table.
5. Jog papers with "portrait" orientation until even across top.	8. Jog papers with "portrait" orientation until even across top.
6. Jog papers with "landscape" orientation until even across top.	9. Jog papers with "landscape" orientation until even across top.
7. Place papers on stack on table.	10. Place papers on stack on table.

Note: Boldface inserts represent a modification of original steps in content task analysis or the addition of new steps into the process.

The data sheet is the employment specialist's best tool to establish criterion. At some point in the successful training of every job task, a cycle will occur in which the employee performs all of the steps correctly, without assistance. This is a critically important event for a number of reasons: 1) this marks the beginning point for establishing criterion; 2) it serves to remind employment specialists or trainers to redouble their focus on topographically correct performance—to set a high standard; and 3) it signals the necessity for the employment specialist to begin taking step-by-step, cycle-by-cycle data. Because the employee has virtually learned the task at this point, it is possible to pick up the data sheet and account for performance on each step of a task.

As close to criterion as this first assist-free performance is, paradoxically it might be the most fragile point of training. The reason is simple—human nature. Trainers naturally want employees to be successful on the cycles that follow the initial unassisted effort. It is understandable that trainers might want to overlook small flaws in performance so as to get on with establishing criterion. Trainers and employment specialists must fight this urge and recommit to a high standard of correctness. Think of this focus as an investment in the future performance of employees. Employment specialists must be careful, of course, to not be so stringent that the errors and flexibility that are acceptable are not considered. However, if trainers set criterion to a point that merely equals the natural conditions of a workplace, then it is likely that the correctness exhibited by the employee will lessen after the employment specialist begins to fade. Therefore, criterion is a balance that is stricter than the expectations of the employer but not so tight that employees are unable to meet the standard.

We recommend that employment specialists share points of criterion with supported employees, employers, and family members. Also, with the completed data sheet safely in the employee's file, employment specialists can rest easier in relation to liability, site visits from funding sources, and personal accomplishment. If performance problems occur after a criterion has been reached, then the first troubleshooting consideration typically is to assume that criterion was set too low. Reestablish training using the Seven-Phase Sequence as a guide for decision making, and take additional data until a new criterion has been met.

Narrative Data Collection Strategies   The strategies used by employment specialists for collecting narrative data on jobsites are much more individually determined than the more formal, prepared data sheets described previously. Narrative data is collected simply by writing down all of the observations of performance, discussions with employers, daily issues, and noteworthy events that comprise the workday of a supported employee. Whereas coded data sheets are used to chart the course of training and productivity, narrative data gives life to the experiences of daily supported employment. We recommend a device that experienced employment specialists often use—a steno notebook for each person they support. The notebook is taken to work each day, and entries of all kinds are recorded in the book. Narrative data can encompass virtually every aspect of a job. Certainly the most critical data to include in such a book would be issues or problems that may have an impact on the success of the employee, such as work requirements, problems with work or co-workers, rule violations, commendations, or messages for family or support people. Of course, narrative data need not be negatively focused. Any information that might relate to the supported employee's success should be included. By maintaining a journal-like account of the job-related issues, employment specialists can use the data as a resource to recall agreements made weeks before, employees and families can verify the decisions and strategies that were made, and managers of employment specialists can get a glimpse into the issues faced on jobsites.

Production Data   A final consideration on data collection concerns production data. Discussions with employment specialists seem to indicate that production data is seldom kept on supported employees. In fact, many job developers purposefully avoid employers who do collect tight production data because it interferes with the learning process. We do not recommend that employment specialists keep production data for the purpose of introducing it to employers—unless, of course, the supported employee is performing much faster than others in the setting. Rather, it simply makes sense for employment specialists to know how quickly employees are performing a task and whether they are progressing in the area of speed. As noted previously in this chapter, production data can easily be gathered during the acquisition phase of a job by simply dividing the number of cycles observed into the data interval. Depending on the type of work performed by the supported employee and the demands of the work setting, employment specialists are encouraged to keep consistent, episodic production data on outcomes such as 1) the number of units produced by type of unit, 2) the number of cycles performed by task/routine, 3) the time per unit/cycle, or 4) the percentage of assigned work completed. If employers rate all employees on tight productivity criteria, then employment specialists should regularly spot check supported employees on the dimensions required by the employer.

Other General Considerations

The following are some general factors that should be considered during the process of data collection in a community employment setting:

- During the first few trials, do not try to keep data on every step. Identify trends and glaring problem areas when you have a chance to write.
- Keep a production log to record impressions, changes, and other related information.
- Use a quality control data collector, if one is available, during the initial trials or for the entire day of each new task.
- Decide what you will record—the symbols you will use—on the data sheet in advance.
- Be sure to record the date, time, and the process or product involved.
- Time data can either be time per trial or time to produce a specified number of units. Use both types of time for different purposes.
- During the acquisition stage, training data also serves as production data, although the trainer might have to complete a separate production report beginning with the first day.
- Study each day's data sheets to check for trends or problems, and make adjustments, if necessary, during the next day's training.
- Keep data sheets organized and as clean as possible. A clipboard with a clear plastic flap keeps data sheets clean and organized.
- File the reports for easy referral. (Mcloughlin, Garner, & Callahan, 1987, p. 149)

A FINAL THOUGHT

As can be seen from this chapter, the planning required to implement systematic instructional procedures is merely an extension of the individualized, person-centered planning that preceded employment. At this phase, however, we are combining our knowledge of the learner, the demands and natural features of the workplace, and sound instructional procedures.

The collection and analysis of employee performance data is a critically important aspect of systematic instruction. Data collection, however, is not an end in itself. The time and energy used to gather performance or production data should be considered an investment. The time spent should yield information that either validates the success of the instructional process (e.g., task or skill acquisition, increases in performance or production rates) or emphasizes specific areas of difficulty that require adjustments or modifications (e.g., reconsideration of content or method, adjustment of informing strategies, task accommodations). We are plotting a path toward ensuring that the individual is maximally successful in becoming a productive and valued employee. To do this, we continue to plan, seek additional information, and modify and enhance our problem-solving skills.

Strategies for Informing, Motivating, and Reinforcing

11

Learning is not attained by chance, it must be sought for with ardor and attended to with diligence.

Letter to John Quincy Adams, Abigail Adams, 1780

After the information regarding the tasks to be performed by the supported employee has been organized, the employment specialist must consider the decisions that will emerge in Phase Six the Seven-Phase Sequence: how to augment or provide additional structure to the natural means used in the setting. This requires a knowledge of the second major component of effective systematic instruction: strategies for training and motivating the employee to perform the job. In this chapter, training—that is, the communication or interpretation of the information organized by the employer or the employment specialist—is considered and reviewed, as is the ingredient of motivation, which is the encouragement of employees to perform tasks to the employer's satisfaction.

INFORMING STRATEGIES

As the employment specialist[1] completes the Job Analysis activity, the natural means to communicate natural ways of learning will become increasingly apparent. Employers use a variety of means to teach new employees to perform their jobs. Those means will range from sophisticated and structured, individualized employee training programs to "sink or swim" conditions in which the employee is expected to come to the job with all of the skills and experiences necessary for unsupported performance. Job developers must begin the training process by asking employers to describe the procedures used to assist new employees to perform their jobs and, when possible, by observing actual training interactions while touring potential jobsites.

---

[1]In discussions regarding the implementation of systematic instruction procedures, we use the terms "employment specialist" and "trainer" interchangeably.

Trainers must consider several components of training strategies in order to offer assistance during Phase Six of the Seven-Phase Sequence. They will need to know the following information:

- Which formats should be used to present information to the employee
- When information should be provided to the employee
- What kinds of assistance should be provided
- How much information should be provided
- Where training should be provided

Which Formats Should Be Used to Present Information to the Employee

Formats deal with the *amount* of information, obtained from the content task analysis, that a trainer presents to an employee each time the task is performed. During job analysis, facilitators will discover that most employers begin training new employees by presenting all of the steps of a method each time a task is to be performed. Traditional human services perspectives have assumed that people with cognitive disabilities and indeed many people with other disabilities were incapable of handling all of the steps of job tasks at once. Therefore, chaining procedures, which presented only one or two steps at a time, became common practice in workshops and, later, on supported employment jobs. Although it is true that chaining procedures offer increased opportunities for practice on small components of job tasks, they rarely are used in natural workplaces. Facilitators should carefully observe during job analysis the natural formats used by employers and discuss options with natural trainers that might be used to solve "information overload" problems.

Types of Formats   A *total task format* involves the performance of all of the steps of the task each time the job cycle naturally occurs. Unless a work setting has a unique way of presenting information to employees, facilitators should encourage the use of a total task format during the initial period of employment. If problems occur in training, then the facilitator can recommend a number of options:

- Move on to clusters or mixed formats.
- Use a chaining procedure to tailor the amount of information presented to the supported employee.
- Consider an "easy to hard" sequence if the task lends itself to such a strategy. This approach is particularly useful when clear productivity demands are a part of job performance. An easy-to-hard sequence might be used in an usher job in a theater, for example. The job would be taught with the natural trainer or support person presenting all of the steps of the method for taking tickets, while another co-worker or the facilitator takes up the majority of the tickets. This allows the supported employee time to receive training without the pressure of high productivity demands.

Cluster formats involve the performance of portions of the task that are later chained together to form the total task. Clusters can be used when either the number of steps or the scope of the task proves to be too much for the employee. For tasks with numerous steps, it is often possible to identify sub-tasks, or groups of steps, that logically fit together. For instance, the job of "cleaning a guest room" in a hotel can be divided into the clusters of bed stripping, bed making, vacuuming, dusting, cleaning the bathroom, and straightening personal items. It may be possible to negotiate an initial focus on one or two of the subtasks for a supported employee who is having difficulty with the total task of cleaning a guest room.

Some tasks have a broad scope, which can prove difficult for some employees. In the case of the job "sweeping a warehouse floor," the task may seem overwhelming to the employee. The employment specialist can suggest that the warehouse floor be divided into smaller sections. The original total task format can then be utilized to teach the employee to clean one section at a time. After one section is complete, subsequent areas can be cleaned in a sequential manner until the entire floor is cleaned. Whether the clusters involve using subtasks or have a smaller scope, the clusters must be rejoined using a chaining strategy.

Forward chaining is the process of presenting the clusters of the task for training purposes in a sequential manner as typically performed in the total task format. *Backward chaining* is the process of presenting the final cluster first, then proceeding backward toward the first cluster. This approach might be useful when employees need to see the completion of a task in order to receive the information or motivation provided by completing the final steps. Facilitators should recommend backward chaining only after trying a forward chaining approach.

Mixed formats are used in training situations that begin with total task or cluster formats and then require that a step or cluster of steps be "pulled out" and taught using "massed trials"—teaching the target step(s) over and over, without delay between performance of the steps. The steps or clusters are later plugged back into the original format as the employee gains proficiency with that part of the task.

Massed-trial presentation of selected steps or clusters usually is artificial to the natural cycle and therefore should usually be considered in Phase Six of the Seven-Phase Sequence. This strategy can be effective in focusing attention on a targeted problem area. Massed-trial training must be negotiated in most employment settings. There are a number of alternatives for increasing the opportunity to practice problem steps using massed-trial training. A general caveat for implementing massed trial training is that there is always a cost to pay for this decision. Employment specialists must carefully consider both the potential gains in instructional power and the costs in the areas of logistics, motivation, confusion, and artificiality. Descriptions of potential strategies and costs follow:

Strategy 1: Stop the natural method at the point that the problem step(s) occur(s) or when the task is complete and practice the problem step for a number of trials.

Cost: This approach can lower production, cause confusion for the employee as to the natural sequence, and cause confusion to other employees in the area.

Strategy 2: Use lunch or breaktimes to practice problem steps.

Cost: This strategy can cause motivational problems because the employee will miss resting and eating times, it may be illegal or improper in relation to labor laws or agreements, and other employees may not understand.

Strategy 3: Come in before the shift or stay after the shift and practice problem steps.

Cost: This approach likely will cause transportation problems for the employee. It may be necessary to pay both the employee and the facilitator for the additional time. The task may not be available for practice after hours. The facilitator's schedule has to be rearranged. The employee may not be motivated to work before or after the shift.

Strategy 4: When feasible, take the task home or to school or replicate the task at home or school and practice the problem step(s).

Cost: It typically is not possible to take a task from work or to accurately replicate the task in another setting. There is liability for any item taken from a workplace. The parts or devices may be needed at the workplace and cannot be taken off site. Significant motivational problems can develop when employees must perform work at home.

Even considering these costs, often it is necessary to find opportunities for increased practice for difficult steps on job tasks. Employment specialists are encouraged to engage employers in determining solutions that best fit each individual work setting and employee. Also, keep in mind that changing formats is only one of a number of strategies that facilitators can use to address problem steps of a task. Additional strategies for modifying or adapting the method, improving training assists, and breaking down content steps are discussed elsewhere in this chapter.

Sequential role play involves presenting artificial approximations of a natural situation in an easy-to-hard format. This format is used for skills that cannot be taught in the natural environment. This approach, described by Gold (1980b) as "organized exposure with feedback" (p. 14), might be used for the tasks such as "how to avoid a difficult co-worker" or "dealing with worksite teasing." When the employment specialist or natural support person is with the employee, these situations usually do not occur. They often arise only when assisting people are not around. It is necessary to practice the method of the task, using one of the formats suggested, in a simulated environment until the employee is able to successfully perform the task. Facilitators must identify a simulated environment, as similar to the natural conditions as possible, that can be handled by the employee. After allowing sufficient opportunity for practice and confidence building, increasingly natural simulations can be provided until the facilitator believes that the employee can handle the real-life situation. By using this format carefully, facilitators can use systematic instruction procedures to assist employees to deal with difficult interactional issues.

Using Systematic Instruction Strategies: A Juggling Act   After the employment specialists have prepared themselves to teach by observing and memorizing the natural training method, breaking the task into natural content steps, and selecting the format for presenting the information, the time has come for communicating the image of correct performance to the employee. Effective communication, which results in topographically correct performance of the steps of the method, is challenging and somewhat like a juggling act. Employment specialists must consider a number of factors simultaneously. Decisions must be made as to when information is to be provided, what kind of information will best convey the method, how much information will be offered, and where the best place to teach the task may be. It is important to remember the method of the task, deal with the employee's motivation and behavior, and screen out any distractions that may exist in the work setting.

As employment specialists consider Phase Two of the Seven-Phase Sequence (i.e., natural means), it is likely that most work settings will not focus on the process or method of job tasks performed by employees but rather on the outcome of the task. This difference of focus requires a decision as to whether and when to offer training information to the person assigned by the employer to teach job tasks to the supported employee. The Seven-Phase Sequence encourages the company's trainer to begin the initial training of supported employees using the natural means used in the setting. Then if problems arise, trainers can suggest ways to focus on all of the factors that affect successful communication of information in Phase Six.

The next few sections target the training issues of *when* information should be offered, *what kind* of information will be provided, *how much* ownership is required of the employee, and *where* to best provide instruction. Each of these factors must occur simultaneously and, as training progresses toward criterion, the responses by the trainer will change. Figure 11.1 provides a model (Leitner, 1986) of how these factors change as the employee approaches criterion.

When Information Should Be Provided to the Employee

This factor requires the employment specialist to consider when it is best to offer information to an employee. The initial decision should always be influenced by the natural means used in each work setting. Most workplaces will offer new employees or current employees learning new jobs information

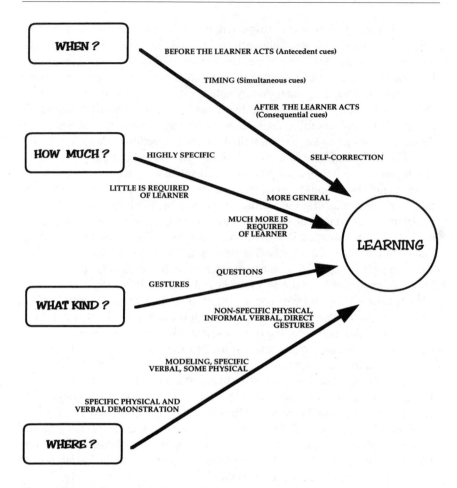

Figure 11.1.   Adjustments in intervention strategies as criterion is approached.

before any performance occurs. This information often is in the form of lengthy explanations or demonstrations of the job by an experienced employee or supervisor. Typically, employment specialists in community workplaces will then wait until *after* a new employee performs the task to provide feedback on any errors that were made. In fact, it is common for trainers and supervisors to leave new employees after the "before" information has been provided. After a short time, the trainer might return for critique and to answer questions from the employee. It is important to realize, however, that the means used by community work settings to teach new employees will vary widely. This chapter offers strategies for analyzing the training naturally provided to employees and for suggesting more effective means for communicating information as problems occur.

Information Provided Before Employee Action   Systematic in-struction procedures that have evolved from the strategies developed by Gold (1980b) also rely on information delivered *before* learner action. The differ-ence between systematic procedures and many natural means used in com-munity work settings is that with systematic instruction the employment spe-cialist recognizes the role that antecedent information plays in communicating correct performance. Information provided before the employee begins per-formance lays the groundwork for the topographical correctness desired in the setting. A critical assumption in systematic instruction is that correct perfor-mance will not occur without clear information provided before employee action. Job tasks are not like sand castles, which can be built at the whim of each person on the beach. Rather, job tasks reflect the culture and demands of each setting and result from specific decisions made by employees or by tradition practiced over time. Employment specialists can use systematic instruction strategies to suggest that employers carefully consider the need for accurate and usable information to be available before employees begin to perform their job tasks.

Information Provided During Employee Action   Natural training strategies rarely take advantage of the performance of a task as a time for offer-ing information for correctness. Perhaps it is because many workplaces follow the adage "It's necessary to make mistakes in order to learn." This perspective encourages allowing time for errors and using training strategies after employ-ee performance to correct the mistakes. As with many adages, however, this approach to training can cause problems for new employees, especially for employees with disabilities who find it difficult to learn tasks.

Rather than view the opportunity to make mistakes as a condition of learning, it is often more helpful to offer employees the opportunity to *make decisions.* Each content step of the training method offers the learner a chance to decide on the correct action to be performed. The person providing instruc-tion can wait to offer information until *after* a decision has been made by the employee but *before* the decision is acted on. This strategy is referred to as *timing* (Gold, 1980b). By using timing, trainers can allow employees to make the decisions necessary for acquisition and, at the same time, avoid the prob-lems associated with waiting until incorrect decisions have been acted on. When trainers wait until the action is completed to offer information, several problems arise:

1. Cycle constancy (see pp. 155–156) can be compromised. When employ-ees are allowed to complete incorrect actions, there is the possibility of a "learning effect" associated with the incorrect rather than the correct actions.
2. Safety concerns are raised. It is simply not ethical to allow an employee to encounter the negative consequence of an injury in order to perform and learn a task.

3. Assists offered after an error has occurred often are in the form of critique rather than information for correct action. This can cause some employees to feel reluctant about training.
4. Continual checking of errors after performance can result in the employee developing a dependence on the trainer. Rather than viewing the trainer as a provider of information, the role may be perceived as offering constant approval.

The use of timing is not without cost, however. It is important to realize that timing is not likely to be a feature of most natural means. Therefore, facilitators should typically consider suggesting the use of timing in Phase Six. The conditions necessary for using timing are as follows:

1. The trainer must be present during the performance of the task.
2. The trainer must carefully observe the performance of each step of the task and be in a position to intervene with information after an incorrect decision has been made but before it has been acted on.
3. The trainer should utilize a "no news is good news" strategy (Gold, 1980b) in relation to the trainer's reaction to the steps of the task performed correctly. This approach allows employees to understand that they are performing correctly when the trainer is silent. In this manner, fading is built into training, and the chances for a dependency relationship are lessened.
4. The trainer should offer information for correctness, rather than critique, when assisting the employee. This allows the employee to view the trainer in a more positive light.

Information Provided After Employee Action As employment specialists observe the natural means used in teaching employees, they often will notice a tendency for natural supporters to focus on correcting the errors. As described previously, powerful systematic instruction procedures tend to avoid the need to correct errors for a number of important reasons. One reason that correction and information naturally occur *after* employee action is that it is expensive to have a trainer observe an employee throughout the acquisition phase of a task. When businesses use this strategy, employment specialists should wait to intervene with suggestions until after problems occur, unless there are safety or behavioral concerns relating to the supported employee. The decision to suggest a change in this area, however, should not be delayed for too long. It is possible for the supported employee and the natural trainer to get frustrated and uncertain about the performance of the task if the teaching strategy continues to focus on correcting errors after performance. It may be necessary for the facilitator to demonstrate timing to the employer or even to substitute for the natural trainer if the issue of information versus correction begins to cast doubt on the supported employee's job performance.

Of course, not all correction is problematic. Errors will occur outside of the opportunity of a trainer to provide correction by using timing procedures. And, as stated previously, error correction after employee action is likely to be natural in most work settings. When observing natural trainers and supported employees, facilitators should look for signs of frustration by either party. If the correction is provided respectfully and is taken well, then it is recommended that the facilitator take no action. If an uncomfortable atmosphere begins to emerge, however, then steps must be taken to avoid problems. The following strategies can be used to correct errors after employee performance:

1. Focus on information for correction rather than simply on critique.
2. Recognize that correcting errors after action might cause a lack of confidence in supported employees.
3. Start the correction by asking the employee to critique his or her own performance.
4. Suggest that continuing error correction after employee performance is an indicator that timing is probably needed.

If the natural trainer decides to use timing but misses an error, then correction must be made after employee action. This can be particularly confusing because the bargain struck when using the strategy of "no news is good news" is that silence is an indicator of correct performance. It is therefore necessary for the trainer to tread carefully when the timing of correcting employee errors is missed. The easiest way to resolve the confusion is for the trainer to assume responsibility for the error in timing. The following three steps are recommended in the case of trainer error when using timing:

1. Apologize to the employee for the trainer's lapse of concentration.
2. Correct the error at the point at which it was made rather than at the point at which it was identified. This may require the trainer to reset the task to the point of the error and perform the steps correctly up to the point at which the error was caught.
3. Point out the natural features of correctness on the step that the employee should have referenced for correctness.

These three steps are particularly useful, perhaps even necessary, for supported employees who do not seem to take correction of errors well and who may respond with inappropriate behavior. It is also recommended for people who have low self-esteem or who are unsure of their ability to complete tasks correctly. Of course, all people appreciate respectful treatment when others do not hold up their end of a bargain.

Self-Correction   There are situations in which a trainer will choose to not use timing, even with employees who seem to require this strategy. As an employee begins to reach criterion on a given task, the trainer typically will need to determine whether the employee can catch errors on certain steps, without assistance from the trainer. Because the use of timing requires the trainer to correct an error before it is acted on, this creates a challenge. The solution is to use a self-correction strategy. When using this approach, the trainer allows the learner to make an error in the hope that the learner will catch the error and learn from the experience. Self-correction meets the concerns of some trainers who worry that the use of timing will not allow for the opportunity for employees to identify the characteristics of an error because the approach focuses solely on correct performance. When considering self-correction as a teaching strategy, trainers should follow these guidelines:

1. Use self-correction only when the trainer believes that more can be learned by making an error than by having it corrected with timing (Gold, 1980b). This implies that the employee has had sufficient information for correctness and the opportunity for consistent practice of the task—in other words, the employee needs to be familiar with the task.
2. Offer naturally appropriate feedback and reinforcement for the employee's correct decision, and explain that it is permissible for the employee to correct errors without the trainer's assistance or permission.
3. If the employee does not catch the error and correct it, then realize that the decision not to use timing was the trainer's error. Therefore, use the strategy described previously for correcting a trainer's error.

What Kinds of Assistance Should Be Provided

Instructional assists are means of giving information about the method or outcome of a job task. Instructional assists may be used to offer information as to the correct action to be performed, to reference natural cues that provide information for correctness, or to correct errors made during performance. Frequently used instructional assists found in natural settings include

*   Demonstration
*   Verbal information
*   Gestures and modeling
*   Physical assists
*   Side-by-side performance
*   Instructional assists that do not require a trainer
    *   Adaptations
    *   Written procedures
    *   Photographs
    *   Videotapes
    *   Slide presentations
    *   Lectures

Each of these types of assists is discussed in the following sections.

Demonstration　Possibly the most common strategy for providing information before employees begin a new job task is to have the trainer demonstrate the method of the task to the new employee. Demonstration allows the trainer to perform the steps of the task in the manner that the employer wants—in other words, with topographical correctness. This approach requires the trainer to carefully follow the acceptable method and the employee to carefully observe the performance.

Even though demonstration is commonly used in community work settings as an instructional strategy, it is not a powerful assist for most individuals. It can be useful in providing general information to the employee about what the job task looks like. It is not, however, an effective strategy for communicating specific information on complex steps of a task. To be effective, the demonstration of the task must be observed by the learner. If the learner is not paying attention, as might happen with some people who have issues relating to their behavior or interest in tasks, then the demonstration is not likely to be very informative. In that case, the trainer should consider another type of instructional assist.

Demonstrations are useful, however. They can be particularly effective in showing the pace of work to an employee. Demonstration also provides a general picture of what the employee is expected to do. Most people prefer to see a task before they perform it. Demonstration also can help break the ice between natural trainers and supported employees. Because the trainer knows the task better than the new employee does, it is a more comfortable place to get started.

The length of a demonstration is an issue for any new employee, especially for supported employees. No one wants to stand and watch someone else perform a job for very long. Because demonstration does not involve the performance of the new employee, longer observations do not result in better information for performance. If it is natural for new employees in a setting to watch an experienced employee work for an extended period, then the facilitator should carefully monitor the supported employee's behavior and interest. If a problem begins to occur, then the facilitator should move to Phase Six and suggest that a different assist be used.

Verbal Information   Verbal assists include any spoken or signed instructions to an employee for the purpose of communicating information about the performance of a job task or other job-related behavior. Along with demonstrations, verbal assists certainly are the most commonly used of all of the teaching cues found in community job settings. These assists are useful in providing information before employee performance; during action when using timing; and following the completion of the task or action to provide critique, information, or reinforcement. Spoken information allows the trainer to specifically explain the details of a step to an employee and to generally describe the bigger picture of the way the task fits into the needs and culture of the company.

Verbal assists are particularly useful for teaching order and discrimination steps but typically are not effective in teaching manipulation skills. This limitation exists because of the complexity of manipulating dynamic steps, many of which require judgment and consistent practice to reach criterion. In order to be effective communicators of discrete information, verbal assists must be succinct, clear, and sharply focused on the step to be taught. Trainers should plan verbal assists for each step of a method, considering information-packed phrases early in teaching and clear, but longer, descriptive sentences as training progresses toward criterion. Facilitators must closely observe whether natural trainers are overwhelming supported employees with verbal information and be prepared to recommend more useful cues.

Information overload is a common problem when using verbal assists. Trainers regularly use language during most of their daily interactions—both at work and at home. Most of these interactions are in the form of conversation. *Conversation* is the general use of language to communicate feelings, experiences, needs, and other issues. *Information* involves the specific use of language to communicate discrete and usable words that can be turned into correct performance by the employee. Trainers, conversely, often need to provide specific information on task performance. Information is like a crystal-clear view of a landscape. Conversation is like a fog that creeps into view and obscures the fine lines of detail and color. A common mistake of trainers is that they allow conversation to cloud the information that is to be communicated.

Trainers, therefore, should allow a pause to occur between one verbal assist and the next to allow the employee to utilize the information. If the employee has difficulty, then the trainer should reduce the amount of verbal information in the assist. Some learners require verbal assists of no more than one word at a time early in training. If natural trainers seem especially verbal during the job analysis, then keep a close watch during the initial hours of training on the first day of work. If the trainer's style does not change or if the employee seems to be struggling with the amount of information being communicated, then facilitators should consider intervening with suggestions in Phase Six of the Seven-Phase Sequence. For some learners, it may be necessary to distinguish verbal information from routine conversation. The trainer can do this by the tone used to convey the information and by the amount of information included in a verbal interaction.

There are other subtle but important problems that can arise when using verbal assists. Gold (1980a) warned trainers that, when trainers use spoken information, employees are more likely to shift their attention from the task to the trainer, out of respect or teaching-induced habit. This may create a problem for supported employees who have difficulty staying focused on the task. It is possible that some employees may find the trainer more reinforcing than the task. By overusing verbal assists, trainers can create a significant distraction to the performance. Trainers must also be careful not to distract an employee with verbal assists when safety is an issue.

Gold (1980b) often characterized his approach to teaching as essentially a nonverbal process. During the late 1970s and early 1980s, human services trainers followed that trend and used training strategies that silenced the trainer. While there continues to be a rationale for considering the individualized and episodic use of nonverbal teaching, we no longer encourage trainers to minimize the use of language in teaching. The most overpowering reason is that silent teaching is almost never found in natural workplaces. The arbitrary use of this strategy would require natural trainers to change their means of teaching, without first verifying the need for such a change. Also, it is likely that the natural motivation provided by well-matched supported employment jobs will overcome the likelihood of the distraction so common in segregated settings. Finally, we may discover that supported employees can learn effectively from verbal assists. By starting naturally, we might avoid the need to use this artificial approach.

Facilitators should consider the costs and benefits of verbal information and carefully monitor the result of teaching using this strategy. It is much better to control this common and natural strategy than to eliminate it from our "bag of tricks." It is equally important, however, to remember that some employees may benefit from a teaching strategy that minimizes verbal interaction at certain times during acquisition and performance. Facilitators can use the Seven-Phase Sequence to amend or structure the natural teaching means in order to control or minimize the use of verbal assists as required by the employee.

Gestures and Modeling Gestures and modeling are considered together in this section, even though they contain different kinds of information. They are similar in that both assists involve the use of the trainer's hands or other body parts to reference or simulate desired behavior related to a job task. Gestures involve information provided by the trainer, primarily using pointing or other general hand signs, that directs the employee's attention to a certain aspect of the task. Often, by the trainer simply pointing at a relevant feature of the task, an employee can figure out the correct action to take.

Modeling also involves body action, typically with the trainer's hands, that simulates the action that an employee should make for correct performance. For instance, a trainer might model the action of smoothing a sheet before it is folded in a laundry. Modeling would occur in the same area as employee performance and should follow the topographically correct performance as required by the employer. In the same job, a gesture might be given by the trainer to point out the hem of the sheet or another feature of the task. Modeling differs from demonstration in that in a demonstration the trainer actually performs the task. When modeling, the trainer simulates the correct movement while the employee continues to perform the task.

Gestures and modeling can effectively communicate information without the use of language or touching. Trainers can simply point to an object or direction that represents the correct action. Gestures are also useful for referencing natural cues. These assists are particularly useful in noisy work settings and for employees who may be easily distracted by an overuse of verbal information. Gestures and modeling allow employees to keep their attention on the task rather than on the trainer. The natural response to a point is to follow it with our eyes to the target. These assists also can be useful for teaching employees who do not understand the language of the trainer or who are not able to interpret verbal assists into action. Finally, gestures and modeling allow the trainer to require much more of the employee and therefore fade from training more quickly. Instructional power can be easily controlled with gestures by moving the gesture farther and farther back from the task and with modeling by allowing the simulated action to become more and more subtle.

Physical Assists   Physical assists involve the trainer touching the employee for the purpose of communicating information for correctness. Most physical assists are in the form of the trainer's hand(s) assisting or supporting the employee's fingers, hands, wrists, or arms. It is also possible to offer assistance by touching an employee's shoulder, back, leg, or head. These assists became popular in the human services field during the 1970s and early 1980s and were considered ways of communicating complex manipulations to people with significant cognitive disabilities who were in settings such as workshops and group homes. As job trainers began to observe the natural training styles of supervisors and co-workers, however, it became clear that physical assists were rarely used between people in community work settings. The impact of this observation seemed to cause job trainers and supported employment providers in general to reduce the emphasis on physical assistance as a strategy for providing information. We believe that, to the degree that it happened, this is unfortunate. Physical assists often are the only reliable means of communicating complex manipulations to people who find it difficult to learn. Even though physical assists can be heavy-handed and are rarely used, facilitators can closely monitor and model as necessary the use of these assists in natural workplaces.

An interesting finding that encourages the acceptance of physical assists has been identified during 2 years of training-based research performed during staff training by Callahan (1995). In this research, human services participants in technical assistance training workshops perform a job analysis in a company in the community, observing the natural means used to teach a lead participant a supported employment task. Participants rarely have noted the use of physical assists by natural trainers. The trainers are given no instruction on systematic teaching strategies or information concerning the impact of the supported employee's disability. When the supported employee arrives at the company for a simulation of the first day of employment, the natural trainer begins teaching the tasks in the manner used to teach any new employee.

The participants consistently have noted the appropriate use of physical assists during these sessions. One possible hypothesis of this behavior by natural trainers is that when a new employee requires more assistance to learn a task, more is provided. The rarity of the use of this form of assist may simply confirm that many community work settings have not had the opportunity to teach and support people who may require physical assists to learn certain steps or tasks.

Physical assists often are effective on manipulation steps of tasks and when safety is an issue. Even when used naturally in the work setting, trainers should use physical assists only when necessary and should be gentle and responsive to employees' needs and reactions to the assists. Trainers can never teach against resistance—only with cooperation from the learner. An employee should never be forced to accept physical assistance. Fading is accomplished by requiring the employee to own more and more of the step. Strategies in which the trainer stands behind the employee and reaches around him or her, whether the employee is standing or sitting, should be avoided. At worst, this can evoke imagery of a lecherous golf pro reaching around a student. Even in the best of circumstances, this strategy implies overbearing control by the trainer.

Side-by-Side Performance This instructional strategy has been derived directly from the natural teaching approaches used in many community workplaces. Side-by-side performance combines a demonstration by the trainer with simultaneous performance by the employee. The demonstration can be paired with any of the other instructional assists described previously. The trainer performs the job task while watching the performance of the employee. Even though timing is possible, it is more difficult because of the necessity for the trainer to halt performance before offering an assist.

This assist offers several advantages to trainers. First, because it is a very common approach, it will feel natural to trainers and co-workers. Second, side-by-side performance allows the trainer the opportunity to model both the pace of the task and complex manipulations during the employee's performance. Third, this assist allows trainers and co-workers to continue to produce while teaching. Facilitators must realize, however, that this strategy tends to result in less attention being paid to the supported employee because of the necessity of trainers to attend to their own work. It is easy for trainers to become involved in the routine of performance and miss errors made by the employee. Employees who require close attention from the trainer for correctness and timing might experience problems with this approach. For employees who are experiencing significant difficulty benefiting from this assist, the facilitator and the trainer can work as a team, with one person demonstrating the task with side-by-side performance and the other offering other instructional assists using timing.

Instructional Assists that Do Not Require a Trainer   There are a number of means available to employers and facilitators for communicating information on task performance that do not require direct interaction with a trainer. There is a legitimate argument as to whether these approaches comprise training strategies or whether they are instructional aides. Commonly used options for providing information, without the presence of a trainer, include

- Adaptations
- Written procedures
- Photographs
- Videotapes
- Slide presentations
- Lectures

Certainly the most common factor among these strategies is the assumption that information on correctness can be communicated to employees without the presence (and therefore the expense) of a trainer. Therefore, these procedures are fairly common in many community businesses. The disadvantage is that the employee has the primary responsibility of translating the information into correct action. For this reason, facilitators must carefully monitor the effectiveness of these trainerless approaches for supported employees. It is recommended that initial training begin by referencing whatever means are typically used for other employees to acquire information on their jobs. If problems occur, then facilitators must move quickly to Phase Six of the Seven-Phase Sequence to resolve any confusion or misinterpretation by the employee.

Except for adaptations, these approaches share a common flaw from the perspective of powerful systematic instruction. In an effort to save money, companies often try to get two outcomes for the price of one. In this case, employers hope that the organization of the information to be presented will double as the training strategy. This is effective in some cases. Carefully developed procedures can be used by skilled employees to produce correct performance; however, the requirements implicit in these procedures—reading, generalization, comprehension—often are the areas with which many people with cognitive disabilities have difficulties. Facilitators are encouraged to consider ways to amend the general procedures to meet individual needs if supported employees experience problems.

Adaptations deserve special attention in the area of training. Although they fall into the area of "trainerless" procedures, adaptations are much more specific to individual problem steps and can be tailored to meet individual employee needs. Although the use of adaptations, including sophisticated technological devices, has become more commonplace in instructional design, specific criteria are necessary to determine the effectiveness of these approaches:

1. There should be documented changes in the behavior of the learner.
2. The [instructional] . . . integrity of the strategy should be verifiable (i.e., did the change in behavior take place as a direct result of the intervention?).
3. The instructional procedures and their associated outcomes should have empirical and social validity. (Garner & Campbell, 1987, p. 129)

Sowers and Powers (1991) offered specific suggestions for the design and implementation of adaptations in community work settings:

1. Identify the process and procedures currently used to perform the required task.
2. During observation, note the steps of the tasks that are difficult for the learner to perform.
3. Select an adaptation that will aid in task performance.
4. Make revisions in the task analysis that reflect the use of an adaptation.
5. Begin training the tasks and routines with the adaptations.
6. Assess the effectiveness of the adaptation.

There is sometimes a tendency among human services personnel to invent adaptations that go far beyond the basic requirements of the task at hand. It is important to remember that the selected adaptation only needs to be sophisticated enough to allow the learner to acquire the targeted skills and competencies. To create overly sophisticated adaptations that require extensive maintenance or special training before use may inhibit their continued use by natural supporters in the workplace.

How Much Information Should Be Provided

In addition to *when* information is to be provided to the employee and *what kind* of information should be provided, the trainer must consider *how much* information to offer. Because this is less concrete than the other concepts, it often is misunderstood by trainers. One way to think about how much information should be provided is to think in terms of ownership. Any step of a task requires ownership of the decisions and actions necessary for correctness. After criterion, the ownership of the task typically will rest completely with the supported employee. During training, however, the decisions and actions necessary for correct performance are shared between the trainer and the employee. Early in training, for instance during a demonstration, the ownership lies mostly with the trainer, as the employee is responsible only for observing the task. As the training progresses, the ownership of the various steps of the task begins to slowly shift toward the employee. The term typically associated with this shift in ownership is *fading*.

Fading involves purposefully diminishing the presence of instructional assists as the employee acquires more and more information about the task and the relevant natural cues. A trainer has successfully faded when the employee no longer depends on the trainer for the acceptable performance of a job task. Successful fading can involve the ongoing assistance by a person in the natural setting, if such assistance is critical to the supported employee having access to a task. For instance, a supported employee who worked in a restaurant had to remember to clean the filter on the dishwasher every 3 days. Because the task was difficult to remember due to the time delay between cycles, a co-worker always helped him remember the first step. However, facilitators should strive to ensure that tasks are "owned" as completely as possible by the employee, especially for core routines (see p. 158).

Fading of instructional cues is essential to the independent performance of a task, even those used by natural trainers. Some instructional cues, such as adaptations, may be picked up by the setting, if used regularly by natural supporters. In these cases, the facilitators must ensure that the assist is either faded completely or, if this is not possible, a continuation of the assist is agreed to and understood by the employer.

The strength of an assist is an important consideration for fading. The relative strength of the various instructional assists—the degree of effectiveness in communicating useful information—differs from person to person. Some people respond well to verbal assists, whereas others may prefer repeated demonstrations. In addition, different steps of a task lend themselves to differing assists. For instance, an order step—knowing what to do next—often can be communicated with a simple gesture or short verbal assist. Discrimination steps—those that require the employee to distinguish the correct orientation, position, or quality of a step—usually can be taught with verbal assists, modeling, or side-by-side performance with the trainer. Manipulation steps require the employee to use dynamic movements while interacting with the task. These steps must be performed consistently and may require brief physical assists by the trainer for correct body position and hand placement on the task.

Experienced trainers experiment with assists and the various types of steps so that they can better anticipate the best assist for each step of a task. By doing this, it will become possible to select the assist that provides sufficient information for quality performance and, at the same time, allows maximum ownership of the step by the employee. Therefore, facilitators should encourage natural trainers to use a variety of assists in order to determine which assists meet this balance.

Strength of Assists and Assist Hierarchies   In the early 1980s, Gold (1980a) and other researchers who studied the strategies and impact of systematic instruction for people with disabilities suggested that instructional assists existed in a hierarchy in relation to their strength or power. A classic ordering was offered by Gold (1980a) in his Hierarchy of Assists, in which he suggested that physical assists were the most powerful and therefore the first to be faded. Next came gestural assists followed by verbal information. Although there may have been logical, and perhaps even some research-based, reasons to develop a hierarchy, the potential for misuse of this concept out-weighs any benefit. Trainers often considered the hierarchies as dogma to be followed rather than as indicators of a general phenomenon. This led to a per-ception that all training and the accompanying data collection had to begin with physical assists, fade to gestural assists, and culminate with verbal assists prior to criterion.

We no longer suggest that facilitators follow an assist hierarchy when planning and fading the instructional assists to be used on jobsites. It makes more sense to focus on increasing the ownership of the various steps of the task by the employee with whatever assists seem to be effective. Trainers can then have access to the entire range of instructional assists (see the following section). Within each type of assist, however, the trainer can give less and less specific information, requiring more and more ownership, as the learner approaches criterion. In this way, fading can continue to be systematically achieved.

Choosing Assists to Initiate Training: A "Least Power" Approach
Based on the preceding discussion, it is recommended that trainers begin teaching by using the instructional assists typically used in the setting, at the power or strength level offered to other employees. If this amount of power is not sufficient, then the facilitator should consider in Phase Six recommend-ing assists with sufficient strength to effectively communicate the informa-tion. This suggestion usually is an educated guess based on a "least power" perspective. That is, the facilitator tries to estimate the amount of power nec-essary to communicate correctness, but no more. If the assist does not result in correct performance, then power can be increased with the subsequent assists by requiring less and less ownership by the employee until correct per-formance is communicated.

Where Training Should Be Provided

The issue of trainer position may, at first glance, seem straightforward: Train-ers must be close enough to the employee to provide information and to inter-vene with timing. With the changes that are occurring in the shift of roles between human services job facilitators and natural trainers, however, the issue becomes more complex. Therefore, this section first addresses the ques-tion of trainer position in relation to the employee and then discusses options for facilitators who may be observing the teaching interaction between sup-ported employees and natural trainers.

Trainer Position   The location of a trainer with respect to the employ-ee will vary as the different types of job tasks vary. Some job tasks are per-formed standing in front of a machine. Others are performed standing while moving about a work area. Office jobs often are performed in a sitting posi-tion, with brief periods of standing. Trainers, whether natural or human ser-vices, must consider the best position from which to offer information. Decisions must be made concerning which side is best to teach from, whether information can be offered from in front of the employee, and whether there is sufficient room for a trainer in the work area. Because many errors occur early in training, it is necessary for the trainer to assume a position close to the employee in order to catch errors as they happen. The gradations of closeness are subtle, however. If the trainer moves too close, then the training interaction will seem unusual. This "hovering" can be uncomfortable to the employee. It can also create dependence on the trainer if the position is maintained throughout the duration of the training.

A removed training position also can create problems. The farther away the trainer moves from the performance, the more difficult it is to intervene with information on correctness using the timing strategy. We recommend that trainers position themselves close to the employee, standing or sitting, in the same manner as the employee. Trainers can then use the various steps of the task to anticipate whether they should move closer or ease away from the task a bit. Because the trainer will quickly know the more difficult steps of a task, these decisions can provide a fairly accurate guess as to the need for closeness.

Generally, trainers should assume the same position, standing or sitting, as the employee. When working with employees who use wheelchairs for mobility, this is particularly important for creating a balanced relationship. Some tasks will not allow for the trainer to assume the same position as the employee. For instance, when teaching an employee to change a light bulb while standing on a step stool, the trainer may feel that it is best to remain on the floor to help in case of a problem. Trainers should try to avoid standing behind an employee and reaching around to provide information. This position is uncomfortable to most employees, seems unusual in natural workplaces, and sends an image of dependence to others in the setting. Trainers can usually find an alternative way of teaching a step by moving to the employee's side or front.

Fading Trainer Position   As training progress from the initial days of performance toward criterion, the position of the trainers also can change. As the employee acquires more and more of the task, trainers can afford to move away from close contact to an observation position in the general work area. As noted previously, the close position of the trainer during training can result in a dependent relationship between supported employees and their trainers. This is understandable because many supported employees previously have been in settings that fostered dependence by surrounding them with protective supports. If trainers in workplaces continue to stay too close during training, then they will find it extremely difficult to fade.

Trainers must consider ways to fade their position, as well as the strength of their assists. They should take every opportunity to back away from employees as soon as their performance warrants. As employees reach criterion, trainers should be positioned well away from the task. For employees who seem to need the presence of the trainer during performance, a graduated fading strategy must be implemented. A supported employee in a restaurant in Syracuse, New York, required a 2-week strategy of gradual fading of the trainer's position in order to feel comfortable enough to work alone. If the trainer had simply left the work area upon criterion, it is likely that the employee would have lost his job.

Facilitator Position

The evolving role of human services supporters has caused a reconsideration of their position in workplaces that now may utilize natural trainers for much of the teaching provided to supported employees. If a co-worker, trainer, or supervisor from the company is providing instruction, then facilitators must decide on the best location from which to observe the training interactions. Even though work settings vary greatly, it is usually possible for the facilitator to find a location that will allow for unobtrusive observation. If the facilitator feels that the introduction and initial interactions of the supported employee and the natural trainer have been smooth, then it is possible to find a comfortable space from which to watch the training. If it is believed that the employee might require immediate Phase Five, Six, or Seven decisions, then the facilitator should stand close to the training in order to offer assistance.

It is also likely that, initially, the roles of trainer and facilitator will be confusing to all parties. The training-based research (Callahan, 1995) referenced previously in this chapter indicates that if the facilitator is too close to the training, then the natural trainer will tend to back off and allow the facilitator to take over. The give and take between trainers and facilitators continues to evolve as more jobs are developed that reference natural features of support. Facilitators are encouraged to give as much attention to their relationship with trainers as they traditionally gave to planning and delivering training strategies.

MOTIVATING AND REINFORCING STRATEGIES

Chapter 10 and the preceding section on systematic instruction positioned the role of more powerful techniques for teaching relative to the needs of individual employees and their unique work settings. It is not our purpose, however, to delve into the approaches commonly referred to as "behavior modification techniques." Rather, in this section we address the "whys" of working:

- Why should employees come to work on time?
- Why should they conform to the culture and rules of the workplace?
- Why should workers work harder and faster?

The answers to these and countless similar questions raise issues that are qualitatively different from those that focus on the "how" of work. Systematic instruction shows its power in dealing with the issues of how a job is to be performed. Motivation and its subset, reinforcement, address the "why" of work.

The concepts of *motivation* and *reinforcement* have confused and preoccupied the human services field for years. Most traditional training approaches seem to depend on these concepts for their primary sources of training power (Gold, 1980a) and to lump the two perspectives together within a single synonymous definition. Although this section does not attempt to describe behavioral interventions or the use of reinforcement procedures, it is important to relate the issues of motivation and reinforcement to the success of supported employees in natural community work settings:

- *Motivation* can be described as all of the naturally existing features of a worksite that promote desire, initiative, cooperation, enthusiasm, and other desired behaviors on the part of employees of the setting.
- *Reinforcement* is the purposeful arrangement of events—to increase the likelihood that a desired behavior in a work setting will occur again.

These definitions have been adapted from the early perspectives of Gold (1980a) to reflect the role of motivation and reinforcement in community employment sites. In the system of instruction presented in this section, reinforcement is considered a subset of motivation. Motivation is a critical natural feature of all employment sites. Just as with natural styles of informing, the approaches of employee motivation used by companies vary widely. The Seven-Phase Sequence asks facilitators to identify the ways in which companies naturally motivate employees and then reference and utilize those strategies in training. If problems develop, then more individualized and powerful motivating or even reinforcing strategies can be implemented in Phase Six.

The Role of "No News Is Good News"

It often seems that human services trainers must pass a preemployment test in which they have to prove their ability to say "Good job!" after every instance of a supported employee's successful performance. Whether it is because of some innate trait or a sense of collective guilt that we share in relation to our traditionally poor expectations for people with disabilities, job trainers find it very difficult to allow an unassisted action to pass without comment. Gold (1972) closely examined the impact of this constant reinforcing and believed that it bred dependency more than it facilitated success. In fact, he accused trainers of needing to give constant reinforcement more than the people with disabilities needed to receive it.

Gold's (1980b) response to continual and arbitrary reinforcement was to suggest that the most effective reinforcers are those found in natural environments. With this perspective, Gold was in line with the Seven-Phase Sequence

10 years before it was conceptualized. Because many people with disabilities have spent major portions of their lives in settings that effectively have addicted them to habitual reinforcement procedures, an intentional strategy to replace these responses had to be developed. For that purpose, Gold suggested that correct performance should be rewarded with silence, along with the trainer's close attention to all aspects of the learner's performance. Gold called this approach "no news is good news."

"No news is good news" acknowledges correct performance through silence and, at the same time, allows the trainer to become less and less a part of an employee's success. This approach strikes a deal with a learner. Information will be offered if an error is made—and in a way that is respectful and helpful. This approach changes the consequences of making errors during acquisition from negative to assisting. Error becomes an acceptable and expected component of all teaching. The consequence of making an error is that the learner receives sufficient information for correctness.

The consequences of making a correct decision also are changed. Rather than receiving artificial—indeed, unnatural—affirmation of each correct action, the employee receives the silent approval of an attentive trainer. This allows the learner to operate on "internal feedback" for acknowledgment of correctness. This also happens to be the same condition for approval that is natural to most community workplaces.

Of course, all people need encouragement and motivation in order to continue to perform quality work. For this reason, facilitators should seek to ensure that all of the natural motivating features of the workplace are available to the employee. In addition, there is certainly nothing wrong with praise and encouragement from the facilitator or from co-workers and supervisors, as long as it does not create dependency. We recommend that training begin with using whatever motivators and reinforcers are natural to the setting. If problems occur with the employee's motivation to work, then increase power by following the suggestions described next.

Using Motivators in a Natural Setting

The use of formal, systematic strategies for reinforcement is rare in community employment settings. Therefore, trainers need to utilize an approach that starts with the most natural motivating strategies and only employs more artificial measures if absolutely necessary. The following steps describe a natural-to-artificial approach for utilizing reinforcers in community jobsites:

1. Use *natural motivators* at a *natural rate*.
2. Use *natural motivators* at an *artificial rate*.
3. Use *artificial motivators* at a *natural rate*.
4. Use *artificial motivators* at an *artificial rate*.

To *increase power,* as in Phase Six decisions, move from step 1 through step 4, in order, *adding additional steps only as necessary.* To *fade,* move from the last step that worked *back to step 1. Examples:*

1. **Using natural motivators at a natural rate**   A job trainer observes the natural procedures of an employment setting during Job Analysis and plans to incorporate and reference these procedures during training and orientation of the new employee. This company utilizes a short pep talk by the supervisor for a team of employees at the end of each day. The trainer ensures that the sessions are attended by the supported employee and spends additional time pointing out the purpose and importance of the meetings to the employee.

2. **Using natural motivators at an artificial rate**   A company pays its employees in cash every Friday. A supported employee is learning to appreciate the role of money in her life. Her enthusiasm for continuing to work lags toward the end of each workday. The job trainer feels that if the employee could be paid daily for a few weeks then the employee could learn to appreciate pay as a natural motivator. The job trainer negotiates with the employer for daily pay for 3 weeks. After that point, the employer and the trainer will consider fading the daily pay to semiweekly and eventually to weekly.

3. **Using artificial motivators at a natural rate**   A company utilizes a formal weekly meeting between the supervisor and each employee as a performance review and motivational strategy. The supported employee becomes extremely nervous, even agitated, at the prospect of these meetings during the first 2 weeks of training. The job trainer negotiates with the supervisor for the job trainer to provide the review each week with the supervisor sitting in providing positive comments. Gradually the job trainer fades his or her comments, and the supervisor begins to be primarily responsible for the feedback, as the employee gets to know the supervisor and his job.

4. **Using artificial motivators at an artificial rate**   An employee is experiencing difficulty in increasing her production rate. After exhausting many other strategies, the job trainer works with the employee in setting very concrete productivity goals for each 30 minutes of work. The job trainer also develops a set of responses designed to encourage performance and to acknowledge quality effort. The trainer closely attends to the employee's productivity by keeping data and relating the results to the employee. As the employee's productivity increases, the trainer gradually fades the degree of supervision and comment until an acceptable level of performance is established.

The Role of Powerful Reinforcers

The approach to instruction described in this chapter does not suggest specific strategies for providing artificial reinforcement when more natural approaches, such as those just suggested, prove to be sufficient. If effective, then individualized job development is accomplished, and if the Seven-Phase Sequence and "no news is good news" is followed by trainers, then most employees, even those with significant behavior challenges, usually will be successful without artificial reinforcement. It would be extremely limiting to suggest that reinforcers and other systematic behavioral interventions not be used by facilitators or employers. After all, the utility of the Seven-Phase Sequence lies in the idea that it is acceptable to use or to suggest more powerful techniques when natural approaches fail to result in successful performance by the employee. Many readers will recognize that interfering behaviors and personal motivation often are greater barriers to employment than most other impacts of disability.

It is critical, however, for facilitators to understand the difference between the roles of providing information and of controlling behavior. Once again, the perspectives of Gold span nearly 2 decades to provide an insight into these concepts. Gold (1980a) suggested that the provision of information could be captured in a concept that he called "content influence." *Content influence* refers to the intention of a trainer, natural or artificial, to focus on knowledge and information about a task or job. By carefully avoiding the pitfall of mixing emotions into the teaching interaction, the relationship between a trainer and a learner can be balanced and respectful. A sort of "yin and yang" whole can emerge from the training experience in which each party depends on the other for success.

Gold saw a very different reality, however, when emotions became either a part of the effort of a learner to acquire information or the sole focus of the interaction between trainers and learners. Gold (1980a) had observed years of efforts to control behavior and found that all attempts, even the most successful and value based, shared a common flaw—the necessity to create a hierarchical relationship with the person to be helped. Gold (1980b) referred to this perspective as "process influence."

Process influence involves the intention of the trainer to focus on feelings about tasks, jobs, or situations rather than on information about the task to be performed. Process influence is involved in virtually any systematic use of powerful reinforcers. In order to effect such behavioral control, the trainer must assume a perspective that is hierarchical to the learner. Behavior control is not a two-way street. If the learner behaves, then a reinforcer is received. If the behavior is unacceptable, then the reinforcer is withheld.

In addition to this unbalanced relationship, there were other problems. Gold recognized that people often had to behave correctly *before* they were offered the information necessary for successful performance. The result of this precondition led to the assumption that people with severe behavior challenges had to behave before they could work. In addition, learners seemed to develop a dependence on the reinforcers used to control behaviors. These factors, coupled with the problems associated with the assumption of the right to control a person's behavior by human services staff, led Gold to seek a way around reinforcement as a primary means of power for training.

It is important, therefore, for facilitators to recognize that if powerful reinforcers must be used to assist people with behavioral or motivational challenges to successfully work in the community, then there is a potential cost to both the supported employee and the employer. As described previously in this text, strategies suggested and modeled by facilitators often become part of the culture of the workplaces that employ people with disabilities. In fact, this is a valued outcome in most cases. If powerful reinforcing strategies are suggested and modeled in workplaces, then we must find an equally systematic way to fade the use of such procedures back to natural conditions. If not, then supported employees with behavior and motivational challenges can become trapped in a loop of continuous control.

The trainer must constantly assess the balance that must exist between the needs of the employee to learn and the desire to teach in as natural a manner as possible. If trainers feel, after exhausting all natural strategies, that an artificial reinforcement strategy is necessary to help people learn and stay in valued natural work settings, then they should consult behavioral strategies available outside of this approach to training and deliver those strategies within a set of values that give the employee a way out and demand the highest levels of respect and concern on the part of those implementing the plan.

A FINAL THOUGHT

Training for employment in integrated community settings requires an awareness of many interrelated factors: the needs, skills, and preferences of the supported employee; the requirements of the job routines and tasks; the culture of the workplace; the quality of completed work; opportunities for interactions with co-workers; and the expectations of the employer. To effectively balance these variables, trainers are encouraged to invest time and energy in planning for this experience. Nevertheless, trainers certainly will have to make changes in the original plan in response to actual workplace conditions and events. Trainers will improve in making these midstream adjustments with experience, but a thorough working knowledge of the workplace and the learner and an understanding of the various informing and motivating strategies will enhance the likelihood of success in employment.

Practical Tips

— 12 —

Practice is the best of all instructors.

Publilius Syrus, First Century B.C.

Facilitating employment for individuals with disabilities is a *process,* not an *event.* In this text we have described a variety of activities, strategies, and processes that contribute to the creation of employment opportunities for people with disabilities: a consistent set of values regarding people with disabilities and the importance of employment, individualized planning, the critical role of appropriately designed supports, the importance of family and friends, the Seven-Phase Sequence, the Vocational Profile, individualized job development strategies, job analysis, and systematic instruction procedures. The time has come to put these procedures into place within the context of individual lives, communities, and workplaces.

This final chapter consists of a potpourri of practical tips that, initially, may seem to be "leftovers" yet that contribute greatly to the overall success of the employment process. Topics covered include the following:

- Planning for the employment experience
- Getting to know the culture of the workplace
- Getting to know the worker
- Analyzing work tasks and routines
- Developing and implementing systematic instruction strategies
- Collecting and analyzing data
- Implementing supports
- Maintaining ongoing supports
- Maintaining your edge as an employment facilitator

PLANNING FOR THE EMPLOYMENT EXPERIENCE

- Clarify those values and beliefs about people that will guide and direct the development, selection, and implementation of services and supports for people with disabilities.

- Include a variety of family, friends, and human services personnel in the activities that surround person-centered planning for employment.
- Maintain an attitude of acceptance, creativity, and flexibility when generating a menu of possible employment roles and locations.
- Assume the role of an advocate for the individual with disabilities when seeking employment opportunities (i.e., emphasize the preferences and goals of the individual when reviewing various options and employment locations).
- Emphasize the critically important features of naturalness when planning for those supports and services that will be available within the workplace.
- Include the person with disabilities in all facets of the decision-making process.
- Use the Vocational Profile as a means of identifying potentially promising worksites.
- Decisions should be made by the individual with disabilities who is the focus of the planning process. Your role is only to offer suggestions and alternatives. Provide honest feedback on the alternatives and their consequences.

GETTING TO KNOW THE CULTURE OF THE WORKPLACE

- If the employer offers an orientation program for new employees (e.g., tour, explanation of benefits, hours), take advantage of this experience. This can be a valuable learning experience for both the employee and the employment facilitator.
- The employment facilitator should schedule specific times to spend in the workplace observing and becoming familiar with the culture of the workplace. Remember that this is a time to observe, to get to know the "lay of the land," and to become acquainted with people.
- Leave your "human services" or "behavior intervention" vocabulary at home. It is important for the employment facilitator to be viewed as an asset to the workplace and the worker without portraying the image of a behavioral technician.
- Ask other workers to share the "tricks of the trade" that may be valuable to the new employee (Moon, Goodall, Barcus, & Brooke, 1986).
- Always maintain a spirit of flexibility, and be prepared for surprises.
- Determine the best sources of formal and informal communication within the organization. To whom do you or the employee go when there is a question to be answered? This information can save you significant amounts of time and effort.
- Dress like the other employees.
- Ask questions. Ask questions. Ask questions.

GETTING TO KNOW THE WORKER

- Take the time and effort to become *personally* acquainted with the individual who will be the focus of the employment facilitation process.
- It is recommended that the employment facilitator arrange for an opportunity to participate in some type of instructional experience with the applicant as part of the "information gathering" process. This experience provides a perspective on how the applicant learns most effectively and which strategies for support may be most effective and expedient.
- Participate with the applicant in non–work-related activities (e.g., visit the individual's home, go to a movie, watch a baseball game, go to a restaurant for dinner). This experience allows the employment facilitator to have an additional perspective on the personal preferences and characteristics of the applicant in a more focused, personalized manner.
- With permission, talk informally with others who have known the individual with disabilities over a number of years (e.g., parents, siblings, extended family, neighbors, friends). These discussions should be very low-key and informal. The purpose is not to dig into the person's intimate past but rather to gain a wider perspective on the life experiences that have contributed to his or her current circumstances.
- Take notes to remind you of the information that you have gained and unanswered questions that you may need to pursue in further detail.

ANALYZING WORK TASKS AND ROUTINES

- Conduct a job analysis for the purposes of recognizing the natural ways, means, and people used by the employer to typically teach and perform the job.
- Observe and note the various approaches that are used to organize information about the job to be performed by the supported employee.
- Formulate a plan for balancing the natural features of support in the workplace with the needs of the employee by using the Seven-Phase Sequence. This formulation process is gradual. Try to maintain a flexible and creative approach to your role as an employment facilitator.
- Develop skill in asking questions in a way that provides information-filled answers.
- The initial job analysis should be viewed as a working document. Once the process of training begins and interactions with the employee have started, the astute trainer will observe components of the job analysis that should be modified (e.g., adding additional steps in completing various tasks or routines).
- The job analysis should emphasize the use of observable descriptors for

worker performance (e.g., *lift* the tray, *turn* the knob to the right, *move* to the sorting machine, *pick up* the paper, *close* the door).

- Write the job analysis as if you were preparing this documentation for someone else to use. This frame of reference will encourage the use of clear language and precise terminology.
- It is, of course, advisable to gain approval for your developed job analysis before it is used to begin the process of systematic instruction. This also provides an opportunity for seeking the guidance and direction of current employees in the workplace—an excellent method for establishing contact with potential sources of natural support.

DEVELOPING AND IMPLEMENTING SYSTEMATIC INSTRUCTION STRATEGIES

- In designing instruction strategies, one of the cardinal rules is *simpler is better.* Quiet, unobtrusive strategies that "blend in" with the activities of the workplace are preferred. Elaborate, technological approaches or sophisticated adaptations should be reserved (if ever used) for situations in which they are absolutely required by the employee.
- Provide effective training that operates under an umbrella of guiding principles—a philosophy embraced by the system—and is dependent on the balance of generic validity and power.
- Acknowledge that there are several components of systematic instruction that will be important to the new employee during the initial phases of the work experience:
  1. Formats for presenting information
  2. When to offer information to the employee
  3. The appropriate quantity of assistance that will be provided
  4. The kinds of assistance that should be provided
  5. Where best to teach the task
- Remember: Systematic instruction is a means to an end, not an end in itself (Nisbet & Callahan, 1987b). In other words, do not let your instructional technology "get in the way" of maximizing the natural features of the workplace.
- The most effective reinforcers are those that 1) occur naturally in the workplace, 2) have the greatest relevance to the needs of the worker, 3) may also be valued by other employees in the workplace, and 4) are the least intrusive to the routines and customs of the workplace.
- Pace precedes speed. "Pace involves performing the component movements . . . at an efficient rate. Once a comfortable pace is established, the rate of production (speed) can be increased by increasing the pace" (Mcloughlin, Garner, & Callahan, 1987, p. 147).

- In providing systematic instruction in a work setting, the first few weeks are the most difficult and demanding. Get plenty of rest and ensure that you are in top shape for the instructional experience (Moon et al., 1986).
- Remember Murphy's Law: *Anything that can go wrong—will.* This is particularly true during the early phases of the instructional process (Mcloughlin et al., 1987).

COLLECTING AND ANALYZING DATA

- Data collection procedures provide a means of assessing the effectiveness of the varied types of supports that have been implemented within the workplace. Once again, however, remember that *simplicity is the key.*
- Collected data should be pertinent to the issues and concerns of the employer (i.e., What kinds of information will demonstrate the degree to which the employee is achieving success in employment?).
- Data collected on employee performance should be pertinent to the quality or quantity standards established during initial discussions with the employer.

IMPLEMENTING SUPPORTS

- Resist the temptation to "step into" discussions between the employee and *his or her* co-workers.
- Maintain confidentiality in the workplace, and protect the dignity of the supported employee.
- The best supports are those that occur naturally in the workplace and that are available to all workers (Nisbet & Callahan, 1987b).
- "Do not get involved in attempting to solve the problems of business and industry; you are there only to facilitate employment. The goal is to promote supports and success for the individual employee" (Mcloughlin et al., 1987, p. 153).

MAINTAINING ONGOING SUPPORTS

- Old employment facilitators never die; they just fade away.
- Co-workers can, in many or most cases, serve as a major source of long-term support for the new employee. Whenever feasible, the employment facilitator should encourage co-workers.
- Any ongoing follow-up supports or services should be maximally unobtrusive. These supports should be delivered in a way that will not jeopardize or compromise the individual's employment or personal dignity.
- Procedures should be implemented to allow the employee to request or

secure support for work and work-related problems or difficulties. Once again, these supports can be those that occur naturally in the workplace or those that are available externally through the agency sponsoring the supported employment initiative.

- Individuals should have the right to approve (or reject) the use of follow-up services in *their* place of employment.
- For many individuals with significant disabilities, ongoing supports may be necessary for the remainder of their work career. Agencies sponsoring the supported employment program should deal with the reality of this issue early in the program development process.
- There are several ways to secure information about a worker's status and progress in the workplace (e.g., observe the worker, ask the employer). Do not ignore the importance of asking the employee how he or she feels that he or she is doing in relation to the demands of the work setting.

MAINTAINING YOUR EDGE AS AN EMPLOYMENT FACILITATOR

- The emotional and physical well-being of the employment facilitator is an often-ignored component of a supported employment program. Take good care of yourself (Provençal, 1987).
- *Be committed to what you are doing.* If being an employment facilitator is merely a job for you, then perhaps you should reconsider your career plans.
- People in the workplace will be watching you and the manner in which you interact with the new employee. Resist any pressure that this may cause you. Act natural, be yourself, and respond to the individual with disabilities in the same manner. Remember the phrase "Nothing special."
- Last, but very significant, remember that you are doing important work.

As you prepare to enter the workplace to secure employment opportunities for one or more individuals with disabilities, remain open to the possibilities that are inherent in the process of creating new options. One important possibility is that you will make mistakes. Ultimately, we can learn from our mistakes. O'Brien (1987b), in fact, went to the extent of referring to error, ignorance, and fallibility as the "three teachers." This is not to say that we should revel in their ignorance and fallibility on a topic or area of concern. At the same time, however, we should commit ourselves to learning from our mistakes in a constructive and positive manner. Consider the following example:

> Two men were walking down the street, and both spied simultaneously a rather large man. The two men turned to each other, and the first said, "Look at that fat man, he needs to go on a diet." The second man replied, "He is fat all right, but what he really needs is to jog!" The two men next went to the subject of their discussion and said, "Hi, how do you feel?" The large man replied, "Well, not so

good." The two men reveled for the moment in their excellent diagnosis and pre- scriptions. The large man continued, "I am the world champion weight lifter, and I have to put on about 20 or 30 pounds so that I can press the amount of weight that it will take to win the next world competition. I won't feel really good until the extra weight is on me and then I know I can win the championship again." (White House Conference on Children, 1970, p. 546)

As in this case, human services professionals frequently hold the view that they must be able to answer any and all questions and find solutions to any and all problems. As the two men in this story learned in a dramatic fash- ion, it is important to be able to say "I don't know." Of equal value is the free- dom that can come from putting forth a new idea that may seem to be "off the wall." If we do not feel comfortable in these areas, then there will be a ten- dency for us to become stagnant, restricted, and regimented in our approach to problems. The Chinese philosophy presented in the *I Ching* in the 12th cen- tury B.C. summarizes this approach: "Before the beginning of great brilliance, there must be chaos. Before a brilliant person begins something great, they must look foolish to the crowd." Take the risk. Remember that one of your best tools as an employment facilitator is your ability to create. Use that tool often and it will maintain a sharp edge.

A FINAL THOUGHT

The practical tips offered in this chapter have a clear focus on maintaining the skills and "edge" of the employment facilitator. Acquiring the skills and knowledge necessary to facilitate employment is a vital step. Applying this information within actual community and workplace settings is another important aspect of the employment facilitator's skill development process. Over time, however, it is critically important for those individuals who are responsible for facilitating employment opportunities for individuals with dis- abilities to make a strong commitment to several important activities:

- Professional growth
- Periodic "value checks," which validate the degree to which your current practices are compatible with your values and beliefs
- Listen to and learn from the experiences of people with disabilities
- Take care of yourself emotionally and physically

We have found these steps to be important aspects of the strenuous and demanding tasks that are the keys to the workplace.

References

Agosta, J. (1994). *Results of the Three Year National Job Coach Study.* Salem, OR: Human Services Research Institute.

Albin, J.M., Rhodes, L., & Mank, D. (1994). Realigning organizational culture, resources, and community roles: Changeover to community employment. *Journal of The Association for Persons with Severe Handicaps, 19*, 105–115.

Americans with Disabilities Act (ADA) of 1990, PL 101-336, 42 U.S.C. § 12101 *et seq.*

Bartholomew-Lorimer, K. (1993). Community building: Valued roles for supporting connections. In A.N. Amado (Ed.), *Friendships and community connections between people with and without developmental disabilities* (pp. 169–179). Baltimore: Paul H. Brookes Publishing Co.

Beeman, P., Ducharme, G., & Mount, B. (1989). *One candle power: Building bridges into community life for people with disabilities.* Manchester, CT: Communitas, Inc.

Bellamy, G.T., Peterson, L., & Close, D. (1975). Habilitation of the severely and profoundly retarded: Illustrations of competence. *Education and Training of the Mentally Retarded, 10,* 174–186.

Bellamy, G.T., Rhodes, L.E., Mank, D.M., & Albin, J.M. (1988). *Supported employment: A community implementation guide.* Baltimore: Paul H. Brookes Publishing Co.

Bellamy, G.T., Rhodes, L.E., Wilcox, B., Albin, J.M., Mank, D., Boles, S.M., Horner, R.H., Collins, M., & Turner, J. (1984). Quality and equality in employment services for adults with severe handicaps. *Journal of The Association for Persons with Severe Handicaps, 9*, 270–278.

Biklen, D. (1988, June). Empowerment: Choices and change. *Newsletter of The Association for Persons with Severe Handicaps,* 1.

Blalock, G. (1988). Transitions across the lifespan. In B.L. Ludlow, A.P. Turnbull, & R. Luckasson (Eds.), *Transitions to adult life for people with mental retardation: Principles and practices* (pp. 3–20). Baltimore: Paul H. Brookes Publishing Co.

Borthwick-Duffy, S. (1994). [Review of Mental Retardation: Definition, classification, and systems of support]. *American Journal on Mental Retardation, 98*, 541–544.

Bradley, V.J. (1994). Evolution of a new service paradigm. In V.J. Bradley, J.W. Ashbaugh, & B.C. Blaney (Eds.), *Creating individual supports for people with development disabilities: A mandate for change at many levels* (pp. 11–32). Baltimore: Paul H. Brookes Publishing Co.

Bradley, V.J., Ashbaugh, J.W., & Blaney, B.C. (Eds.). (1994). *Creating individual supports for people with developmental disabilities: A mandate for change at many levels.* Baltimore: Paul H. Brookes Publishing Co.

Brown, L., Albright, K., Udvari-Solner, A., Shiraga, B., Rogan, P., York, J., & Van Deventer, P. (1986). *The Madison strategy for evaluating the vocational milieu of a worker with severe intellectual disabilities.* Madison: University of Wisconsin and Madison Metropolitan School District.

Brown, L., Branston, M., Baumgart, D., Vincent, L., Falvey, M., & Schroeder, J. (1979). Using the characteristics of current and subsequent least restrictive environments as factors in the development of curricular content for severely handicapped students. *AAESPH Review, 4*, 407–424.

Brown, L., Branston, M., Hamre-Nietupski, S., Johnson, F., Wilcox, B., & Gruenwald, L. (1979). A rationale for comprehensive longitudinal interactions between severely handicapped students and other nonhandicapped students and other citizens. *AAESPH Review, 4*, 3–14.

Brown, L., Branston, M., Hamre-Nietupski, S., Pumpian, I., Certo, N., & Gruenwald, L. (1979). A strategy for developing chronological age appropriate content for severely handicapped adolescents and young adults. *Journal of Special Education, 13*, 81–90.

Brown, L., Nietupski, J., & Hamre-Nietupski, S. (1976). The criterion of ultimate functioning and public school services for severely handicapped students. In M.A. Thomas (Ed.), *Hey don't forget about me: Education's investment in the severely, profoundly and multiply handicapped* (pp. 2–15). Reston, VA: Council for Exceptional Children.

Brown, L., Nisbet, J., Ford, A., Sweet, M., Shiraga, B., York, J., & Loomis, R. (1983). The critical need for nonschool instruction in education programs for severely handicapped students. *Journal of The Association for the Severely Handicapped, 8*, 71–77.

Brown, L., Shiraga, B., York, J., Kessler, K., Strohm, B., Rogan, P., Sweet, M., Zanella, K., Van Deventer, P., & Loomis, R. (1984). Integrated work opportunities for adults with severe disabilities. *Journal of The Association for Persons with Severe Handicaps, 9*, 262–269.

Brown, L., Udvari-Solner, A., Frattura-Kampschroer, L., Davis, L., Ahlgren, C., Van Deventer, P., & Jorgensen, J. (1991). Integrated work: A rejection of segregated enclaves and mobile work crews. In L.H. Meyer, C.A. Peck, & L. Brown (Eds.), *Critical issues in the lives of people with severe disabilities* (pp. 219–228). Baltimore: Paul H. Brookes Publishing Co.

Brown, L., Udvari-Solner, A., Shiraga, B., Long, E., Davis, L., Verban, D., Van Deventer, P., & Jorgensen, J. (1987). The Madison strategy for evaluating the vocational milieu of a worker with severe intellectual disabilities. In L. Brown, A. Udvari-Solner, L. Frattura-Kampschroer, L. Davis, & J. Jorgensen (Eds.), *Educational programs for students with severe intellectual disabilities* (Vol. XVII, pp. 1–372). Madison, WI: Madison Metropolitan School District.

Button, C. (1992, October–November). P.L. 102-569: A new season for the Rehabilitation Act. *Word from Washington.*

Callahan, M. (1986). *What happened when Try Another Way met the real world?* Gautier, MS: Marc Gold & Associates.

Callahan, M. (1991a). Common sense and quality: Meaningful employment outcomes for persons with severe physical disabilities. *The Journal of Vocational Rehabilitation, 1*(2), 21–28.

Callahan, M. (1991b). *Final report for United Cerebral Palsy Associations' three year demonstration project on supported employment.* Washington, DC: United Cerebral Palsy Associations.

Callahan, M. (1992). Job site training and natural supports. In J. Nisbet (Ed.), *Natural supports in school, at work, and in the community for people with severe disabilities* (pp. 257–276). Baltimore: Paul H. Brookes Publishing Co.

Callahan, M. (1993). *The seven phase sequence: Balancing naturalness and individual employee needs.* Gautier, MS: Marc Gold & Associates.

Callahan, M., & Mast, M. (1994). *The vocational profile: A process for matching individuals to jobs which make sense.* Gautier, MS: Marc Gold & Associates.

Chadsey-Rusch, J. (1992). Toward defining and measuring social skills in employment settings. *American Journal on Mental Retardation, 95,* 316–327.

Chappell, T. (1993). *The soul of a business: Managing for profit and the common good.* New York: Bantam Books.

Culver, J.B., Spencer, K.C., & Gliner, J.A. (1990). Prediction of supported employment placements by job developers. *Education and Training in Mental Retardation, 25,* 237–242.

Defazio, N., & Flexer, R.W. (1983). Organization barriers to productivity, meaningful wages, and normalized work opportunities for mentally retarded persons. *Mental Retardation, 21,* 157–163.

Dennis, R.E., Williams, W., Giangreco, M.F., & Cloninger, C.J. (1993). Quality of life as context for planning and evaluation of services for people with disabilities. *Exceptional Children, 59,* 499–512.

Donnellan, A.M., & Cutler, B.C. (1991). A dialogue on power relationships and aversive control. In L.H. Meyer, C.A. Peck, & L. Brown (Eds.), *Critical issues in the lives of people with severe disabilities* (pp. 617–624). Baltimore: Paul H. Brookes Publishing Co.

Dufresne, D., & Laux, B. (1994). From facilities to supports: The changing organization. In V.J. Bradley, J.W. Ashbaugh, & B.C. Blaney (Eds.), *Creating individual supports for people with developmental disabilities: A mandate for change at many levels* (pp. 271–280). Baltimore: Paul H. Brookes Publishing Co.

Ellison, R. (1952). *The invisible man.* New York: Random House.

Fabian, E.S., Edelman, A., & Leedy, M. (1993). Linking workers with severe disabilities to social supports in the workplace: Strategies for addressing barriers. *Journal of Rehabilitation, 59,* 29–34.

Fabian, E.S., Luecking, R.G., & Tilson, H.P. (1995). Employer and rehabilitation personnel perspectives on hiring persons with disabilities: Implications for job development. *Journal of Rehabilitation, 61*(1), 42–49.

Ferguson, M. (1976). *The aquarian conspiracy: Personal and social transformation in the 1980s.* Boston: J.P. Tarcher, Inc.

Ferguson, P.M., Ferguson, D.L., & Jones, D. (1988). Generations of hope: Parental perspectives on the transitions of their children with severe retardation from school to adult life. *Journal of The Association for Persons with Severe Handicaps, 13,* 177–187.

Ford, A., & Mirenda, P. (1984). Community instruction: A natural cues and corrections decision model. *Journal of The Association for Persons with Severe Handicaps, 9,* 79–87.

Forest, M., & Pearpoint, J. (1992). Families, friends, and circles. In J. Nisbet (Ed.), *Natural supports in school, at work, and in the community for people with severe disabilities* (pp. 65–86). Baltimore: Paul H. Brookes Publishing Co.

Galloway, C. (1982). *Employers as partners: A guide to negotiating jobs for people with disabilities.* Sonoma, CA: Times Mirror Publishing Group.

Garner, J.B., & Campbell, P.H. (1987). Technology for persons with severe disabilities: Practical and ethical considerations. *Journal of Special Education, 21,* 122–132.

Gaylord-Ross, R. (1986). The role of assessment in transitional, supported employment. *Career Development for Exceptional Individuals, 9,* 128–134.

Gaylord-Ross, R., & Browder, D. (1991). Functional assessment: Dynamic and domain properties. In L.H. Meyer, C.A. Peck, & L. Brown (Eds.), *Critical issues in the lives of people with severe disabilities* (pp. 45–66). Baltimore: Paul H. Brookes Publishing Co.

Gaylord-Ross, R., Forte, J., Storey, K., Gaylord-Ross, C., & Jameson, D. (1987). Community-referenced instruction in technological work settings. *Exceptional Children, 54*, 112–120.

Gerry, M.H., & Mirsky, A.J. (1992). Guiding principles for public policy on natural supports. In J. Nisbet (Ed.), *Natural supports in school, at work, and in the community for people with severe disabilities* (pp. 341–346). Baltimore: Paul H. Brookes Publishing Co.

Giangreco, M.F., & Putnam, J.W. (1991). Supporting the education of students with severe disabilities in regular education environments. In L.H. Meyer, C.A. Peck, & L. Brown (Eds.), *Critical issues in the lives of people with severe disabilities* (pp. 245–270). Baltimore: Paul H. Brookes Publishing Co.

Gold, M. (1972). Stimulus factors in skill training of the retarded on a complex assembly task: Acquisition, transfer, and retention. *American Journal on Mental Deficiency, 76*, 517–526.

Gold, M. (1976). Task analysis of a complex assembly task by the retarded blind. *Exceptional Children, 43*, 78–84.

Gold, M. (1980a). *Did I say that?* Champaign, IL: Research Press.

Gold, M. (1980b). *Try Another Way training manual.* Champaign, IL: Research Press.

Gold, M.W. (Producer). (1982). *A look at values* [Videotape]. Gautier, MS: Marc Gold & Associates.

Greenspan, S. (1994). [Review of Mental Retardation: Definition, classification, and systems of support]. *American Journal on Mental Retardation, 98*, 544–548.

Greenspan, S., & Shoultz, B. (1981). Why mentally retarded adults lose their jobs: Social competence as a factor in work adjustment. *Applied Research in Mental Retardation, 2*, 23–38.

Gretz, S. (1992). Citizen participation: Connecting people to associational life. In D.B. Schwartz (Ed.), *Crossing the river: Creating a conceptual revolution in community and disability* (pp. 11–30). Cambridge, MA: Brookline Books.

Grossman, H.J. (Ed.). (1973). *Manual on terminology and classification in mental retardation.* Washington, DC: American Association on Mental Deficiency.

Grossman, H.J. (Ed.). (1977). *Manual on terminology and classification in mental retardation* (Rev. ed.). Washington, DC: American Association on Mental Deficiency.

Grossman, H.J. (Ed.). (1983). *Classification in mental retardation* (3rd rev.). Washington, DC: American Association on Mental Deficiency.

Guess, D., Benson, H.A., & Siegel-Causey, E. (1985). Concepts and issues related to choice-making among persons with severe disabilities. *Journal of The Association for Persons with Severe Handicaps, 10*, 79–86.

Hagner, D.C. (1992). The social interactions and job supports of supported employees. In J. Nisbet (Ed.), *Natural supports in school, at work, and in the community for people with severe disabilities* (pp. 217–239). Baltimore: Paul H. Brookes Publishing Co.

Hagner, D.C., Cotton, P., Goodall, S., & Nisbet, J. (1992). The perspectives of supportive coworkers: Nothing special. In J. Nisbet (Ed.), *Natural supports in school, at work, and in the community for people with disabilities* (pp. 241–256). Baltimore: Paul H. Brookes Publishing Co.

Hagner, D., & Dileo, D. (1993). *Working together: Workplace culture, supported employment, and persons with disabilities.* Cambridge, MA: Brookline Books.

Hagner, D., Rogan, P., & Murphy, S. (1992). Facilitating natural supports in the workplace: Strategies for support consultants. *Journal of Rehabilitation, 58*, 29–34.

Halpern, A. (1993). Quality of life as a conceptual framework for evaluating transition outcomes. *Exceptional Children, 59*, 486–498.

Hanley-Maxwell, C., Rusch, F.R., Chadsey-Rusch, J., & Renzaglia, A. (1986). Reported factors contributing to job termination of individuals with severe disabilities. *Journal of The Association for Persons with Severe Handicaps, 11*, 45–52.

Hasazi, S.B. (1991). An exchange on personal futures and community participation: An interview with John McKnight and Ronald Melzer. In L.H. Meyer, C.A. Peck, & L. Brown (Eds.), *Critical issues in the lives of people with severe disabilities* (pp. 537–541). Baltimore: Paul H. Brookes Publishing Co.

Heber, R. (1959). A manual on terminology and classification in mental retardation. *American Journal of Mental Deficiency, 64*(Suppl).

Heber, R. (1961). A manual on terminology and classification in mental retardation (2nd ed.). *American Journal of Mental Deficiency,* (Suppl).

Henderson, M., & Argyle, M. (1985). Social support by four categories of work colleague: Relationships between activities, stress, and satisfaction. *Journal of Occupational Behavior, 6*, 229–239.

Hunter, J., & Bellamy, G.T. (1976). Cable harness construction for severely retarded adults: A demonstration of training technique. *AAESPH Review, 1*, 2–13.

Individuals with Disabilities Education Act (IDEA) of 1990, PL 101-476, 20 U.S.C. § 1400 *et seq.*

Jacobson, J.W. (1994). [Review of Mental Retardation: Definition, classification, and systems of support]. *American Journal on Mental Retardation, 98*, 539–541.

Jorgenson, C.M. (1992). Natural supports in inclusive schools: Curricular and teaching strategies. In J. Nisbet (Ed.), *Natural supports in school, at work, and in the community for people with severe disabilities* (pp. 179–215). Baltimore: Paul H. Brookes Publishing Co.

Jung, C.G. (1953). Collected works: Vol. 4. The theory of psychoanalysis. In J. Jacobi (Ed.), *Psychological reflections: A Jung anthology* (p. 83). New York: Pantheon.

Kendrick, M. (1994). Public and personal leadership challenges. In V.J. Bradley, J.W. Ashbaugh, & B.C. Blaney (Eds.), *Creating individual supports for people with developmental disabilities: A mandate for change at many levels* (pp. 361–372). Baltimore: Paul H. Brookes Publishing Co.

Kennedy, M., Killius, P., & Olson, D. (1987). Living in the community: Speaking for yourself. In S.J. Taylor, D. Biklen, & J. Knoll (Eds.), *Community integration for people with severe disabilities* (pp. 202–208). New York: Teachers College Press.

Kiernan, W.E., & Stark, J.A. (1986). The adult with developmental disabilities. In W.E. Kiernan & J.A. Stark (Eds.), *Pathways to employment for adults with developmental disabilities* (pp. 3–8). Baltimore: Paul H. Brookes Publishing Co.

Klein, J. (1992). Get me the hell out of here: Supporting people with disabilities to live in their own homes. In J. Nisbet (Ed.), *Natural supports in school, at work, and in the community for people with severe disabilities* (pp. 277–339). Baltimore: Paul H. Brookes Publishing Co.

Knoll, J.A., & Racino, J.A. (1994). Field in search of a home: The need for support personnel to develop a distinct identity. In V.J. Bradley, J.W. Ashbaugh, & B.C. Blaney (Eds.), *Creating individual supports for people with developmental disabilities: A mandate for change at many levels* (pp. 299–323). Baltimore: Paul H. Brookes Publishing Co.

Kregel, J., & Wehman, P. (1989). Supported employment: Promises deferred for persons with severe handicaps. *Journal of The Association for Persons with Severe Handicaps, 14*, 293–303.

Leitner, R. (1986). *Adjusting intervention in relation to criterion.* Gautier, MS: Marc Gold & Associates.

Levy, J.M., Jessop, D.J., Rimmerman, A., & Levy, P.H. (1992). Attitudes of Fortune 500 corporate executives toward the employability of persons with severe disabilities: A national study. *Mental Retardation, 30,* 67–75.

Luckasson, R., Coulter, D.L., Polloway, E.A., Reiss, S., Schalock, R.L., Snell, M.E., Spitalnik, D.M., & Stark, J.A. (1992). *Mental retardation: Definition, classification, and systems of supports.* Washington, DC: American Association on Mental Retardation.

Luckasson, R., & Spitalnik, D. (1994). Political and programmatic shifts of the 1992 AAMR definition of mental retardation. In V.J. Bradley, J.W. Ashbaugh, & B.C. Blaney (Eds.), *Creating individual supports for people with developmental disabilities: A mandate for change at many levels* (pp. 81–96). Baltimore: Paul H. Brookes Publishing Co.

Mallory, B.L. (1995). The role of social policy on life-cycle transitions. *Exceptional Children, 62*(3), 213–223.

Mann, T. (1924). *The magic mountain.* New York: Vintage Books.

Mast, M., & Callahan, M. (1994). *The vocational profile and the profile meeting: A process, not a form.* Gautier, MS: Marc Gold & Associates.

McCallion, P., & Toseland, R.W. (1993). Empowering families of adolescents and adults with developmental disabilities. *Families in Society: The Journal of Contemporary Human Services, 17,* 579–587.

McGaughey, M.J., Kiernan, W.E., McNally, L.C., Gilmore, D.S., & Keith, G.R. (1995). Beyond the workshop: National trends in integrated and segregated day and employment services. *Journal of The Association for Persons with Severe Handicaps, 20*(4), 270–285.

McGee, J.J., Menousek, P.E., & Hobbs, D. (1987). Gentle teaching: An alternative to punishment for people with challenging behaviors. In S.J. Taylor, D. Biklen, & J. Knoll (Eds.), *Community integration for people with severe disabilities* (pp. 147–183). New York: Teachers College Press.

McKnight, J. (1987). Regenerating community. *Social Policy, 17,* 54–58.

McKnight, J. (1990). *Beyond community services.* Chicago: Northwestern University, Center for Urban Affairs and Policy Research.

Mcloughlin, C.S., Garner, J.B., & Callahan, M. (1987). *Getting employed, staying employed: Job development and training for persons with severe handicaps.* Baltimore: Paul H. Brookes Publishing Co.

McMillan, D.L., Gresham, F.M., & Siperstein, G.N. (1993). Conceptual and psychometric concerns about the 1992 AAMR definition of mental retardation. *American Journal on Mental Retardation, 98,* 325–335.

Moon, M.S., Goodall, P., Barcus, M., & Brooke, V. (Eds.). (1986). *The supported work model of competitive employment for citizens with severe handicaps: A guide for job trainers.* Richmond: Virginia Commonwealth University, Rehabilitation Research and Training Center.

Moon, M.S., Inge, K.J., Wehman, P., Brooke, V., & Barcus, J.M. (1990). *Helping persons with severe mental retardation get and keep employment: Supported employment strategies and outcomes.* Baltimore: Paul H. Brookes Publishing Co.

Mount, B. (1987). *Personal futures planning: Finding directions for change.* Unpublished doctoral dissertation, University of Georgia, Athens.

Mount, B., Beeman, P., & Ducharme, G. (1998a). *What are we learning about bridge-building?* Manchester, CT: Communitas, Inc.

Mount, B., Beeman, P., & Ducharme, G. (1988b). *What are we learning about circles of support?* Manchester, CT: Communitas, Inc.

Murphy, S., & Rogan, P. (1994). *Developing natural supports in the workplace: A practitioner's guide.* St. Augustine, FL: Training Resource Network.

Nietupski, J., Verstegen, D., & Hamre-Nietupski, S. (1992). Incorporating sales and business practices into job development in supported employment. *Education and Training in Mental Retardation, 27*, 207–217.

Nisbet, J., & Callahan, M. (1987a). Achieving success in integrated workplaces: Critical elements in assisting persons with severe disabilities. In S.J. Taylor, D. Biklen, & J. Knoll (Eds.), *Community integration for people with severe disabilities* (pp. 184–201). New York: Teachers College Press.

Nisbet, J., & Callahan, M. (1987b). *The vocational strategy.* Gautier, MS: Marc Gold & Associates.

Nisbet, J., & Hagner, D. (1988). Natural supports in the workplace: A reexamination of supported employment. *Journal of The Association for Persons with Severe Handicaps, 13*, 260–267.

O'Brien, J. (1987a). Embracing ignorance, error, and fallibility: Competencies for leadership of effective services. In S.J. Taylor, D. Biklen, & J. Knoll (Eds.), *Community integration for people with severe disabilities* (pp. 184–201). New York: Teachers College Press.

O'Brien, J. (1987b). A guide to life-style planning: Using The Activities Catalog to integrate services and natural support systems. In B. Wilcox & G.T. Bellamy (Eds.), *A comprehensive guide to The Activities Catalog: An alternative curriculum for youth and adults with severe disabilities* (pp. 175–189). Baltimore: Paul H. Brookes Publishing Co.

O'Brien, J. (1988). *Personal futures planning: A workshop for people searching for new appreciations of people with developmental disabilities.* Decatur, GA: Responsive Systems Associates.

O'Brien, J., & Lyle, C. (1988). *Framework for accomplishment.* Atlanta: Responsive Systems Associates.

O'Brien, J., & Mount, B. (1991). Telling new stories: The search for capacity among people with severe handicaps. In L.H. Meyer, C.A. Peck, & L. Brown (Eds.), *Critical issues in the lives of people with severe disabilities* (pp. 89–92). Baltimore: Paul H. Brookes Publishing Co.

O'Brien, J., & O'Brien, C.L. (1992). Members of each other: Perspectives on social support and people with severe disabilities. In J. Nisbet (Ed.), *Natural supports in school, at work, and in the community for people with severe disabilities* (pp. 17–63). Baltimore: Paul H. Brookes Publishing Co.

O'Brien, J., & O'Brien, C.L. (1993). Unlikely alliances: Friendships and people with developmental disabilities. In A.N. Amado (Ed.), *Friendships and community connections between people with and without developmental disabilities* (pp. 9–39). Baltimore: Paul H. Brookes Publishing Co.

O'Brien, J., & O'Brien, C.L. (1994). More than just a new address: Images of organization for supported living agencies. In V.J. Bradley, J.W. Ashbaugh, & B.C. Blaney (Eds.), *Creating individual supports for people with developmental disabilities: A mandate for change at many levels* (pp. 109–140). Baltimore: Paul H. Brookes Publishing Co.

O'Connell, M. (1988). *The gift of hospitality: Opening the doors of community life to people with disabilities.* Evanston, IL: Northwestern University, Center for Urban Affairs and Policy Research.

Ohio Safeguards. (1990a). *Personal histories: Suggestions for studying and recording them.* Chillicothe, OH: Author.

Ohio Safeguards. (1990b). *What have we noticed as we've tried to assist people one person at a time?* Chillicothe, OH: Author.

Parent, W., Kregel, J., Metzler, H.M.D., & Twardzik, G. (1992). Social integration in the workplace: An analysis of the interaction activities of workers with mental retardation and their co-workers. *Education and Training in Mental Retardation, 27,* 28–38.

Pealer, J., Landis, S., & Winnenberg, J. (1992). *The community living paper: Promoting life in the community for Ohio's citizens with developmental disabilities.* Chillicothe, OH: Ohio Safeguards.

Peck, C.A. (1991). Linking values and science in social policy decisions affecting citizens with severe disabilities. In L.H. Meyer, C.A. Peck, & L. Brown (Eds.), *Critical issues in the lives of people with severe disabilities* (pp. 1–5). Baltimore: Paul H. Brookes Publishing Co.

Perske, R. (1987). Foreword: The legacy of Marc Gold. In C.S. Mcloughlin, J.B. Garner, & M. Callahan (Eds.), *Getting employed, staying employed: Job development and training for persons with severe handicaps* (pp. vi–viii). Baltimore: Paul H. Brookes Publishing Co.

Perske, R. (1993). Introduction. In A.N. Amado (Ed.), *Friendships and community connections between people with and without developmental disabilities* (pp. 1–6). Baltimore: Paul H. Brookes Publishing Co.

Pomerantz, D.J., & Marholin, D. (1977). Vocational habilitation: Time for a change. In E. Sontag, N. Certo, & J. Smith (Eds.), *Educational programming for the severely and profoundly handicapped* (pp. 129–141). Reston, VA: Council for Exceptional Children.

Provençal, G. (1987). Culturing commitment. In S.J. Taylor, D. Biklen, & J. Knoll (Eds.), *Community integration for people with severe disabilities* (pp. 67–84). New York: Teachers College Press.

Rafelson, B., & Wechsler, R. (Producers), & Rafelson, B. (Director). (1970). *Five easy pieces.* [Film]. (Available from Columbia Pictures.)

Rehabilitation Act Amendments of 1992, PL 102-569, 29 U.S.C. § 701 *et seq.*

Rehabilitation Act of 1973, PL 93-112, 29 U.S.C. § 701 *et seq.*

Rhodes, L., & Drum, C. (1989). Supported employment in the public sector: Procedural issues in implementation. *Journal of The Association for Persons with Severe Handicaps Studies, 14,* 197–204.

Rhodes, L., Mank, D., Sandow, D., Buckley, J., & Albin, J. (1990). Supported employment implementation: Shifting from program monitoring to quality improvement. *Journal of Disability Policy Studies, 1,* 1–17.

Rhodes, L.E., Ramsing, K.D., & Bellamy, G.T. (1988). Business participation in supported employment. In G.T. Bellamy, L.E. Rhodes, D.M. Mank, & J.M. Albin (Eds.), *Supported employment: A community implementation guide* (pp. 247–261). Baltimore: Paul H. Brookes Publishing Co.

Rogan, P., Hagner, D. (1990). Vocational evaluation in supported employment. *Journal of Rehabilitation, 57,* 45–51.

Rogan, P., Hagner, D., & Murphy, S. (1993). Natural supports: Reconceptualizing job coach roles. *Journal of The Association for Persons with Severe Handicaps, 18,* 275–281.

Rucker, L. (1987). A difference you can see: One example of services to persons with severe mental retardation in the community. In S.J. Taylor, D. Biklen, & J. Knoll (Eds.), *Community integration for people with severe disabilities* (pp. 109–128). New York: Teachers College Press.

Rusch, F.R., Chadsey-Rusch, J., & Johnson, J.R. (1991). Supported employment: Emerging opportunities for employment integration. In L.H. Meyer, C.A. Peck, & L. Brown (Eds.), *Critical issues in the lives of people with severe disabilities* (pp. 145–169). Baltimore: Paul H. Brookes Publishing Co.

Rusch, F.R., Hughes, C., Johnson, J.R., & Minch, K.E. (1991). Descriptive analysis of interactions between co-workers and supported employees. *Mental Retardation, 29,* 207–212.

Rusch, F.R., Johnson, J., & Hughes, C. (1990). Analysis of co-worker involvement in relation to level of disability versus placement approach. *Journal of The Association for Persons with Severe Handicaps, 15,* 32–39.

Schalock, R.L., Stark, J.A., Snell, M.E., Coulter, D.L., Polloway, E.A., Luckasson, R., Reiss, S., & Spitalnik, D.M. (1994). The changing conception of mental retardation: Implications for the field. *Mental Retardation, 32,* 181–193.

Schuler, A.L., & Perez, L. (1991). Assessment: Current concerns and future directions. In L.H. Meyer, C.A. Peck, & L. Brown (Eds.), *Critical issues in the lives of people with severe disabilities* (pp. 101–106). Baltimore: Paul H. Brookes Publishing Co.

Schuster, J.W. (1990). Sheltered workshops: Financial and philosophical limitations. *Mental Retardation, 29,* 235–239.

Schwartz, D.B. (1992). *Crossing the river: Creating a conceptual revolution in community and disability.* Cambridge, MA: Brookline Books.

Shafer, M.S., Banks, P.D., & Kregel, J. (1991). Employment retention and career movement among individuals with mental retardation working in supported employment. *Mental Retardation, 29,* 105–110.

Shafer, M.S., Rice, L.S., Metzler, H.M.D., & Haring, M. (1989). A survey of nondisabled employees' attitudes toward supported employees with mental retardation. *Journal of The Association for Persons with Severe Handicaps, 14,* 137–146.

Simmons, T., & Flexer, R. (1992). Business and rehabilitation factors in the development of supported employment programs for adults with developmental disabilities. *Journal of Rehabilitation, 58,* 35–42.

Sinott-Oswald, M., Gliner, J.A., & Spencer, K.C. (1991). Supported and sheltered employment: Quality of life issues among workers with disabilities. *Education and Training in Mental Retardation, 26,* 388–397.

Smull, M.W., & Bellamy, G.T. (1991). Community services for adults with disabilities: Policy challenges in the emerging support paradigm. In L.H. Meyer, C.A. Peck, & L. Brown (Eds.), *Critical issues in the lives of people with severe disabilities* (pp. 527–536). Baltimore: Paul H. Brookes Publishing Co.

Snow, J. (1992). On dreams, gifts, and services. In D. Wetherow (Ed.), *The whole community catalogue* (pp. 64–65). Manchester, CT: Communitas, Inc.

Sowers, J., & Powers, L. (1991). *Vocational preparation and employment of students with physical and multiple disabilities.* Paul H. Brookes Publishing Co.

Speight, S., Myers, L., Cox, C., & Hughes, P. (1991). A redefinition of multicultural counseling. *Journal of Counseling and Development, 70,* 29–36.

Taylor, S. (1988). Caught in the continuum: A critical analysis of the principle of the least restrictive environment. *Journal of The Association for Persons with Severe Handicaps, 13,* 41–53.

Taylor, S.J. (1987). Continuum traps. In S.J. Taylor, D. Biklen, & J. Knoll (Eds.), *Community integration for people with severe disabilities* (pp. 25–35). New York: Teachers College Press.

Test, D.W., Hinson, K.B., Solow, J., & Keul, P. (1993). Job satisfaction of persons in supported employment. *Education and Training in Mental Retardation, 28,* 335–344.

Wehman, P., & Kregel, J. (1995). At the crossroads: Supported employment a decade later. *Journal of The Association for Persons with Severe Handicaps, 20*(4), 286–299.

Weiner-Zivolich, J.S., & Zivolich, S. (1995). If not now, when? The case against waiting for sheltered workshop changeover. *Journal of The Association for Persons with Severe Handicaps, 20*(4), 311–312.

West, M.D., & Parent, W.S. (1992). Consumer choice and empowerment in supported employment services: Issues and strategies. *Journal of The Association for Persons with Severe Handicaps, 17*, 47–52.

West, M.D., Revell, W.G., & Wehman, P. (1992). Achievements and challenges I: A five year report on consumer and system outcomes from the supported employment initiative. *Journal of The Association for Persons with Severe Handicaps, 17*, 227–235.

Wetherow, D. (Ed.) (1992). *The whole community catalogue.* Manchester, CT: Communitas, Inc.

White House Conference on Children. (1970). Report to the president. Washington, DC: U.S. Government Printing Office.

Willer, B., Scheerenberger, R.C., & Intagliata, J. (1980). Deinstitutionalization and mentally retarded persons. In A.R. Novak & L.W. Heal (Eds.), *Integration of developmentally disabled individuals into the community* (pp. 3–20). Baltimore: Paul H. Brookes Publishing Co.

Williams, R.R. (1992). Natural supports on the fly: Between flights in Chicago. In J. Nisbet (Ed.), *Natural supports in school, at work, and in the community for people with severe disabilities* (pp. 11–16). Baltimore: Paul H. Brookes Publishing Co.

Wilson, S.W., & Coverdale, M.C. (1993). Partnerships at work and in the community. In A.N. Amado (Ed.), *Friendships and community connections between people with and without developmental disabilities* (pp. 327–350). Baltimore: Paul H. Brookes Publishing Co.

A

Vocational Profile Form
Profile Summary
Profile Meeting Form

VOCATIONAL PROFILE FORM

1. **Identification Information**

   a. **Name:**

   b. **Date of birth:**

   c. **Social Security #:**

   d. **Address:**

   e. **Telephone:**

   f. **Marital status:**

   g. **Current occupation/status:**

2. **Residential/Domestic Information**

   a. **Family (parent/guardian, spouse, children, siblings):**

   b. **Extended family:**

   c. **Names, ages, and relationships of people living in same residence:**

      1.   **Age:**   **Relation:**

      2.   **Age:**   **Relation:**

      3.   **Age:**   **Relation:**

      4.   **Age:**   **Relation:**

      5.   **Age:**   **Relation:**

   (If more than five, then use back of form.)

d. Residential history:

e. Family support available:

f. Description of typical routines:

g. Friends and social group(s):

h. Description of neighborhood:

i. Location of neighborhood in community:

j. Services near home:

k. Transportation availability:

     l. General types of employment near home:

     m. Specific employers near home:

3. **Education Information**

     a. History and general performance (from school records, interview data, observations):

     b. Vocational programming/performance:

     c. Community functioning programming/performance:

     d. Recreation/leisure programming/performance:

4. **Work Experience Information**

     a. Informal work performed at home:

b. Formal chores performed at home:

c. Informal jobs performed for others:

d. Sheltered employment:

e. Paid work:

5. Summary of Present Level of Performance

   a. Domestic skills:

   b. Community functioning skills:

   c. Recreation/leisure skills:

   d. Academic skills (reading, math, time, money):

   e. Motor/mobility skills:

   f. Sensory skills:

   g. Communication skills:

   h. Social interaction skills:

   i. Physical/health-related skills and information:

   j. Vocational skills:

6. Learning and Performance Characteristics

   a. Environmental conditions that the applicant likes best:

   b. Instructional strategies that work best:

c. Amount of support typically required to learn and participate:

d. Environments/strategies to be avoided:

7. Preferences

a. Type of work that the applicant wants to do:

b. Type of work that applicant/family always wished could be obtained:

c. Type of work that parent/guardian feels is appropriate:

d. What the applicant most enjoys doing:

e. Observations of the kinds of work that the applicant likes to do best:

f. Observations of social situations that the applicant likes best:

8. Connections

a. Potential employers in family:

b. Potential employers among friends:

c. Potential employment sites in neighborhood:

d. Business/employer contacts for leads:

9. Flexibility/Accommodations that May Be Required in the Workplace

a. Accessibility assistance, rehab technology, personal care:

b. Habits, idiosyncrasies, routines:

c. Physical/health restrictions:

d. Behavior challenges:

e. Degree and type of negotiation required:

10. Other Important Information

    a. Primary disability classification of physical impairment (record one):

    b. Age of onset of primary disability (either specific age or, if unavailable, narrow to either Developmental [birth to 21], Adult Onset [22 or older], or Unknown):

    c. Documented secondary disability:

    d. Pattern of physical involvement (one response only):

        __ Monoplegia __ Paraplegia __ Double hemiplegia
        __ Hemiplegia __ Diplegia __ Quadriplegia
        __ Unknown

    e. If cerebral palsy is primary or secondary disability, record by type:

        __ Spasticity __ Rigidity __ Tremor __ Mixed
        __ Athetosis __ Dystonia __ Hypotonia

PROFILE SUMMARY

Date begun: _____

Date completed: _____

Date for home visit: _____

Interviews:

| **Name** | **Relation to applicant** | **Date** |

1.

2.

3.

4.

5.

Profile development notes:

PROFILE MEETING FORM

Name of applicant: _____ Site: _____

Date of meeting: _____ Employment facilitator: _____

Provider: _____

People attending:

    Name   Relation to applicant

    1.

    2.

    3.

    4.

    5.

    6.

A.   Ideal Employment Situation(s) (This section describes the characteristics of an ideal job situation based on all of the information gathered during the profile activity.):

    Conditions:

    Preferences:

    Contributions:

B. Job Development/Prospecting List (The following lists are to be used for job development purposes. They are used to match the applicant's profile information to types of employment and to potential employment sites. This information must be compiled with input by the applicant, parents/guardians, friends, and service agency staff.):

Types of Jobs (This list targets the job categories, duties, or job titles that are consistent with the Ideal Employment Situation.):

1.	6.
2.	7.
3.	8.
4.	9.
5.	10.

Specific Employers (This list targets specific employers in the applicant's local community who are consistent with the information developed in the Profile, in the Ideal Employment Situation, and in the Types of Jobs sections.):

Name of employer	Address/location	Contact/referral
1.		
2.		
3.		
4.		
5.		
6.		
7.		
8.		
9.		

Name of employer	Address/location	Contact/referral
10.		
11.		
12.		
13.		
14.		
15.		
16.		
17.		
18.		
19.		
20.		

B

Vocational Profile Form
Profile Summary
Profile Meeting Form
Completed

VOCATIONAL PROFILE FORM

1. **Identification Information**

    a. **Name:** *Jenna McAllister*

    b. **Date of birth:** *August 8, 1976*

    c. **Social Security #:** *123-45-6789*

    d. **Address:** *226 Bowery St., Leavittsburg, Indiana 39624*

    e. **Telephone:** *(517) 555-2963*

    f. **Marital status:** *Single*

    g. **Current occupation/status:** *Jenna is a high school student. She is nearing graduation, and she has never had any employment experiences or vocational programming in her curriculum. Her parents want her to have a job before she graduates.*

2. **Residential/Domestic Information**

    a. **Family (parent/guardian, spouse, children, siblings):** *Jenna lives at home with her mother and father. She has one brother, who is away at college in another state.*

    b. **Extended family:** *Jenna's natural grandparents all are living. Her mother's parents are retired, and they live within 20 miles of her home. Her father's parents live in Indianapolis, 40 miles away. Both of her parents have siblings who live within a short distance of her home. Her father's brother, Max, is Jenna's favorite relative. Max often takes Jenna to swimming lessons at the YMCA.*

    c. **Names, ages, and relationships of people living in same residence:**

    1. *Alice McAllister*   **Age:** *51*   **Relation:** *Mother*

    2. *Wesley McAllister*   **Age:** *50*   **Relation:** *Father*

    d. **Residential history:** *Jenna has lived with her family in her* *current house for 8 years. Prior to that, they lived in a suburb of Chicago.*

e. Family support available: *Both of Jenna's parents are willing to provide whatever initial supports that she needs in order to get and hold a job. This includes calling on potential employers, providing transportation, and even paying for a job trainer for a short period of time. Mr. and Mrs. McAllister have played an integral part in Jenna's schooling, and they regularly advocate for quality services.*

f. Description of typical routines:

7:00 A.M.	Wake up with assistance from mother
7:15	Bathe, dress, and prepare for school (with partial assistance from mother)
7:45	Eat breakfast
8:15	Leave for school (parents transport)
8:30	Begin school day
3:30 P.M.	Return home
4:00	Physical therapy with in-home therapist
5:00	YMCA for swimming (usually with parent/uncle)
6:00	Return home and prepare for dinner
6:30	Dinner with parents
7:15	Homework
8:00	Watch television or play video games
9:00	Bedtime

g. Friends and social group(s): *Jenna is very close to her parents and her brother. She does not maintain frequent contact with fellow students from school. Her parents encourage and assist her to participate in regular community activities, but her closest relationships are with family.*

h. Description of neighborhood: *Jenna lives in a middle-class neighborhood in Leavittsburg, a suburban community. The houses are from 5 to 10 years old. The lots are large, and the streets give the impression of being rural. There are no sidewalks, and the nearest services are 5–10 minutes away by automobile.*

i. Location of neighborhood in community: *Bowery Street is approximately 2 miles from the commercial center of Leavittsburg. The neighborhood also is near several other small communities.*

j. Services near home: *Shopping, library, professional services, government offices, schools, parks and recreation sites, and a small mall.*

k. Transportation availability: *There is no public transportation in Leavittsburg. The school district provides a bus for students. Jenna's mother does not work, and she has a minivan that has been modified to accommodate Jenna's wheelchair. She is willing to transport Jenna, initially, for any important reason.*

l. General types of employment near home: *As indicated in item j, there are ample types of employment in Leavittsburg and in neighboring communities. A detailed inventory of specific employment sites will be compiled before the profile meeting.*

m. Specific employers near home: *A detailed inventory will be compiled prior to the profile meeting. This inventory will be conducted by automobile by following main traffic arteries away from Jenna's home.*

3. Education Information

a. History and general performance (from school records, interview data, observations): *Jenna has attended special education for her entire student life. Jenna was diagnosed with cerebral palsy when she was a toddler. Her parents sought help from the local school district when she was 4 or 5 years old. They enrolled her in a preschool program for kids with disabilities. Her school records indicate that she was cooperative and pleasant, and her IEPs reflect a traditional, deficit-reducing curriculum. Even though she has consistently made good grades, her parents question the effectiveness of her curriculum. Jenna can read 20-25 familiar words, she can print her name, she can count and identify numbers up to 100, and she has mastered a number of nonfunctional skills on her IEPs.*

b. Vocational programming/performance: *Jenna has received no structured vocational programming. She has been required to perform routine chores in school and at home. She cheerfully completes her chores on time and with little prodding.*

c. Community functioning programming/performance: *Jenna's school program has not included a community functioning domain. The extent of community programming has involved occasional field trips to points of interest in the local area. Her parents, however, have always tried to get Jenna involved in her community. She belongs to the YMCA, a girl scout troop, and a computer users group.*

d. Recreation/leisure programming/performance: *Jenna regularly swims at the YMCA, she uses the Leavittsburg library, and she attends girl scout meetings. The school district encourages participation in the Special Olympics, and Jenna has competed since she was 8 years old. She sometimes is reluctant to attend other recreational events for only people with disabilities sponsored through her high school. Her IEP identifies several school-related recreation skills involving mostly board games and physical development tasks.*

4. **Work Experience Information**

   a. Informal work performed at home: *Jenna does basic chores in her room. She folds and puts away her clothes after they are washed. She also puts away her electronic games and other recreational items.*

   b. Formal chores performed at home: *Jenna is not required to perform any formal chores at home. Her parents have considered including home chores on her next IEP.*

   c. Informal jobs performed for others: *Jenna has not performed any work for others except for her Uncle Max. Max occasionally will involve Jenna in helping him with his hobby, metal working. Jenna has helped clean the shop with a ShopVac and has helped assemble certain items.*

   d. Sheltered employment: *None.*

   e. Paid work: *Except for her weekly allowance of $4 per week, Jenna has not received pay for work.*

5. **Summary of Present Level of Performance**

a. Domestic skills: *Jenna participates while being dressed. She is able to snap and button if the buttons are not too small. She is able to bathe herself using a grab bar to assist in getting into and out of the tub. She can brush her teeth and comb her hair. Jenna is not required to make her bed, but she is expected to keep her electronic games, tapes, and other recreational items picked up and stored properly. Jenna does not prepare meals, but she can independently feed herself, except for cutting meat.*

b. Community functioning skills: *With transportation assistance, Jenna is able to gain access to most community environments. She accompanies her parents on most of their outings not related to business. Because of her physical disability and the lack of sidewalks in her neighborhood, Jenna does not range too far from home on her own. Most of the shopkeepers in Leavittsburg know and speak to Jenna when she is in town.*

c. Recreation/leisure skills: *Jenna enjoys swimming, electronic games, watching videos and TV, and anything to do with computers. She is able to swim without assistance across the pool at the YMCA. She can start and operate her father's computer to play games, and she can operate her VCR and television.*

d. Academic skills (reading, math, time, money): *Jenna can read 20-25 familiar words in her environment. Reading and math tests indicate that she is currently at the 2.0–2.5 grade level. She is aware of the importance of money, and she can recognize several smaller bills and all coins. She is not able to count money, however. She knows to wait for change from a clerk. Jenna can recognize the time on her digital watch, and she is just learning to tell time on a clock with hands.*

e. Motor/mobility skills: *Jenna has cerebral palsy, which affects her mobility and her ability to walk. On certain occasions, she uses hand crutches with forearm braces for stability, whereas at other times she uses her wheelchair for mobility. She walks very slowly yet confidently with crutches. She prefers to use her wheelchair, but she has difficulty efficiently pushing and maneuvering because of the physical involvement required of her hands and arms. Her chair is a state-of-the-art, lightweight model that is easily folded and carried.*

f. Sensory skills: *Jenna can see and hear, and she has full use of all other sensory areas.*

g. Communication skills: *Jenna is able to communicate effectively in complete sentences. Her cerebral palsy affects her enunciation and the speed at which she speaks. She is able, however, to communicate in a manner that is understandable to anyone who takes care to listen closely.*

h. Social interaction skills: *Jenna is an extremely likable and cooperative young woman. She typically is in a good humor, and she smiles often. Most of her academic reports cite her pleasant behavior as one of her most outstanding competencies. Jenna is a bit shy around strangers, possibly because of her fear that others might not understand her. Most of her recreation and leisure is performed alone.*

i. Physical/health-related skills and information: *Jenna enjoys excellent health, and she rarely is sick, even with colds. Her cerebral palsy affects her ability to move her arms and manipulate small objects, though not in a significant manner. Her movements are controlled but slow. She is able to reach out in front of her body and grasp or pick up objects that are light. Her finger and hand control is slow and sometimes a bit shaky, but she is accurate when given the chance to work slowly.*

j. Vocational skills: *Specific vocational skills have not been determined at this time because of lack of opportunity; however, her disposition, enthusiasm, and willingness to stick to a task will be appreciated by employers.*

6. **Learning and Performance Characteristics**

a. Environmental conditions that the applicant likes best: *Jenna enjoys working inside in clean conditions. She likes the out-of-doors in warm weather and may consider a job outside in the summer. She also prefers to work sitting in her wheelchair rather than standing or sitting in a regular chair.*

b. Instructional strategies that work best: *Jenna's parents feel that she needs the opportunity to independently perform tasks in* *order to learn. They cite her ability to use the home computer, VCR, TV, and electronic games as proof. Her teachers feel that repetition of small tasks is necessary. Regardless of the task, instruction must establish acquisition before focusing on speed. Jenna doesn't seem to benefit from written information, but she responds well to visual cues.*

c. Amount of support typically required to learn and participate: *At this point in life, Jenna needs a structured, planned approach to instruction. A trainer or teacher must be prepared to reassess teaching strategies and to keep data on teaching sessions. Jenna probably can learn many social and nonspecific tasks by observing others, but complex tasks require a systematic approach.*

d. Environments/strategies to be avoided: *Jenna has clearly expressed her desire to work in a sitting position. Other situations should be avoided. In addition, strategies that push speed or rapid performance should be delayed until a task is mastered. Artificial reinforcement should not be used until it is clear that it is needed. Jenna gets a great deal of personal satisfaction from tasks that she likes.*

7. Preferences

a. Type of work that the applicant wants to do: *She has expressed interest in "computer work" and office work and might like to try a plant nursery in the spring and summer.*

b. Type of work that applicant/family always wished could be obtained: *Jenna's parents agree with her choices in that they don't feel that food service and janitorial jobs would be appropriate. They seem particularly interested in any kind of employment that would involve computers.*

c. Type of work that parent/guardian feels is appropriate: *Jenna's parents are unsure of this. Her mother believes that she has an excellent memory, once she has learned a task. Her father notes Jenna's friendliness and acceptance by others. They believe that these characteristics will be beneficial on the job—regardless of the type.*

d. What the applicant most enjoys doing: *She enjoys the approval of others, especially adults. She likes to be able to* *choose her own tasks. She loves most electronic games and mag-azines and posters of flowers.*

e. Observations of the kinds of work that the applicant likes to do best: *Jenna's parents and teachers agree that her preferences are consistent with their observations. Her teachers also indicate that she will work on complex puzzles for as long as they will allow her to do so.*

f. Observations of social situations that the applicant likes best: *Jenna is most comfortable with people whom she knows well. She tends to remove herself from groups, especially from groups of people with disabilities. She likes situations best that involve one or two other people with whom she has a relationship.*

8. **Connections**

    a. Potential employers in family: *Jenna's father owns a small designing and construction firm. He works out of his home, and he feels that Jenna might do better with others. There are several aunts and uncles in the area. Of these, Max is the most likely candidate for providing a job. Max is very close to Jenna, and he also owns a dry cleaning shop in a nearby community.*

    b. Potential employers among friends: *Jenna's mother is active in social and volunteer circles in Leavittsburg. She knows the head librarian at the local library, the personnel director at the hospital, and numerous other potential employers. Her father has many connections in the construction industry and in the related business. He has said that he would be willing to become actively involved in developing jobs for Jenna.*

    c. Potential employment sites in neighborhood: *The nearest potential employment sites are in the commercial center of Leavittsburg. This area is not far by car, but it is not any closer to Jenna's home than two or three other small communities in the area.*

    d. Business/employer contacts for leads: *Jenna's mother and father both are well-connected in their community, and they both* *are willing to make contacts on her behalf. Her father's contacts may be useful. Her parents indicate that their relatives also will help to make contacts with potential employers.*

9. **Flexibility/Accommodations that May Be Required in the Workplace**

   a. Accessibility assistance, rehab technology, personal care: *Potential employment sites for Jenna will need to be wheelchair accessible. She also likely will benefit from rehab technology services to make her work station efficient. She needs some help with toileting and eating, but she should not require a full-time personal care attendant on the job.*

   b. Habits, idiosyncrasies, routines: *Jenna doesn't have any unusual behaviors that would require accommodation by an employer.*

   c. Physical/health restrictions: *The most critical concern in this area involves the limitations that Jenna experiences in mobility, standing, lifting, stooping, reaching, and climbing. Either a work station would need to be modified to minimize such actions, or a job that does not require these actions would need to be developed.*

   d. Behavior challenges: *Jenna's easy temperament and friendly attitude present few if any behavioral challenges. She will balk at work that she perceives to be too difficult or rapidly paced. She also might require motivation to keep working when she gets tired or frustrated.*

   e. Degree and type of negotiation required: *Negotiation is likely to be required in several areas: 1) the need for rehabilitation technology, 2) the need for assistance in toileting and eating and 3) the likelihood that Jenna's productivity will be significantly below typical expectations for a long time. Job developers must recognize and answer these concerns before calling on employers.*

10. Other Important Information

a. **Primary disability classification of physical impairment (record one):** *Cerebral palsy*

b. **Age of onset of primary disability (either specific age or, if unavailable, narrow to either Developmental [birth to 21], Adult Onset [22 or older], or Unknown):** *Developmental*

c. **Documented secondary disability:** *Mental retardation*

d. **Pattern of physical involvement (one response only):**

___ Monoplegia   ___ Paraplegia   ___ Double hemiplegia
___ Hemiplegia   ___ Diplegia   _X_ Quadriplegia
___ Unknown

e. **If cerebral palsy is primary or secondary disability, record by type:**

_X_ Spasticity   ___ Rigidity   ___ Tremor   ___ Mixed
___ Athetosis   ___ Dystonia   ___ Hypotonia

PROFILE SUMMARY

Date begun: _10/23/96_

Date completed: _1/6/97_

Date for home visit: _11/5/96_

Interviews:

Name	Relation to applicant	Date
1. *Alice McAllister*	*Mother*	*10/30*
2. *Wesley McAllister*	*Father*	*10/30*
3. *Max McAllister*	*Uncle*	*11/12*
4.		
5.		

Profile development notes:

PROFILE MEETING FORM

Name of applicant: _Jenna McAllister_   **Site:** _Leavittsburg_

Date of meeting: _1/10/97_   **Employment facilitator:** _Michael Callahan_

Provider: _Association for Citizens with Disabilities_

People attending:

Name	Relation to applicant
1. _Alice McAllister_	_Mother_
2. _Wesley McAllister_	_Father_
3. _Mike Callahan_	_Employment facilitator_
4. _Gerald Chang_	_Provider representative_
5. _Max McAllister_	_Uncle_
6. _Pam Walters_	_VR counselor_

A.   Ideal Employment Situation(s) (This section describes the characteristics of an ideal job situation based on all of the information gathered during the profile activity.):

> **Conditions:** _Accessible, low stress, day shift—4 hours maximum to start, repetitive job duties, regular contact with co-workers_

> **Preferences:** _Work with computers, deliver items in a large office or other workplace, data entry, plant nursery in spring and summer_

> **Contributions:** _Friendly, pleasant, dependable, enthusiastic, good memory, liked by others, can deliver quality on data entry_

B.   Job Development/Prospecting List (The following lists are to be used for job development purposes. They are used to match the applicant's profile information to types of employment and to potential employment sites. This information must be compiled with input by the applicant, parents/guardians, friends, and service agency staff.):

> **Types of Jobs** (This list targets the job categories, duties, or job titles that are consistent with the Ideal Employment Situation.):

> **1.** *Product delivery*   **6.** *Water plants*

> **2.** *Data entry*   **7.**

> **3.** *Message delivery*   **8.**

> **4.** *Greeting*   **9.**

> **5.** *Usher*   **10.**

> **Specific Employers** (This list targets specific employers in the applicant's local community who are consistent with the information developed in the Profile, in the Ideal Employment Situation, and in the Types of Jobs sections.):

Name of employer	Address/location	Contact/referral
1. *Computer City*		
2. *Sears*		
3. *Macy's*		
4. *Leavittsburg Botanical Gardens*		
5. *K-Mart*		
6. *Leavittsburg Hospital*		
7. *Wal-Mart*		
8. *UA Sixplex Theaters*		
9. *Local Office of Social Security*		

Name of employer	Address/location	Contact/referral
10. *Leavittsburg Nursery*		
11. *Local Board of Education*		
12. *State Univ. of Leavittsburg*		
13.		
14.		
15.		
16.		
17.		
18.		
19.		
20.		

C

Job Analysis Form

JOB ANALYSIS FORM

Participant: Provider:

Company: Comp. phone #:

Address: Contact:

Date job begins: Site:

Job title: Immed. supervisor:

Provider: Provider phone #:

Core routines   **Episodic routines**
(identified by employer):   (identified by employer):

Job-related routines   **Important cultural aspects**
(identified during Job Analysis):   (and possible accommodations
                                     based on info in Profile):

Job summary:

Job facilitator:

1. **The Way in Which Job Tasks Typically Are Performed**
    a. **Method**
        The facilitator should observe the manner in which each job is performed by typical employees in the setting. This is accomplished by assuming an unobtrusive observation position and carefully watching the employee(s) perform their duties. The facilitator should strive to make a "mental videotape" to be used later as a standard of correct performance and as a way to assist the supported employee to perform in a natural manner.

Job observed	Employee observed	Date & time
1.		
2.		
3.		
4.		
5.		

    b. **Content**
        The employment facilitator should ask whether the employer has step-by-step procedures for the job tasks observed above. If so, then these procedures should serve as the initial content task analysis for each task. If not, then the facilitator should write content steps that would be appropriate for an average employee in the workplace. These content steps should be presented to an appropriate decision maker in the company for approval and refinement. Attach step-by-step procedures to this form.

    c. **Specific requirements identified by employer** (Check only critical items; fully describe the extent of the demand and outline possible adaptations/accommodations believed to be problematic for targeted employee.)

Physical demands:	Sensory/communication demands:
__ Lifting	__ Vision
__ Standing	__ Hearing
__ Continuous movement	__ Speaking
__ Rapid movement	__ Judgment

__ Walking   **Academic demands:**
__ Climbing   __ Reading
__ Stooping   __ Writing
__ Crawling   __ Math

General strength/endurance requirements:

Pace of work:

Potentially dangerous components of job:

Critically important components of job:

Established learning curve or probationary period for job:

d. **Worksite considerations**

Special clothing, uniforms, safety equipment required:

Tools to be used:

Equipment to be operated:

Materials to be handled:

Special terms used at worksite:

Description of environmental conditions of worksite:

2. **The Means Used by the Employer to Train and Support New Employees**
    a. **Description of the company's orientation procedures**
        Ask to review any written documents that describe typical orientation procedures. Discuss with a supervisor or decision maker the flow of typical procedures. Ask employees about their experiences. If possible and if it is believed to be necessary, ask to be taken through an orientation.

    b. **Description of the company's procedures for initially training and supporting new employees**
        Follow the suggestions in 2a, above. In addition, ask for training from the employer on at least one of the tasks to be performed by the supported employee. Use this training as an opportunity to assess the capacity and flexibility of the employer in reference to the needs of the supported employee.

    c. **Description of specific strategies used by the employer**
        1. **Who typically provides new employees with training?**

        2. **Availability of company trainer assigned to employee:**

        3. **Availability of co-workers/supervisors as trainers:**

4.　Description of strategies used by employer:

5.　Important rules stressed by employer and co-workers:

6.　Unwritten rules unique to the setting:

7.　Potential for use of adaptations, modifications in worksite:

8.　Willingness of co-workers/supervisors to provide support and assistance:

d.　The "culture" of the workplace
　　1.　Employer's concern for quality:

　　2.　Employer's concern/need for productivity:

　　3.　Flexibility/rigidity observed:

3. Personnel: Managers, Supervisors, Co-workers
    a. Supervisors of employee

        1.   Title:

        2.   Title:

    b. Co-workers of employee
        1.   Position:

        2.   Position:

        3.   Position:

        4.   Position:

    c. Employee social groups and nonwork activities:

    d. Leaders and potential allies among co-workers and
        supervisors:

4.　Job Description

Schedule:

# of days of work per week:

Days:	Hrs	—
	Hrs	—
	Hrs	—
	Hrs	—
	Hrs	—

Sequential chronology of typical workday (include all job tasks):

Type of job task (core, episodic, job-related):

Name of job task:

How often performed:

Content steps/skills: **Strategy for facilitation**
                                         (including instructional and
                                         natural cues and adaptations):

Name of job task: **Page ___ of ___**

Content steps/skills: **Strategy for facilitation**
(including instructional and
natural cues and adaptations):

D

Job Analysis Form
Completed

JOB ANALYSIS FORM

Participant: *Jenna McAllister*   **Provider:** *ACD*

Company: *Leavittsburg Hospital*   **Comp. Phone #:** *(601) 555-4211*

Address: *Leavittsburg, IN*   **Contact:** *Abby Long*

Date job begins: *July 20, 1997*   **Site:** *Leavittsburg*

Job title: *Delivery Tech*   **Immed. supervisor:** *Tina Hernandez*

Provider: *Michael Callahan*   **Provider phone #:** *(601) 555-6999*

Core routines
(identified by employer):

1. *Deliver computer printouts to departments*

Episodic routines
(identified by employer):

1. *Receive and catalog supplies*
2. *On-call, while at work, for special deliveries to patient rooms*

Job-related routines
(identified during Job Analysis):

1. *One break*
2. *Clock in and out*
3. *Set up bar-code scanner*

Important cultural aspects
(and possible accommodations based on info in Profile):

1. *Wear uniform (hospital blues)*
2. *Wear security badge*
3. *Wash hands with disinfectant soap*

Job summary:
  Jenna will deliver computer printouts to as many as 54 departments on 12 floors of the hospital. She will work for the Transport Department, and her supervisor will be Tina Hernandez. She will start on the day shift, 5 days per week, from 8:00 A.M. until

12:30 P.M. She will be paid $6.00 per hour to start. Jenna will get a 15-minute break at 9:30.

Job facilitator: *Nadine Wilcox*

1. **The Way in Which Job Tasks Typically Are Performed**

   a. **Method**

   The facilitator should observe the manner in which each job is performed by typical employees in the setting. This is accomplished by assuming an unobtrusive observation position and carefully watching the employee(s) perform their duties. The facilitator should strive to make a "mental video-tape" to be used later as a standard of correct performance and as a way to assist the supported employee to perform in a natural manner.

Job observed	Employee observed	Date & time
1. *Printout delivery*	*Alan Grier*	*7/21/97, 9:45–11:45 AM*
2. *I.V. delivery*	*Alan Grier*	*7/22/97, 1:30–3:00 PM*
3. *Cataloging supplies*	*Anya Brinker*	*7/22/97, 9:30–11:30 AM*
4. *Special deliveries*	*Alan Grier*	*7/23/97 (throughout full day)*
5.		

   b. **Content**

   The employment facilitator should ask whether the employer has step-by-step procedures for the job tasks observed above. If so, then these procedures should serve as the initial content task analysis for each task. If not, then the facilitator should write content steps that would be appropriate for an average employee in the workplace. These content steps should be presented to an appropriate decision maker in the company for approval and refinement. Attach step-by-step procedures to this form.

c.   **Specific requirements identified by employer** (Check only critical items; fully describe the extent of the demand and outline possible adaptations/accommodations believed to be problematic for targeted employee.)

Physical demands:

_X_ **Lifting** (Max. 10 lbs.)
__ **Standing**
__ **Continuous movement**
__ **Rapid movement**
__ **Walking**
__ **Climbing**
__ **Stooping**
__ **Crawling**

Sensory/communication demands:

__ **Vision**
__ **Hearing**
__ **Speaking**
_X_ **Judgment** (Identify correct dept.)

Academic demands:

__ **Reading**
__ **Writing**
__ **Math**

General strength/endurance requirements:

This job requires employees to lift at least 10 pounds and to deliver the data forms in a timely manner, throughout the shift.

Pace of work:

Employees are required to work steadily, and the pace of work is moderate. There is little "downtime," as there is always something waiting to be done in the Transport Department. Supervisors expect employees to report if they are out of work.

Potentially dangerous components of job:

Employees must maintain a high standard of hygiene, especially hand washing. Strict standards and cautions are set for contact with blood and materials that contain blood. Employment in hospitals typically carries with it the possibility of infection by contagious diseases.

Critically important components of job:

Timely and accurate delivery of data forms to the various departments. Availability, on call, for special deliveries.

Established learning curve or probationary period for job:

The hospital maintains a 90-day probationary period in the Transport Department.

d.   Worksite considerations

Special clothing, uniforms, safety equipment required:

Employees in the Transport Department must wear "hospital blues," provided by the department. Closed-toe shoes, such as athletic shoes, are required. Hats may not be worn. Security badges must be worn at all times.

Tools to be used:

No tool use is required for this job.

Equipment to be operated:

This position requires the use of a Lightpen bar-code scanner, used for data input of all deliveries. The employee must enter his or her name, employee number, date, and department number each day.

Materials to be handled:

Jenna will handle bundles of computer printouts, approximately 1 1/2" thick. These items are delivered to various departments throughout the hospital. Occasionally, she will handle other lightweight items, which can be placed in the basket of her scooter.

Special terms used at worksite:

Each department name is a unique term, particular to hospitals. She eventually will need to learn 54 department names. "Daily Printouts" — the computer information to be delivered to departments.

Description of environmental conditions of worksite:

All of the work is performed inside of the hospital, which is kept at a constant temperature of 76 degrees. The Transport Department is in the basement of a twin-tower, 19-floor teaching hospital. There are seven separate banks of elevators. The hospital uses signs rather than painted lines for reference and directions. The halls all are approximately 10 feet wide. The entire hospital is well-lighted. The burn unit requires special clearance for entry by the head nurse of the unit.

2. **The Means Used by the Employer to Train and Support New Employees**

   a. **Description of the company's orientation procedures**
   Ask to review any written documents that describe typical orientation procedures. Discuss with a supervisor or decision maker the flow of typical procedures. Ask employees about their experiences. If possible and if it is believed to be necessary, ask to be taken through an orientation.

   The Transport Department provides new employees with a 2-day orientation common to all hospital employees. Employees attend classes on hospital personnel policies, benefits, safety procedures, CPR, and basic patient care. After completing these classes, new delivery techs are assigned to an experienced employee for 1 or 2 days. The new tech accompanies the co-worker on deliveries throughout the hospital and assists him or her to compile a "cheat sheet" for finding departments. New employees are introduced to reception staff in the departments by the co-worker. After the

*orientation period, the new employee is given a verbal quiz
by the supervisor to determine whether additional support is
needed. If so, then this is arranged on an individual basis by
the supervisor.*

b. **Description of the company's procedures for initially training
and supporting new employees**
Follow the suggestions in 2a, above. In addition, ask for
training from the employer on at least one of the tasks to be
performed by the supported employee. Use this training as
an opportunity to assess the capacity and flexibility of
the employer in reference to the needs of the supported
employee.

*The Transport Department uses an experienced employee
in a mentor-like role for the first few weeks of work. The
relationship begins during the orientation and continues on
an as-needed basis for up to 3 weeks. The co-worker is
responsible for getting his or her own work done, and the
new employee asks for assistance, after starting to work
independently following orientation. The training basically
involves demonstration and verbal explanations. Beginning
early in the first day of work, the co-worker begins to
encourage the new employee to make the deliveries and
offers feedback on performance.*

c. **Description of specific strategies used by the employer**

   1. Who typically provides new employees with training?

   Experienced employees, assigned by the supervisor.

   2. Availability of company trainer assigned to employee:

   *The hospital does not have specialized trainers; however,
   each new employee has a co-worker assigned to him or
   her.*

   3. Availability of co-workers/supervisors as trainers:

   *The Transport Department supervisor is available to all
   employees on an individual basis, to be determined by the*

supervisor. It is not usual for co-workers to be assigned as ongoing trainers, however, staff have been observed to offer informal assistance to each other often during the workday.

4. Description of strategies used by employer:

This department relies primarily on demonstration and verbal explanations to teach new employees their jobs. They also use written "cheat sheets" as reminders for department locations and route finding.

5. Important rules stressed by employer and co-workers:

The most important rules involve patient interactions and safety and health precautions. These rules are stressed in orientation, and their violation can involve dismissal from the hospital.

6. Unwritten rules unique to the setting:

Possibly the most commonly discussed unwritten rule is that employees must be busy at all times during work hours. It seems that, historically, workers in the Transport Department would lounge about between calls for assistance. Recently, however, workers have been directed to seek out work from their supervisor any time there is a lull. It is critical to appear to be busy at all times.

7. Potential for use of adaptations, modifications in worksite:

The most likely adaptation for Jenna is the use of a three-wheeled, battery-powered scooter for ambulation. This should present no problem, as many patients use such devices in the hospital. The Transport Department supervisor seems willing to consider any adaptations that would allow Jenna to better perform her job.

8. **Willingness of co-workers/supervisors to provide support and assistance:**

Co-workers were willing during Jenna's nonschool vocational experience to provide her with assistance and support. The supervisor seems very supportive and willing to assist. In general, employees in the Transport Department help each other whenever needed.

d. **The "culture" of the workplace**
1. **Employer's concern for quality:**

Quality is perhaps the most important concern in the Transport Department. It is crucial that the daily printouts be delivered to the correct area. In addition, if equipment is needed on a patient floor, then the delivery must be correct.

2. **Employer's concern/need for productivity:**

The transport supervisor expects steady, dependable performance rather than blazing speed. She constantly stresses accuracy over speed in her description of the job.

3. **Flexibility/rigidity observed:**

The rules of the hospital are quite clear and rigid, especially concerning safety precautions and patient care; however, the Transport Department seems to offer a good deal of flexibility in the way a job gets done. Each employee brings an individual style to the procedures established by the supervisor.

3. Personnel: Managers, Supervisors, Co-workers

   a. Supervisors of employee

      1. *Tina Hernandez*   **Title:** *Transport Department Supervisor*

      2. *Alan Grier*   **Title:** *Assistant Supervisor, Transport*

   b. Co-workers of employee

      1. *Alan Grier*   **Position:** *Assistant Supervisor*

      2. *Maria Vasquez*   **Position:** *Delivery Tech*

      3. *Elton Williams*   **Position:** *Transport Tech*

      4. *Anita Costner*   **Position:** *Transport Tech*

   c. Employee social groups and nonwork activities:

The employees of the Transport Department seem to be a close-knit group and socialize with each other rather than with other employees. They meet after work on Tuesday nights at a local diner. They also participate in company-sponsored sports activities. They have a bowling team during the winter and a volleyball team in the summer.

   d. Leaders and potential allies among co-workers and supervisors:

Alan Grier, assistant supervisor, clearly is the emotional leader in the department. He bridges the gap between management and direct employees. He also has shown interest during Jenna's nonschool vocational experience, which preceded this job.

4. **Job Description**

    Schedule:

    # of days of work per week: *5*

    Days: *Monday–Friday*   **Hrs** *8:00ᴀᴍ–12:30ᴘᴍ*
                                                      Hrs –
                                                      Hrs –
                                                      Hrs –
                                                      Hrs –

Sequential chronology of typical workday (include all job tasks):

7:45 Report to worksite, use toilet

7:55 Clock in

8:00 Get daily assignment from supervisor

8:05 Load basket and begin delivery rounds

9:30 Break

9:45 Continue delivery rounds

11:30 Check with despatcher for specialty deliveries orequipment deliveries

11:35 Make deliveries

12:30 Clock out

12:40 Meet taxi at transport entrance

4. **Type of job task** (Core, episodic, job related): *Core*

Name of job task: *Delivery Tech*

How often performed: *Every day, during morning hours*

Content step/skills: **Strategy for Facilitation**
(including instructional and natural
cues and adaptations):

   1. *Report to area supervisor for duty or additional assignment.*

   2. *Receive department sheet containing delivery routing.*

   3. *Locate cart with daily printouts.*

   4. *Locate first department on list and match to department in cart.*

   5. *Scan bar code with scanner to enter employee code and time.*

   6. *Load first department in basket on scooter.*

   7. *Check department off of delivery routing sheet.*

   8. *Repeat steps 4 and 5 until basket is loaded.*

   9. *When basket is loaded, proceed to first department.*

10. *At appropriate department, enter, and locate reception person.*

11. *Locate department's daily printout from basket.*

12. *Scan the bar code to enter time delivered.*

13. *Exit department.*

14. *Repeat steps 9–13 until basket is empty.*

15. *Return to Transport Department for restocking, and repeat steps 1–15.*

Name of job task: **Page ___ of ___**

Content steps/skills: **Strategy for facilitation**
                                   (including instructional and
                                   natural cues and adaptations):

Index

Page numbers followed by "*f*" indicate figures; those followed by "*t*" indicate tables.